The Future of the Left

The Future of the Left

Edited by James Curran

Polity Press & New Socialist

© New Socialist, 1984

First published 1984 by
Polity Press, Cambridge, in association with Basil Blackwell, Oxford.

Editorial Office:
Polity Press
PO Box 202, Cambridge, CB1 2BT, UK.

Basil Blackwell Ltd
108, Cowley Road, Oxford, OX4 1JF, UK.

Basil Blackwell Inc.
432 Park Avenue South, Suite 1505, New York, NY 10016, USA.

British Library Cataloguing in Publication Data
The Future of the Left.
1. Socialism——Great Britain
I. Curran, James
335'.00941   HX244

ISBN 0-7456-0003-4
ISBN 0-7456-0004-2 Pbk

Also included in the Library of Congress Cataloging in Publication lists

Typeset by Katerprint Co. Ltd, Oxford
Printed in Great Britain by Billing and Sons Ltd, Worcester.

Contents

CONTENTS

List of Contributors

ANTHONY BARNETT is a writer and journalist.

TONY BENN is MP for Chesterfield and NEC member of the Labour Party.

KEN COATES is Reader in Adult Education at the University of Nottingham.

PHILIP COHEN is Research Fellow at the Institute of Education, London University.

ANNA COOTE is Deputy Editor of Diverse Productions, Channel 4.

JAMES CURRAN is Head of the Department of Communications at Goldsmith's College, University of London.

DAVID EDGAR is a playwright.

STUART HALL is Professor of Sociology at the Open University.

DAVID HELD is Lecturer in Politics at the Open University.

STUART HOLLAND is MP for Vauxhall, Lambeth and Opposition Spokesperson for Overseas Development and Cooperation.

RICHARD HYMAN is Reader in Industrial Relations at the University of Warwick.

GARETH STEDMAN JONES is Fellow in History at King's College, University of Cambridge.

MARY KALDOR is Senior Research Fellow of the Science Policy Research Unit, University of Sussex.

JOHN KEANE is Lecturer in Politics at the Polytechnic of Central London.

NEIL KINNOCK is Leader of the Labour Party.

COLIN LEYS is Lecturer in Political Studies, Queen's University, Canada.

DOREEN MASSEY is Professor of Geography at the Open University.

BEN PIMLOTT is Lecturer in Politics at Birkbeck College, University of London.

LYNNE SEGAL is Lecturer in Psychology at Middlesex Polytechnic.

GÖRAN THERBORN is currently visiting Professor of Sociology at the University of Nijmegen, Holland.

HILARY WAINWRIGHT is a writer and researcher at present working in the Poplar Planning Unit of the GLC.

JOHN WESTERGAARD is Professor of Sociological Studies at the University of Sheffield.

RAYMOND WILLIAMS is Fellow of Jesus College and former Professor of Drama at the University of Cambridge.

Introduction

JAMES CURRAN

Fleet Street's political commentators are unanimous in urging the Labour Party to move back into the middle ground of British Politics. The arguments they advance appear persuasive and compelling. The Labour Party crashed to its worst defeat since 1918, they argue, partly because its left-wing policies put off potential supporters and because Labour failed to come to terms with the profound social changes that have moved Britain to the right. Fewer blue-collar workers, increasing affluence and a consequent decline of working-class identification have all eroded Labour's popular base. This is allegedly why Labour's 1983 election disaster was merely the culmination of a steady haemorrhaging of votes since the early 1950s. Unless Labour moves with the times, it will cease to be a national opposition party and be permanently confined to its declining industrial fastnesses in the north of England and Celtic fringe.

An extraordinary convergence of scholarly opinion has bolstered this bleak analysis. Professor Ivor Crewe argues, on the basis of survey evidence, that many Labour voters at the last general election voted Labour despite its policies. Similarly, Professor Eric Hobsbawm eloquently proclaims that Labour Party activists have pushed the party into a position where it is out of touch with its supporters. Although writing from very different ideological perspectives, both reach the conclusion that the Labour Party needs to shift to the right, possibly even to the extent of making an electoral pact with the Alliance to form a broad anti-Thatcher coalition.

This book provides alternative interpretations of the seismic changes that have transformed British politics, and

alternative prescriptions for responding to them. Göran
Therborn empirically challenges many of the premises on
which the new received wisdom is based. 'There is no direct
sociological or socio-historical explanation for the current
travail of the British Labour Party,' he claims, since the left
has triumphed electorally in many other countries in Western
Europe which have been experiencing similar social changes
to those in Britain. Labour's failure is exceptional and should
be attributed, he argues, mainly to the deficiencies of the
British Labour Party and of its leadership during its period of
decline.

John Westergaard also takes issue with the argument that
Labour's decline is the inevitable consequence of social
changes in post-war Britain. While the decline of class
sentiment, the contraction in the number of manual workers,
and the growth of home ownership have all militated against
the Labour Party, the balance of social change, in Westergaard's view, should potentially favour the left. About
two-thirds of the country are dependent on routine jobs
allowing little discretion and variety, carrying few increments in pay or opportunities for promotion and, by
comparison with the career-class, limited security. The 'job
class' still have a shared interest, in common with some
members of the 'career class', in opposing the 'power-house
of control and wealth at the top'. The growth of the public
sector has also created a large group of workers who have yet
to be effectively mobilized in support of the Labour Party.

In a similar vein, Richard Hyman argues that the revisionist case for moving right (and some left variants of it) is
rooted in a mythical view of the past in which political
consciousness and Labour loyalty are assumed to have arisen
spontaneously out of the situation in which manual workers
found themselves. In reality the British working class,
Hyman argues, has always been sectionalized and fragmented: social ideals and a sense of shared identity were only
developed imperfectly and with difficulty through debate
and active campaigning.

Common to all three of these contributors is the view that
Labour's failures in office, combined with the failure to
project a credible and appealing socialist alternative in

opposition, are the principal reasons for Labour's decline. This is a theme developed more fully by Tony Benn who argues that the record of Labour administrations' involvement in the politics of the cold war and monetarist management of the economy, combined with a disastrous split between Labour MPs and party activists, undermined support for the party. He goes on to outline a different kind of electoral coalition from those who have been urging a pact with the Liberal-SDP Alliance. This last proposal is attacked by Anthony Barnett in his chapter on the grounds that it would entail returning to the set of unsuccessful policies and bankrupt values whose manifest shortcomings helped to propel Margaret Thatcher into office.

Writing from a different (though only partially contradictory) position, three further contributors argue that Labour's crisis is rooted in profound cultural changes in post-war Britain. According to Gareth Stedman Jones, the alliance between the organized working class and the progressive middle class that sustained the broadly defined left for most of this century has now been decisively ruptured. Stedman Jones examines not only changes within the working class but also within the middle class where an evangelical tradition of philanthropy from an unassailed privileged position has increasingly given way to a sense of reduced status and class resentment. Only by allying the two parts of the class coalition in a new way, Stedman Jones argues, will it be possible to reconstruct Labour's electoral base.

In a similarly pessimistic mood, Stuart Hall attributes Labour's crisis to the steady erosion of Labour values and identities against the background of political failure and changes in the composition of the working class. The way in which the new right has successfully constructed a mobilizing ideology contrasts depressingly, he argues, with Labour's unwillingness to express an alternative view of the future, to engage strategically in the battle of ideas, and to become involved in activity that is not directed solely towards Parliament and the council chamber.

Philip Cohen also sees Labour's loss of support among the young working class as a consequence of the disintegration of a whole political culture. Collectivist values and Labour loyalties are no longer being transmitted from one generation to the next in the way that they used to be. Yet, neither the youth sections of the organized left nor the new culturalist politics have succeeded in compensating for this. In these circumstances, he argues, it is essential that the Labour Party constructs a new youth politics that relates to the central concerns of young people, particularly their desire to become independent of their parents.

The price of Labour's electoral failure has been incisively documented by Kaldor, Gamble, Cripps and other distinguished economists who have charted the decline of Britain's economy since Thatcher took office in 1979. For this reason, we have focused in this book on another aspect of Thatcherism – the rise of the authoritarian state. David Edgar shows how right-wing pressure groups and the increasing influence of the American new right have promoted social authoritarianism at the expense of liberal economics within the Conservative Party. The effects of this shift, among other factors, are examined by Colin Leys in an essay that challenges some fashionable sloganizing on the left about Thatcher's police state. Authoritarian trends in Britain, he argues, predate Thatcher: they are also limited in scope, strongly contested and often condemned by the British people. Yet strong pressures are building up, he warns, for a significant shift towards a law-and-order state.

Defending the liberties threatened by Thatcherism and extending real freedom of choice is the central theme developed by Neil Kinnock in the section of the book concerned with strategies for rebuilding the left in Britain. 'In every policy that we compile, publicize and practice,' Neil Kinnock concludes, 'we have to show that our central objective is the development of freedom and that our chosen method for linking need and provision is democracy.'

To achieve this, argue David Held and John Keane, it is necessary to distance Labour from the statist and bureaucratic forms of social democracy with which it has become associated in the past. State power needs to be reformed and restricted, and the British left should draw upon the ideas developed by the left in Sweden, Germany and elsewhere for democratizing the economic process as well as institutions like schools, hospitals and housing estates.

A similar theme is developed, though from a different perspective, by Doreen Massey, Lynne Segal and Hilary Wainwright. The olympian pessimism of detached theorists ignores, they argue, the concrete ways in which the new left in many local authorities have pioneered new forms of local democracy and backed new initiatives projecting an alternative socialist vision of the future. At the same time, the left is actively building new electoral coalitions in their localities to defend these initiatives, and using the resources of the community to strengthen and give voice to the industrial and extra-parliamentary activity needed to rebuild the left in Britain.

The scale of recovery needed in electoral terms remains, nonetheless, enormous. Labour needs to achieve very much more than the come-back so far achieved, in a remarkably brief period, under its new leader. It has to secure double the highest swing ever recorded since 1945 to secure even a bare majority in the Commons.

Furthermore, the anti-Conservative forces are currently disastrously split, with Labour taking third or lower place in 292 constituencies at the last general election. This is prompting some people within the Labour Party to think wistfully about an electoral accommodation with the Alliance as the only feasible means of shifting the Conservatives from office at the next election. This strategy is attacked by both Ben Pimlott and Raymond Williams in this book, though for partially different reasons. An electoral arrangement, Pimlott maintains, would benefit the Alliance considerably more than the Labour Party. It is also unacceptable, Williams concludes, because it would mean abandoning the struggle to transform belief and opinion and force Labour instead to adapt to the popular ground on which it has already lost.

Both contributors argue that Labour should go back to the drawing board to develop and refine its policies. They are in tune with the general tenor of most essays in this book and not with the initial, defensive reaction of many members of

the left to Labour's election disaster. Some of Labour's
half-formed policies do need to be changed: to call merely for
their projection with greater conviction is not an adequate
response.

The last section of this book is therefore devoted to
considering how the Labour Party might develop policies in
a number of key areas. Neil Kinnock calls, in an important
essay, for a major reconstruction of the EEC in terms of
developing joint economic activity, transforming the institutions of the EEC, and moving towards the creation of
Europe as a nuclear free zone. Stuart Holland argues for an
updated version of the alternative economic strategy involving a planned joint reflation of Western economies by
socialist governments. Mary Kaldor puts the case for
reforming NATO as a policy of transition from Atlanticism
to non-alignment. I set out a programme for reconstructing
Britain's mass media against the background of the new
communications revolution. Ken Coates surveys how to
strengthen people's freedom, rights and democratic control
in their workplace. Finally, Anna Coote outlines a strategy
for organizing work and public resources in a way that will
enable men and women to jointly share responsibility for
bringing up children.

Most of these essays first appeared in *New Socialist*. Nearly
all of them have been revised for publication in this book. In
addition, three unpublished essays by Neil Kinnock, Ken
Coates and myself have been included to fill what would
otherwise have been major gaps (though some inevitably
remain to be plugged perhaps in a sequel to this book).

Since the publication of this book coincides with my
retirement as editor of *New Socialist*, I should like to thank all
those who made possible the launch and development of the
magazine. Its transformation from the initial blueprint of a
tiny quarterly magazine into a bi-monthly – now monthly –
with a substantial circulation was only possible because it was
a truly collaborative effort to which many have crucially
contributed. In particular I should like to thank Ros Franey
for all her work as production editor as well as her invaluable
help in putting this book together.

Part 1
Whistling in the Void

1

Marching into History?

GARETH STEDMAN JONES

After five years of apparently terminal illness, the Labour Party appears to be up and about again. Under an energetic and personable new leader and sobered down by the experience of its worst electoral defeat since 1931, Labour again finds itself – somewhat to its surprise – recognized as the principal opposition party in a traditional two-party system. The press has temporarily dropped its talk of the millions disfranchised under the present electoral laws. Mr Healey and Mr Benn once again sit on the same platforms, the challenge of the constituency left has been localized, Michael Foot and Peter Tatchell have withdrawn from the fumbling engagements they were forced to fight out on the front pages of the *Sun*, and the SDP has, for the moment, lost its momentum. And perhaps most important, the Conservative government has at last obligingly begun to create issues around which the Labour Party could begin to construct a new alliance:

(1)   the entrenched racism of Home Office, police and Conservative legislators that daily afflicts two million black citizens;

(2)   the mounting costs of a Conservative approach to 'law and order', in which endemic back-street violence and petty robbery receive perfunctory investigation while the police devote ever more of their time, under the cover of helmets and riot shields, attempting to hold down spasmodic waves of anger and frustration – in large part a creation of Conservative policy itself;

(3)   the disfranchisement of millions of voters in Labour-controlled cities;

(4)   a vendetta against trade unionism culminating in a

spiteful and petty infringement of constitutional rights
in the Cheltenham affair;

(5)   the cuts in education and health;

(6)   silence and complacency about the continuing subordination of women;

(7)   the unpopularity of cruise missiles and anxiety about
Britain's 'special relationship' with Reagan's United
States;

(8)   the aimless despair of the unemployed.

Whether the Labour Party could make these issues into focal
points of a general public campaign, however, still remains
doubtful. It is difficult not to believe that there is something
rather artificial – or at least very contingent – about the
Labour recovery so far. More effective leadership and better
campaigning issues, if Labour people have the imagination to
develop them, are still likely to be inhibited and held back by
the inherited constitution of the party and the habits of mind
which have accompanied it. I will argue in this essay that the
crisis experienced by the Labour Party in the last few years
has been a structural one. Moreover, it is necessary to
remember that nothing has fundamentally changed since the
last election. If the Labour Party is to recover a position
which it has attained at various points in its history – that of
being both the party which can convincingly address major
national issues, and of being the vehicle of aspiration of the
oppressed – it can only do so by building new constituencies
for itself. But to do this it must, above all, better understand
its own history. The reason why it must understand its own
history is to avoid attempts to perpetuate or nostalgically try
to recapture it. The purpose of a better understanding of that
history is precisely to emancipate itself from its grip. Only
then could the Labour Party become the credible vehicle of
progress, change and social justice which the anti-Conservative majority in this country would like it to be.

Of course, history of a kind has not been absent from the
debate of the last few years. But the history on offer has
generally been of the 'golden age' variety and, curiously,
both right and left have been at one in the dating of that
'golden age' – the Labour governments of 1945–51.

Political memories are short. In the late 1950s and early 1960s, the predominant tone of discussion of 1945 was critical. For the right, it had identified the party too closely with obsolete 'shibboleths' like nationalization and the 'cloth cap' image; for the left, it had represented a failure to capture the 'commanding heights' of the economy and a capitulation to market forces, the civil service and the cold war – in either scenario, it had generated 'thirteen wasted years' of Tory rule. But, in the light of the failures and frustrations of the Wilson and Callaghan years, the post-war Labour government has come to be seen in increasingly benign terms. It has come to be associated with a magical moment to which all sections of the party have yearned to return: 1945 has been summoned up as much by social democrats as by Tony Benn; 1951 is the time from which everything started to go 'wrong' for Jeremy Seabrook and it is the point at which Eric Hobsbawm's 'forward march of Labour halted'. The talismanic character of that epoch has been as evident in the television drama of Trevor Griffiths, as it has been in appeals to ageing working-class voters at election times: an Islington Social Democratic election address two years ago claimed that 'a vote for Eden is a vote for trusted Labour Leaders like Clem Attlee, Hugh Gaitskell and George Brown'.

The appeal of 1945 is not primarily based upon an assessment of its policies, but rather upon a nostalgia for the social and political alliance upon which it was based. If the 1970s and 1980s have witnessed the fragmentation of Labour's alliance – between Parliamentary Labour Party (PLP) and constituency activists; between constituency activists and Labour voters; between TUC and Labour governments; and between trade union activists and ordinary workers – then 1945 represents the time when all these different elements appeared to pull in the same direction. The post-war Labour government was relatively free from fundamental clashes between government and the TUC or between PLP and conference. It was a time when individual constituency membership reached its peak, as did the Labour Party's percentage of the popular vote. It was the high tide of the 'labour movement' in all the peculiarly British connotations of that phrase, in which a 'working-class party' committed to 'socialism' gained, and for a time held, the support of the clear majority of the nation.

While there is general agreement that changes in British society since the 1950s have in some sense been responsible for the gradual disintegration of the 1945 consensus, the discussion of what kinds of changes have been responsible, and how, has tended to be crude and one-sided. Generally, both the Marxist left and the social democratic right have focused overwhelmingly upon changes in the distribution of wealth, income and power and shifts in the social structure – as if such changes have found or should have found quasi-automatic correlates in the state of British politics in general and Labour politics in particular. Such an approach first surfaced in the writings of Crosland and the social democratic revisionists of the 1950s. Crosland's revision was not so much of Marxism as of traditional Fabianism.[1] Rather than tracing a Fabian evolution from competitive capitalism to collectivism, Crosland substituted an evolution from capitalism to a mixed economy based upon equality of opportunity and the social security afforded by the welfare state. Such an argument was reinforced in the early 1960s in the writings of Goldthorpe and Lockwood in which it was suggested that Labour's traditional corporate working-class base was cracking up under the impact of affluence.[2] On the other hand, in the gloomier atmosphere of the 1970s, the assumption of a welfare state and full employment creating real classlessness and equality of opportunity became increasingly hard to sustain. Already the researches of Richard Titmuss in the 1950s had shown that it was the middle, rather than working class, who had derived disproportionate benefit from the welfare state.[3] Peter Townsend's poverty survey and the studies of Frank Field have documented the increasingly regressive trend in fiscal policy since the 1950s and have dramatized the inability or unwillingness of successive governments to reform the social security system in such a way as to remove or even significantly ameliorate the actually existing forms of poverty which have continued or even increased in the last decade.[4] There has been no 'fundamental shift in the balance of power and wealth in favour of working people and their families' since the 1940s, nor have the more modest aims of increasing equality of opportunity through institutional reform been as significant as their proponents hoped. According to the recent study of social mobility by John Goldthorpe, chances of social mobility between social groups in proportional terms have not increased, even though in numerical terms a greater proportion appeared to move because of the increase in service and non-manual occupations in the long post-war era of relatively full employment and economic growth.[5] (For further discussion of these issues, see chapter 7.)

The point of mentioning such studies is not to argue that the right was wrong and the left was right or vice versa, but rather to suggest that there is no obvious way in which the course of British politics since 1951 could be deduced from them. Changes in the social realm necessarily form a large part of the raw material out of which different political languages and practices may be forged or reforged. But such changes are not bearers of essential political meaning in themselves. They are only endowed with particular political meanings so far as they are effectively articulated through specific forms of political discourse and practice. There are no simple rules of translation from the social to the political. Relatively minor phenomena may be endowed with enormous significance, while major secular changes may be invested with no particular significance at all. Thus the 'objective' realities of class discerned by social surveys and sociological analysis do not have any unambiguous bearing upon the fate of class-oriented political parties. The nineteenth-century shift in popular politics from Chartism to Gladstonian liberalism did not occur because the country had become in some Marxist or sociological sense less class-defined. The final breakaway and popular success of the social democrats occurred, not in a bland period of social peace such as the 1950s, but amidst the din of riot sirens and the dismantling of the very social services which theorists of this tendency had originally taken to be a presupposition of the viability of their politics. Similarly, actual poverty (however defined) and the 'discovery' of poverty are two different things. Poverty has always been there to be discovered, but only in certain political and ideological contexts did its discovery become an explosive issue. Hence the impact made by Booth and Beveridge, compared with the general indifference towards the findings of Townsend.

The same criticism could be applied to Eric Hobsbawm's interesting essay, 'The Forward March of Labour Halted?'.[6] Hobsbawm, among other reasons, has ascribed Labour's crisis to a growing sectionalism in the trade union movement and the growth of public sector employment. According to his argument, this has meant that trade union struggles have increasingly taken the form of strikes against the public as consumers, rather than against private employers, and have thus divided the labour movement against itself. Although, as a description of the 1979 'winter of discontent', this portrayal undoubtedly captures something of what did happen, it is by no means clear that this is primarily to be seen as a simple reflex of the post-war growth of the state sector. Other sections of the labour movement and the general public were far worse hit by the miners' strikes of the early 1970s and yet, politically, the results were the reverse of 1979.

All this suggests that we need different ways of asking why the Labour Party has been in a mess. The whole idea of a 'forward march of Labour' is something of an optical illusion or, more specifically, part of the social democratic mythology of Labour in the 1940s: an understandable one at the time, encapsulated very well in Francis Williams' *Magnificent Journey*. It is no less ephemeral than Harold Wilson's less sympathetic canard of the 1960s – for a time earnestly debated by media academics – that Labour had become 'the natural party of government'. If we are to understand the history of the Labour Party, we must understand it in terms of a number of discontinuous conjunctures which enabled it to achieve particular and specific forms of success at rather widely separated points of time, rather than as a continuous evolutionary movement which at a certain point mysteriously went into reverse.

Historically, it appears that Labour's electoral viability as a majority party has depended upon a social alliance between the organized section of the working class and the professional middle class broadly defined. Since approximately one-third of the working class has throughout the twentieth century either voted Conservative or not voted at all, Labour has only been able to form majority governments when it could achieve alliance with sections of the population not by nature predisposed to look with any particular favour to a party too closely tied to the trade union movement. Labour has never divided the nation in any simple vertical sense. Despite the efforts and occasional successes of Labour leaders like Herbert Morrison, the Labour Party has never been able to achieve a stable alliance between the organized working class and lower middle class, except when it has also attracted significant support from social groups above them. The constituencies to which the Labour Party has wished to appeal are not very different from that of the pre-1914 progressive alliance espoused by the Liberal Party. Labour's definition of 'working people' has generally reiterated the emphases of pre-war progressivism. According to Ramsay MacDonald:

> The true separation in society is the moral and economic line of division between the producer and the non-producer, between those who possess without serving and those who serve, whereas the separation between the professional classes and labour has made the line of division a purely psychological one which is not without its reason in the different modes of life of the two classes, but which nevertheless is mischievous and ought to be obliterated.[7]

This is not to suggest, however, that the terms of the combination or its centre of gravity have remained the same. The cases of John Burns and Arthur Henderson in the period before 1918 suggest that the liberal progressive alliance could never have embodied the undeferential proletarian note sounded by Ernest Bevin in the 1940s, and the barely disguised contempt for the intellectual capacities of the working class expressed by Edwardian progressives was replaced by Gaitskell's 'humility' as the correct outward stance to be adopted by the Oxbridge-educated Labour leaders in their dealings with the TUC. Moreover, the Labour Party has managed to appeal to sections of the working class not reached by the Liberals, while conversely never securing the same success among rural workers, free trade businessmen and a rump of Whig magnates.

Looked at in these terms, it is clear that Labour between the wars never came near to forming the necessary alliance to achieve a majority. Despite the existence of the mainly middle-class Independent Labour Party, and the adhesion of otherwise politically homeless pacifists and feminists after 1918, Labour was not able to attract significant electoral support outside areas where industrial trade unionism was strong (mining, heavy industry, textiles). While Labour ousted the Liberals as the major opposition party, it did so more by driving former Liberals towards the Conservative Party than by attracting them into its own ranks. MacDonald's party may have been moderate and constitutional, but it was neither by character nor inclination effectively reformist. It only became so under trade union influence in the 1930s after the débâcle of 1931 with *Labour's Immediate Programme* of 1937. Even so, however, there was no sign of Labour's 'forward march' in the 1930s. It was the conjuncture of the war that gave it its unique opportunity to reconstitute the old progressive alliance under its own name.

If the Second World War did generate a new alliance between the organized working class and professional middle-class progressivism, this was not least because, in policy terms, the progressives were in the saddle. As Paul Addison has written of reconstruction in *The Road to 1945*, 'in every area of policy-making the main principles of advance had been defined before 1939 by non-party experts'.

What is important to stress here is not so much the character of the policies of 1945 – which are well known – as the unspoken social premises upon which the alliance was based. Dunkirk radicalized the thinking of the old service class, but only to reinforce their sense of the working class as the object of compassion or reform. Their outlook was summed up in extreme form by Beatrice Webb writing of Beveridge in 1940:

> Beveridge realises that if the war is to be won, and still more
> if the industrial state of Britain is to be saved from decay,

planned production and consumption has to be undertaken. But as of old, Beveridge is obstinately convinced that he and his class have to do the job, and the Trade Unionists have to be ignored and the wage earner ordered to work . . . he agrees that there must be a revolution in the economic structure of society; but it must be guided by persons with training and knowledge.[8]

This sort of diktat was the one thing the trade unions would not accept after the experience of 1914–18 and Bevin on their behalf protected the formal structure of free collective bargaining throughout the Second World War. But the assumption of social reform and post-war reconstruction for the welfare of, rather than by the agency, power and intelligence of, the working class remained deeply ingrained. Even the Solomon of the left socialism of the day, Harold Laski, reproduced the assumption when he wrote unguardedly of 'the pride every citizen of this country is bound to have in the amazing heroism and endurance of the common people'. Moreover, the organized working class kept its side of the bargain. Once its essential interests were secured by the preservation of free collective bargaining during the war, the reversal of the 1927 Trades Disputes Act, and the commitment to social security and full employment, it made little concerted attempt to challenge the policy of the post-war government. Keynes's reasons for his distrust of the inter-war Labour Party – 'I don't believe that the intellectual elements of the Labour Party will ever exercise adequate control' – were not vindicated.[9] Fiscal policy, American loans, the cold war, the public corporation approach to nationalization, the preservation of the existing constitution, and Britain's imperial role – all testified to a continuity of assumptions from the days of pre-1914 progressive liberal imperialism. Globally and nationally, the post-war Labour government was the last and most glorious flowering of late Victorian liberal philanthropy.

Perhaps this provides some clue to Labour's difficulties in reconstituting its social alliance from the 1950s onwards. For one thing was certain, once Britain's global role contracted and its caste-like social structure began to loosen up, that alliance could never successfully be put together again on the same terms. As was stressed at the beginning of this chapter, emphasis upon the minimal or even regressive character of the redistribution of wealth and income since 1945 misses the social changes of the period which have been more important in shaping the pattern of politics. More important than any changes in relative shares were the long years of relatively full employment and rising real wages, the gradual evaporation of Britain's independent position, and the secular decline of class consciousness both among middle and working classes.

Class consciousness in twentieth century Britain has been a conservative rather than a revolutionary phenomenon. The consciousness of the working class in the period from 1900 to 1950 – summed up more by music-hall, cinema, sport, pubs, working-men's clubs and distinctions of accent, residence and dress than by chapel, trade unionism or labour politics – was the consciousness of the separateness of a caste rather than of the hegemonic potentialities of a particular position in production.[10] Among the organized working class – apart from a revolutionary minority which formed and led the Communist Party – it was the consciousness of an estate with definite interests to defend and advance within the existing polity. Among the professional middle classes, it was the ethic of service, of intelligence and expertise in pursuit of humanitarian ends, of a civilizing mission both at home and abroad. Removed from the daily worries of domestic toil by the continuing, if diminishing, availability of servants, the progressive middle classes possessed the consciousness, both locally and nationally, of being notables, untiring in the pursuit of good causes but expecting in return a deference due to their position as experts, teachers, scientists, doctors, civil servants or preachers. The potential terms of alliance between such people and organized labour between the wars was most vividly exemplified in the teaching professions, in the relationship between tutor and class in University Extension and the Workers' Educational Association. Apart from canvassing and some educational work, the least frictional point of rapport between local professionals and working-class Labour stalwarts was to be found in the organization of treats and multifarious acts of benevolence for the benefit of the slum-land poor. Toynbee Hall has as much claim to be counted among the ancestors of the Labour Party as methodism, Taff Vale or William Morris.[11] The career of Clement Attlee exemplifies the point.

After 1951, the type of class consciousness encapsulated in the 1945 victory began to dissolve both among the working and professional classes. Most commentaries on this process have concentrated upon changes in working-class living standards and life style, but certainly of equal importance for the fate of the Labour Party was the way in which these changes impinged upon the professional wing of the alliance. To the extent that the professional classes had given their allegiance to a trade union-based party in the first half of the century, it was premissed upon a representation of trade unionism as the vehicle of the poor and the underprivileged. In many ways the attitudes of this stratum were a continuation in a more or less secularized form of Christian evangelical impulses deriving from the late nineteenth century. Seen in this light, the changes of the 1950s and 1960s were undermining. Not only was Christianity itself a fading force among the educated middle classes, but trade unions and the indigenous working class were no longer associated with the poor and underprivileged. While real differentials might not have narrowed, there was undoubtedly a narrowing in perceived styles of consumption. Much of the self-esteem of the old professional middle class stemmed from their sense of difference from the working class and of helping the labour movement from an unassailed privileged position. The perception therefore of a working class owning cars, televisions and washing machines and even being able to follow them on package holidays to the Mediterranean was corrosive of a sense of evangelical mission. In the same way, the generalization of an ethic of undifferentiated consumerism projected by advertising and oiled by hire purchase – culminating in the 1960s in a chic but socially amorphous youth culture signified by jeans and pop-music – was an incitement to a sense of injured or lost notable status. Mortgage relief and country cottages could not repair this felt

loss of position, and the expansion of higher education and
the advance of comprehensive schools made it all to vulnerable too Black Paper talk of 'declining standards'.

But by the end of the 1960s it was anyway no longer
possible to speak of the professional classes as a unitary
group. The enormous post-war expansion of the state and
service sector had produced increasing differentiation among
the professional classes themselves. The traditional professions were joined by social workers, polytechnic lecturers
and whole new grades of state and municipal employees.
Many of these new positions were occupied by women.
Divisions, partly of generational outlook, opened up both
between and within professions. Old demarcations of status
and etiquette came under attack. New forms of radicalism
appeared among students, social workers, lecturers, school
teachers and, to a lesser extent, among doctors and lawyers.
Lines of distinction between professional associations and
trade unions that had formerly been clear began to blur.
CND, the Vietnam Solidarity Campaign, ecological concerns, life style and community politics, new leftism and
diffuse forms of Marxism, the students' movement and,
most fundamentally, the women's movement, divided this
class against itself. The hierarchical distinctions of the 1940s,
still vigorous in the Indian summer of the 1950s, have not
regained their self-assurance in the aftermath of the euphoric
anti-authoritarian thrust of 1966–72. Meritocratic ambition
and vanguardist illusion commingled uneasily with democratic and egalitarian sentiment in this groundswell of opinion
and agitation. Dependence on the public sector inoculated
large sections of this constituency against Toryism, but
concerns about the costs, inefficiencies and injustices of the
public sector destroyed most of the residual idealism about
the welfare state. The difficulties of providing any clear
political profile to the preoccupations of this sector as a whole
is reflected in the editorial difficulties of the *New Statesman*
since the departure of Kingsley Martin, in the conflicts
exposed by the *Time Out* dispute, and in the schizophrenia of
The Guardian exemplified by the uneasy conjunction of Posy
Simmons and Peter Jenkins. It would be comforting to
interpret the conflict as a simple battle between left and right,

to align the hardcore SDP to the affronted dignity of the traditional professional sector, to associate Bennism with the assertive stridency of the new left. But such a dichotomy would be false. Simple sociological correlates will not work. It would be fairer to say that in so far as either Bennism or the SDP represent coherent positions, each plays in different ways upon elements of evangelism, elitism, egalitarianism and populism, both new and old, from across the whole spectrum of professional groups.

Among the organized working class, long years of a buoyant labour market – particularly in the South and the Midlands – led to a gradual erosion in the authority of the trade union leadership to speak on its behalf. Plant bargaining tended to displace national agreements, shop-steward committees became the most vital embodiment of trade union effectiveness and unofficial strikes became increasingly numerous, often challenging both traditional managerial prerogatives and the authority of trade union officials. If cohesive consciousness among the professional stratum has fragmented, the fragmentation has been even more acute among the organized working class. In the 1940s, Ernest Bevin, both as trade union leader and as member of a Labour cabinet, could talk unselfconsciously about the organized working class as 'our people'.[12] But from the 1950s onwards, the automatic equation between trade unionism, Labour voting and a cluster of labour movements, loyalties became increasingly hard to make.

Trade unionism has always been associated first and foremost with free collective bargaining, but never, until recently, only that. From the days in which trade union organization risked the threat of sacking and blacklisting and in which channels of working-class self-expression were severely limited, trade unionism had been invested with all kinds of moral and political labour-movement aspirations. However, now that the Tories of the 1950s had come to accept social security and full employment, and the vast majority of British employers had come to accept trade union channels of negotiation, the link between trade unionism and political loyalty became less compelling. While the left applauded the rise of shop stewards and unofficial strikes as signs of shop-floor emancipation from the 'bossism' of right-wing trade union leaders, they remained largely oblivious of the increasingly tenuous connection between wage militancy and working-class politics. Trade union leaders themselves accepted with more or less good grace the decentralization of trade union power as a means of adapting the structure of unionism to the novel possibilities of the labour market. Moreover, trade unionism became increasingly generalized as the appropriate form of bargaining for every type of employee group, if they were to maintain their relative position in a ladder of wages and salaries. In an increasingly inflationary situation, those who held back, and those too weak to organize, lost out. In the process, the distinctively proletarian connotations of trade unionism, and its cultural penumbra, receded and public representation of the trade unions shifted from that of a potential class threat to that of a powerful sectional set of vested interests.

Trade unionists found it increasingly difficult to talk with any conviction on behalf of the politics of their members – a problem, it emerged in the 1970s, not just of general secretaries, but of shop stewards as well. Only in defence of the lowest common denominator of trade union politics – the defence of free collective bargaining on behalf of those already organized – could trade unions count on mass support, whether against *In Place of Strife* or Heath's *Industrial Relations Act*. But this was an issue which divided state administration and the leadership of all three political parties from trade unionists, rather than a divide between workers and capitalists, Labour and Conservative. On an issue raising trade union questions of a more fundamental labour movement and class type – the struggle to gain recognition at Grunwick's – trade union support was uneven and the trade union movement went down to an ominous defeat. Already, in the Common Market referendum, it was clear that the majority trade union position was not accepted by large sectors of the membership. It was only a matter of time before Tories – and most notably Thatcher – began to appeal with some success to trade union members over the heads of their representatives, and employers attempted directly to address the shop-floor in defiance of agreed negotiating procedures and shop-steward mediation. Finally, the archaism of official trade union fictions about the views of their members were cruelly and irrevocably exposed in the half-hearted consultation procedure employed by the TGWU in the deputy leadership battle. Whatever validity the trade union bloc vote had once possessed, it had now disappeared with the public admission of the cumulative detachment of trade union membership from class consciousness and Labour loyalty – an equation which the pre-war Labour Party could regard with some justification as axiomatic.

It is not right, however, to view this disintegration in purely negative terms any more than some might bemoan the passing of an old professional ethic. What the changes of the 1950s and 1960s suggested was that the working class as a whole had become far more permeable to practices and ideas from outside its own political and cultural inheritance; and among younger thinking workers, this meant they could often become more readily engaged in politics in other than their purely trade unionist or labour-movement personae. The fairly rigid demarcations between the political and industrial sides of the Labour Party were already beginning to break down in the early 1950s, when the Bevanites began to appeal to a rank and file left within the trade union section against the policies of right-wing trade union leadership. The lines crossed more seriously when Gaitskell attempted to revise clause four and the trade unions took their revenge with a brief espousal of unilateralism.

More significant were the types of popular politics and cultural movements which grew up wholly outside the constitutional and bureaucratic procedures of the pre-existing labour movement. CND, Anti-Apartheid, Vietnam Solidarity, diffuse forms of libertarianism and pop-culture and, finally, the women's movement were not confined in their impact to the youth of the professional classes; they attracted significant elements of proletarian support as well. Radical students were not altogether wrong in believing that their activities might have an exemplary effect on other sectors of society. The actions on the Upper Clyde and the wave of factory occupations in the early 1970s possessed no precedent in trade union rule-books. The growth of single-issue campaigns was yet another indication of the non-coincidence of class ascription and political engagement. Of course, this situation has given new opportunities to the right as well as to the left. But there is nothing predetermined in the form through which such changes have found and will find political expression. The phenomenon of punk music, with its spectrum of political positions from extreme left to extreme right, exemplifies the politically protean character of the young working-class movement of the present.

Finally, it is quite wrong to treat developments within either the professional or working classes over the past three decades in abstraction from the politics of the Labour Party itself. Neither politics in general nor the Labour Party in particular can be regarded as a passive victim of social change. Social alliances do not simply happen, they are brought into being and re-created by the construction and periodic reconstruction of a common political discourse. The alliance constructed between the professional classes and the organized working class of the 1940s, as I have argued, was of a type which could not be rebuilt on the same terms. It was the revisionist right of the 1950s who first discerned this situation, but only understood it in narrowly economistic terms. Although they called rightly for a greater emphasis upon democracy and equality, their conception of these demands was narrowly hemmed in by their acceptance of the managerial ethos of the welfare state and the public corporation and their allegiance to the cold-war priorities of American foreign policy. The left could point to the cultural poverty of this vision and its State Department deference, but provided little in the way of a positive domestic counter-strategy. In the 1960s and 1970s, its intellectual and political energies were focused increasingly upon the progress of anti-imperialist movements abroad, while 'Labourism' was left to fester at home.

In the meantime, however, one last effort had been made by the Labour leadership to renegotiate the terms of the social alliance upon which Labour's viability as a majority party was based. Wilson, with his Panglossian talk of an arrest to industrial decline and a new society which would emerge from the 'white heat of technology' and the sweeping of dead wood from the board-rooms, did momentarily capture the imagination of the contending constituencies upon which the Labour Party was based, and in 1964 managed to poll 44 per cent of the popular vote. Unfortunately, however, it was only talk. The contradictions of this strategy, with its utter acceptance of existing economic power relations, both national and international, which it imagined could be transformed by paper-planning and rhetoric rather than controls, and not least its increasingly blatant political and moral vacuity, rendered the whole fragile concoction vulnerable to the first slight buffeting. Thereafter, there was a political vacuum in the leadership of the Labour Party, and the different social constituencies upon which it was based were left to go their separate ways, bereft now even of the residual political integrity that the party had retained until Wilson.

In the PLP the increasingly predominant professional strata, whose guiding philosophy was now technocratic rather than moral (even in the revisionist sense of Crosland), attacked the trade union side in the name of a productivism devoid of any larger political purpose. This move was stymied at the end of the 1960s by old-style operators of Labour's political machine in the name of a pragmatism equally devoid of any longer-term programme. From this impasse, the Labour Party has never recovered. In 1974, it was the trade union statesmanship of Jack Jones rather than any new initiative from the political leadership which provided what strategy there was. The breakdown of this 'social contract' from the time of the IMF loan and its predictable outcome in 'a winter of discontent' severed what remained of the residual attachments among large sections of middle and working classes alike, and the scene was set for Thatcher, Bennism and the SDP.

In what way a socialist politics could reconstruct an alliance between the working and professional classes, and whether the Labour Party could again be the medium of such an alliance, are questions to which it would be foolish to attempt a confident answer in the present situation. But one formal conclusion at least suggests itself in the light of the preceding analysis. This is that the Labour Party will never be able to make a credible appeal to either of its former constituencies unless it attempts to ally them in a new way by taking account of the profound changes wrought by the welfare state, the mixed economy and national decline, both upon the forms of consciousness and the relative material situation of each.

At the beginning of the twentieth century, when trade unions first formed a political party, whatever 'social security' was available to the working class outside the Poor Law, narrowly depended upon the strength of their collective organizations. Even after the social reforms inaugurated by the Liberal government of 1906, trade union institutional bargaining power and its capacity for political mobilization and the channelling of political allegiance remained crucial. If money wages did not simply fall in line with prices in the inter-war years, and if the unemployed, however miserable their dole payments, were not simply condemned to the workhouse, this was primarily because trade unions in conditions of manhood suffrage represented an irremovable obstacle to the revanchist schemes of Conservative politicians, bankers and employers. It was, therefore, not surprising that consciousness among workers grew naturally out of, and was strongly defined and limited by, trade union membership. The union was a lifeline, both locally and nationally, against employers and the state; and out of the necessary solidarity which trade unions entailed grew many of the larger loyalties and values which held the labour movement together.

The advent of the welfare state, the acceptance of the normality of trade union bargaining, and concomitant changes in the pattern of employment gradually and unevenly transformed this situation. A gulf opened up between trade unionism and the crusade against poverty, for poverty was now either of a wageless type which had to be fought at the level of the state or of a low-wage type effectively beyond the purview of the ordinary bargaining process. Or, to put it less politely, poverty, which remained extensive, was mainly the lot of ethnic minorities and single-parent families (i.e. women) and was thus not an overriding priority for a party whose appeal was pitched to white male organized workers. But even among indigenous workers of this type, the wage packet now formed only part of the social wage and the male wage only a diminishing part of the organized worker's family income. Consciousness no longer derived overwhelmingly from union involvement. If anything, the reverse was becoming true. Political consciousness, generally derived from other sources, could take the form of union militancy. It was not so much that trade union experience bred militancy, but rather that new forms of social and political discontent, not shaped primarily in the workplace, found a form of expression – and often a cramped form – through trade unions. In this sense, the precipitants of political activism among workers were not so different from those present among broad sectors of the professional classes, no longer so conscious of their gentility and no longer so averse to expressing their occupational grievances through trade unions.

In the face of these changes, the preservation of the pre-existing constitutional structure of the Labour Party – with its primary representation of working-class interests by indirect trade union means – has maintained an ever more inappropriate demarcation between its two principal constituencies and has stifled the emergence of forms of politics which could draw in new ones. If the Labour Party is ever to reverse its present involution, it will have to rethink the social alliances upon which it could be based in terms of what they now potentially share in common.

At the moment, the emergence of new and potentially unifying strategies is still thwarted by an enduring major premiss of Labour Party thinking: the perception of one part of its constituency as a homogeneous proletarian estate whose sectional political interest is encompassed by trade unions, and of the other part as a heteroclite aggregate of idealists, notables or entrists to be humoured, promoted or circumvented. This ingrained assumption has survived intact through all the recent constitutional reforms and continues to inform both right and left, whether justified in the language of tired pragmatism, liberal progressivism or mechanical Marxism. It is this premiss, still embodied in the structure and constitution of the Labour Party, which has inhibited a believable appeal to today's real poor or oppressed (blacks, women, the unemployed), has produced unreal and unworkable solutions to Britain's economic plight, and deflected to the sidelines what should be a central socialist debate about the distribution of non-material goods (knowledge, democratic control, environment, quality of life) of interest to all its potential constituencies. Unfortunately, it is not possible to discuss these substantive issues here. All that can be suggested as a formal precondition to such a discussion is that in the present grim situation of the country, Labour will not be able to construct a socialist politics that addresses this situation as long as its inherited thinking and practices continue to be deformed by the largely unquestioned acceptance of an anachronistic and now disastrous social distinction between mental and manual labour.

NOTES

[1] C.A.R. Crosland, *The Future of Socialism* (1956).
[2] J. Goldthorpe and D. Lockwood, 'Affluence and the British Class Structure', *Sociological Review* (1963), and *The Affluent Worker in the Class Structure* (1969).
[3] R. Titmuss, *Essays on 'The Welfare State'* (1958), and *Income Distribution and Social Change* (1962).
[4] F. Field, *Low Pay* (1973); P. Townsend, *Poverty in the United Kingdom* (1979).
[5] J. Goldthorpe, *Social Mobility and Class Structure in Modern Britain* (1980).
[6] E. J. Hobsbawm et al, *The Forward March of Labour Halted?* (1981).
[7] Cited in R. Lyman, *The First Labour Government 1924* (1958); and see also on this period, R. McKibbin, *The Evolution of the Labour Party 1910–1924* (1974).
[8] Cited in P. Addision, *The Road to 1945* (1977), and see also J. Harris, *William Beveridge, a Biography* (1977).
[9] For this strand of liberal progressivist thinking, see, in particular, P. Clarke, *Liberals and Social Democrats* (1981).
[10] For an analysis of the genesis of this type of working-class culture see G. Stedman Jones, *Languages of Class* (1984) ch. 4.
[11] For a depiction of the mid-Victorian pre-history of this middle-class evangelism, see G. Stedman Jones, *Outcast London*, 2nd edn, (1984); and for the way in which it defined the ethos of adult education, see Sheila Rowbotham, 'Travellers in a Strange Country', *History Workshop Journal*, 12 (1981).
[12] On Bevin, see A. Bullock, *The Life and Times of Ernest Bevin*, 2 vols. (1960, 1967).

2

The Crisis of Labourism

STUART HALL

There are worrying signs that the Labour movement is simply not willing to grasp, or is incapable of grasping, the seriousness of the position into which it has fallen. Crises are not reversed simply by thinking about them. But to recognize that they exist – and to try to analyse why they are occurring – is the first, essential requirement for overcoming them. Simply to deny their existence is to exhibit the political nous of the ostrich.

In place of the radical re-appraisal which this seems to require, however, what one hears is the troubling noise of a great deal of whistling in the dark: the solid affirmation, against all the evidence, that 'we can still win', 'things will turn our way', 'unemployment will deliver the vote to us in the end' or, at best, 'we are going through a difficult patch, but Labour is going to form the next government'. As Gramsci once observed, you must turn your face violently towards things as they really are. The reality for Labour is that it is only just holding its own in popularity with the electorate, in circumstances which ought to be favourable. More seriously, it does not seem capable of forming a credible alternative or making a decisive political impact on the electorate. And without a major revival, there can be no realistic possibility of another Labour government this decade, let alone of socialism this century.

'Things' are not automatically turning Labour's way. The short-term electoral indicators point the other way – in a situation of extreme political volatility. The two-party electoral mould has been shaken by the 'unthinkable' Labour/SDP split; and the party's morale has clearly been deeply affected by it. These short-term reversals only compound the long-term political and ideological trends which have now been moving steadily against Labour for some years, as shown in the erosion of its popular base and solid class character, especially since the mid-1970s.

Many people will say this is gross exaggeration, founded on an inexcusable pessimism. With scandals and banana skins liberally strewn everywhere, surely the Tory magic is at last dispersing? The authoritarian face of Mrs Thatcher, now more or less permanently on view, lacks a great deal of its former immediate populist appeal. Postponing elections, taking away basic civil rights, demolishing councils because you do not like their political complexion is not the most obvious route to sustained popularity in a democracy. For a time Mrs Thatcher and her government seemed virtually error-proof, swimming with every tide. If the tides have not turned, have they not, at least, manifestly ebbed?

On the Labour side, there has been a partial upturn in the opinion polls. Some of the splits and divisions have been healed. The left in the constituency parties is both more vigorous and in much better heart. The Benn victory at Chesterfield was a welcome bonus. There is a new, younger, more vigorous leadership, with a positively boyish, enthusiastic new face at the helm. If one listens hard, one can almost hear the ranks of Labour closing – not always a pretty sound in the labour movement. Is the crisis over, then? Perhaps it never existed. Is Labour poised for political revival? Is it ready to run the country? Is it once more *the* alternative party of government? Does it show evidence of once more becoming a popular political force?

These are dubious propositions. First, despite the revival, Labour is still a very long way behind. To win a majority it would have to capture every seat where it lay second in the 1983 election: a formidable challenge. The SDP may not be the threat it was, but the split in the anti-Thatcher forces is exceedingly damaging structurally and wears a look of permanence. It is a situation designed to provide a structural bloc against movement to the left – which is why Dr Owen (who has gravitated so far rightward he has virtually disappeared over the western horizon altogether, powered by an insatiable political envy) takes such fiendish delight in it.

And 1988 is a long time away in British politics. Meanwhile the Thatcherites, by their sheer bloody-minded determination to press on, will continue to set the terms, define the parameters, establish the benchmark of 'political reality'.

Then there is the new leadership. It wears a more attractive face but it is still untested. So far, it lacks political weight and authority. And it shows little sign as yet of becoming a popular political force, as opposed to a (not very successful) electoral machine. Apart from the issue of the health service, the leadership has shown little understanding of the need to confront the real basis of Thatcher populism in the country at large. Its perspective is still narrowly confined to the terrain of the labour movement and the daily accommodations of policy which its contradictory structure require.

More significantly, the new Labour leadership still lacks a really sound grasp of the parameters of Labour's crisis or the ascendancy of Thatcherism, which should be rooted in a searching analysis of Labour's own record over the past two decades. Neil Kinnock is solidly in touch with the well-springs of Labourist culture – and that is important. But he has no feel for the language and concerns of the new social movements – and that is dangerous. He has embraced Eric Hobsbawm's analysis (as set out in 'Labour's Lost Millions', *Marxism Today*, October 1983), give or take the ambiguities about alliances with the Alliance. But he does not understand the politics of putting together a new social alliance – a new historical bloc of forces, which is Hobsbawm's real point.

These aspects constitute important enough problems of strategy and development for Labour. But, essentially, the problem has not gone away because it did not in the first place consist of a temporary loss of electoral popularity. That was symptom, not cause. What is at issue is the disintegration of the historic social democratic programme of Labour, pursued in and out of government since the war. What has 'turned' is that underlying consensus in the political culture around the historic compromise struck in the post-war years, which has underpinned British politics and which gave Labour its legitimate claims of office as the alternative party of government. Gone are the conditions which enabled Labour governments in office to convince the electorate that they could keep the capitalist economy alive *and* pay off there social and industrial constituencies: Labour's historic compromise with labour. It cannot be done in times of economic recession. What 'went' was the solidity of the political formations around that compromise – Labourism as a particular constellation of social forces. We may or may not agree on how far that social basis for Labourist politics has eroded, or what new constituencies there are for radical political change. But there cannot be serious argument about the scale of the problem. It is not simply attributable to the misplaced pessimism of a few free-floating intellectuals.

The complacent view of Labour's crisis is held in place by the consoling illusion that it all happened with the Falklands and, therefore, that 1983 was the backwash of a brief but passing phase. This view is historically incorrect and hence politically misleading. Strategically, the election of 1979 was a more significant turning point than 1983, though the scale of the disaster was less manifest. 1979, in turn, was the product of a major reversal culminating in the middle of the Callaghan government – the 1975–9 period. *Those* were the years when the basis of post-war reformism was destroyed. There, the first turn into monetarism occurred – led by Labour, not by the Tories. It was then that the oil hike exposed the vulnerability of the British economy. By that time trade union unpopularity was far advanced – and nowhere was it so unpopular as inside the Labour Cabinet. That was where the savaging of public expenditure began. Those were the conditions in which the re-education of the Labour leadership in the 'new realism' of managing a capitalist crisis was completed.

They were also the circumstances in which Mrs Thatcher emerged – to capitalize on the crisis, put her finger on the experiences of the people and disperse Labour's exhausted programme to the four corners of the political wilderness. Against that backcloth, she engineered the fatal coupling of the anti-Labourist, anti-statist, anti-equality, anti-welfare spirit with the revitalized gospel of the free market. Thus the qualitatively new and unstable combination of 'Thatcherism' – organic national patriotism, religion of the free market, competitive individualism in economic matters, authoritarian state in social and political affairs – began to cohere as an alternative social philosophy. It was then that the seepage of Labour's popular support quickened into a torrent. In its wider sense the crisis is not of Mrs Thatcher's making alone. Historically, Labour is deeply implicated in it.

Take the question of politics and class. The left is convinced that too much 'analysis' will lead to the growth of a post-class politics in which Labour abandons its historic mission to represent the working class. But no one can pretend that the British class structure still mirrors the portrait drawn by Engels in 1844 or that, then and now, the relationships between class, party and political representation have ever been simple or one-way. The relevance of the class issue to British politics does not require us to say that class formations do not change, since palpably they do. And when they do, the strategies and dynamics of class politics will also shift, leaving those organizations transfixed in earlier structures to one side like beached whales. After all, such shifts have occurred before within the history of British capitalism. Labour, 'Labourism' as we know it and modern trade unionism are all the product precisely of one such shift in the 1880–1920 period. We may again be at a similar watershed.

No one, looking around Britain today, would deny the pertinence of class relations. (Beatrix Campbell's recent book, *Wigan Pier Revisited*, offers a remarkable analysis of the newly emerging contours of class, poverty and gender in modern Britain today.) No one seriously concerned to analyse the nature of present class formations could fail to recognize the changing class composition of our society: the decline of certain traditional sectors and the growth of new sectors; the shift in patterns of skill; radical recomposition as a result of the new gender and ethnic character of labour; the new divisions of labour resulting from changing technologies, and so on. Likewise, no one would deny the enormous variety of class circumstances and experiences, the internal divisions and sectionalisms and the differential cultures which contemporary British society exhibits; the emergence of new social forces leading to what Marx once called 'the production of new needs'. But nor can we afford to ignore the many pressures and forces emerging from contradictions in social life which are, like everything in Britain, inscribed within class but do not have a simple class *vs*. class origin.

This range of political questions are issues which touch us as social consumers rather than as producers, more pertinent to domestic life, the neighbourhood or locality than the 'point of production'. Democratic questions which affect us as citizens rather than class subjects, issues of personal and sexual politics which influence the structures of our everyday life now constitute the *social politics* of our era. They are backed by strong constituencies and movements in which, of course, working people have a stake but they do not necessarily move according to the tempo of the industrial class struggle. The articulation of these arenas of struggle with the changing rhythm of traditional class politics is the political challenge confronting Labour and the labour movement today. What an increasing majority of people feel is not that all these lines converge naturally in and around Labour but – quite the reverse – that there is now the most massive disjuncture between where the real movements, issues and subjects of politics are and the ways in which they are traditionally represented in the political market-place.

There is not – and never has been – *the* given unity of *the* working class in Britain, which Labour could simply 'reflect' in its programmes. There have only been the divisions and fracturings we would expect under an advanced capitalist division of labour. Underlying these are certain shared conditions of exploitation which provide the contradictory raw materials from which the complex unity of a class could possibly be constructed; and out of which a socialist politics *could* be forged. How else are we to unite the very different needs, demands and ideas within the class and constitute those necessary bridges and alliances with other sectors which are currently essential to any popular political ascendancy? Where, for example, would a socialist strategy be without having, at its centre, the needs and demands of the many disadvantaged groups and communities at the receiving end of the Thatcher recession? Yet Labour can neither win elections nor lead the country into the next decade as the party of disadvantaged minorities alone. They have to become part of a wider popular strategy.

Now, what is the common political programme which resonates with both these experiences and outlines a political strategy capable of uniting them within a programme for socialism? Could we develop such a programme on the basis of the current division between waged and unwaged? Or without addressing the contradiction between the defence of the working conditions of the employed and the need of the unemployed for jobs? Could we retain the leap-frogging between high and low-paid workers on which the whole economistic trade union strategy of the 1960s and 1970s depended, or attempt to construct a political alliance between the two extremes without disturbing the divisions between black and white or men and women?

People sometimes speak as if all we have to do to construct a new social alliance is to add up the demands of everybody who happens to be in the room at the time. The fact is that because of the variety of social experiences and the uneven consequences of a capitalist recession, these different needs and demands are often genuinely contradictory. They have to be subsumed and 'reconciled' within some larger programme, which only a party aiming to become a mass political force is capable of putting together. They also have to retain their integrity within that programme, if the alliance is to be anything more serious than a marriage of electoral convenience. These are the strategic political questions which lie behind Labour's so-called 'recovery'. They require a strategy of renewal, a fundamental and permanent recasting which is certainly not yet on the labour movement's agenda.

Unemployment is another key issue. The problem here is that very few people put much faith in Labour's capacity to reverse the trend. On this, as on so many other questions, Mrs Thatcher so far continues to win the battle for hearts and minds; and those who command the definitions command the credibility. A deep fatalism has, therefore, settled over the country in this respect, which is part of the fashionable adductation to the Thatcherite world view that goes under the name of the 'new realism'. The new realism is really a capitulation to the belief that, after all, market forces *are* economic reality and there is no point arguing with or seeking to modify or influence the laws of supply and demand. Unemployment is, therefore, the responsibility of world trends, outside our capacity to influence. The problem is that this ideologically motivated 'explanation' contains a tiny, rational core. Some part of unemployment is indeed the consequence of a deep, capitalist world recession. Some of it is also structural; located in the endemic structural weakness of the British economy and in the restructuring of our economic base which is progressing – unevenly, as it always does under capitalism – at a very rapid rate under conditions of recession.

Of course, something can be done to reverse the trend of mass unemployment and deindustrialization. But, to be convincing, the short-term measures have to be credible and concrete, and the long-term strategy has frankly to acknowledge and address the structural problems. Labour has so far done neither convincingly. 'Jobs' and 'more welfare' are the pious hopes to which the so-called 'Alternative Economic Strategy' was reduced before it altogether disappeared – a paper tiger. In the long term – while microchips eat people's jobs, word processors themselves show secretaries the way to the local dole office and miners are forced to base their claims to a decent life on the strategy of mining pits until the sea begins to seep through the pit floor – Labour has nothing strategic to say about the strategy for economic revival.

In this climate of fatalism, a trace of the old recividism appears: 'what we need are more jobs but those can only be provided if industry becomes more competitive and more profitable. Therefore, do not rock the boat.' Of course, as long as capitalist imperatives prevail, there is a sort of logic in saying that more jobs will depend on the revival of capitalist industry. That is the logic in which reformism is always caught. In fact, of course, there is no historical evidence for the belief that recession produces an automatic turn to the left. Fascism has emerged as often out of such circumstances as socialism. Neither is inevitable. The outcome depends ultimately on how the struggle is conducted.

The problem about expecting unemployment to serve as an electoral conveyor belt is that Labour's alternatives run headlong into the brick wall of an ideological campaign which Thatcherism has already largely won. This has successfully imprisoned common-sense thinking about the economy on the horns of the following dilemma: the only way to reduce unemployment is to increase public spending, but this will inevitably lead to inflation. We are trapped between the millstones of dislike of unemployment and fear of inflation. Thatcherism has effectively encapsulated all the economic alternatives within the terms of this brutal 'either/or'. It is part of a wider strategy, which it has also conducted with masterly effect. It has two prongs.

The first point in the 'new realism' consists of convincing people that the nation has been living beyond its means, paying itself too much, expecting perks and benefits it can't afford, and indulging in all that consumption, permissive-ness, and pleasure. Very un-British! Realities must be faced! Expectations are out of control and must be lowered. In that campaign, British masochism is a powerful ally. When the economy is not being represented in terms of the household budget ('you can't buy more at the shops this week than you have in the kitty'), then it is likened to the British weather. One good summer has to be paid for, in psychic currency, by at least five winters of discontent.

The second prong of the strategy is to disconnect, in the popular mind, the word 'public' from its association with anything that is good or positive, and to harness it instead to a chain of negative associations which automatically connect it with everything that is nasty, brutish, squalid and bureaucratic – and to exalt, in its place, the private market as the sole criterion of The Good Life.

This has been the strategic ideological project of the new right. It consists, first, of the struggle to disorganize the left; to interrupt the social-democratic consensus which has dominated and defined the political settlement between left and right since the war. Second, it aims to command popular conceptions of what is 'good for the country'. And third, it seeks to reverse every sign and signal pointing towards leftish or social-democratic solutions and move them in the oppo-site direction.

In 1945, it seemed that the only way to get less well-off people decent health care was to break the circuit of money and market in health and establish a public form of provision. In 1983, the aim is to make it seem inevitable that the only decent health service people can get is that which they pay for themselves. This is much more than eroding the welfare state – a thing not wholly unknown to Labour governments. It is also, as the Social Affairs Unit (the 'think tank') pamphlet put it, 'breaking the spell of the welfare state' – dismantling it ideologically as a constant reference point, an inevitable fact of the political scene that is taken for granted. The historical project of Thatcherism is to reconstruct and redefine the political terrain, to alter the balance of political forces and to create a new kind of popular common sense, in which the market, the private, possessive, competitive 'man' (*sic*) are the only ways to measure the future.

'Hard-headed' Labour politicians dismiss all this as ideological window–dressing (and ideology is not serious politics), or as mere manipulation ('the Tories don't really believe it'). But the light that shines in Mr Tebbit's eye – or the one that has gone askew in Sir Keith's – is the light of the salvationist, the 'born again'. They regard the catechism of capitalism, so tarnished and discredited among the young in the 1960s and 1970s, as the Sermon On The Mount. It is a creed to live by, to bring up children by; a faith which will move capitalist mountains; the salvation of the civilized world – the 'Free West'. For such things, Mr Heseltine is willing to commit nuclear suicide. Mrs Thatcher clearly commands the gift of translating this vision into the home-spun idioms of daily life. She has the populist touch. But the stake in the struggle remains the popular will. Why is Labour, then, politically illiterate about it?

One explanation is that Labour understands perfectly well, but is incapable of organizing, a popular political and ideological struggle of this kind. It can mobilize the vote, provided it remains habitually solid. But it shows less and less capacity to connect with popular feelings and sentiments, let alone transform them or articulate them to the left. It gives the distinct impression of a political party living on the capital of past connections and imageries, but increasingly out of touch with what is going on in everyday life around it.

A second reason is that it has always been deeply suspicious of the self-activation of the working class. It is often the actual base for, but not the organizing centre of, local or national campaigns. It has become an electoral rather than a political machine. Extra-parliamentary activity – politics and campaigning in any political space other than that directed to the House of Commons or within the confines of the formal electoral system – produces in its leadership the deepest traumas and the most sycophantic poems of praise for parliamentarism. Yet it is precisely the confinement within the parliamentary mould and Labour's containment within a formal definition of the 'political' which has been its undoing.

Does not possess the material means.

A further explanation is that it does not possess the material means with which to wage this kind of popular political/ideological struggle. Of course, it has to operate in the public terrain where the media are either entirely colonized by the populist right – like the popular press – or so solidly grounded in right-wing, neo-liberal assumptions that to start a conversation on radio or an interview on television from any other baseline is literally unthinkable these days.

But, even within the media as they currently exist, Labour commands no intellectual presence. It has never acquired a proper legitimacy. And that is partly because – apart from the handful of experts who advise its committees on policy matters – it has not organized a core of 'organic intellectuals'. Labour, then, still looks like a party which has never heard of the strategy of a 'war of position' – that is, struggling for leadership and mastery over a whole number of different fronts in the course of making itself the focal point of popular aspirations, the leading popular political force.

Focal point of popular aspiration

An even more worrying possibility is that Labour does not believe such a struggle to be necessary because it does not take mass political-ideological struggle seriously. Anti-Marxist as it is in its political culture, Labourism is profoundly 'economistic' in outlook and ideology. It really does suppose that economic facts transmit themselves directly into working-class heads, without passing through the real world. Working-class consciousness is as automatic as self-

programming underground trains: once Labour, always
Labour. And yet the clear signs are that political automatism
is certainly at an end – if ever it existed.

Automatism was grounded on the assumption that
Labour's political support is rooted in the material circumstances of the class Labour claims to represent: 'the culture of
the working class is the culture of Labour'. But is it, in that
obvious, immediate sense? The consequences of uneven
economic restructuring, long-term economic change and
short-term deindustrialization are bearing down directly on
these traditional Labour communities, whether occupational
ones like mining, or ecological ones like Bermondsey. The
heartland of the Labour vote, the backbone of its traditional
support, the traditionalist roots of its loyalists have been
profoundly disaggregated. The traditional vanguard sectors
are also increasingly a dwindling proportion of the modern
working class, though not for that reason insignificant or less
important. The pattern of support in urban areas, where
Labour has traditionally amassed giant majorities, is changing both in scale and political character. Unemployment is
savaging the given structure of skills; technical developments
are fragmenting occupational communities. The age, gender
and ethnic structure of Labour's potential social support in
the country is changing rapidly and profoundly and, so far
we can see, permanently.

Changes of these kinds fragment the class culture of the
party as a political formation. They give rise to new
constituencies, new demands. They generate new tensions,
demand new forms of organization, changing the social
infrastructure of Labour politics. One has only to think of the
profound shift in the character of industrial conflict from the
private to the public sector, and add to that the social
composition and character of social strata which, from this
point of view, have represented the vanguard of the class in
action against Thatcherism, to catch a glimpse of how out of
date is the typical Labour view of the connections between
party and class.

Far from guaranteeing Labour's inevitable return to popular ascendancy, the inevitability of Labourism – its auto-

matism – is now Labour's most serious blockage to establishing a hegemony in these conditions.

What is at stake is no more and no less than 'the people'; the popular will. Stuck at the end of a strategy of 'social democracy from above' for so long, 'the people' are taking a terrible revenge on Labour. Decades of blocked votes, things sewn up in back rooms, deals done in compositing meetings, localities where Labour mafias have ruled the roost like small-time Borgias, a view of politics which depends on mobilizing the respectability rather than the radicalism of the working class (and in the actual contradictory nature of class consciousness both exist, to be mobilized by different political forces), the engineering or hydraulic view of electoral politics – these have become deeply ingrained in the culture of Labourism. But the times are changing.

As a consequence, some Labour voters are nodding at the canvassers when the knock on the door comes – but slipping, sliding, eroding, drifting into uncharted paths as soon as they go away, and they meet and talk in the pub, on the job, in families, with mates, hanging out the washing, calculating the pennies and the kids' chances in a micro-chip world of permanent unemployment. Are they really recidivist Tories at heart? No. Are they Labour's automatic electoral fodder? It would be unwise for Labour to bank on it.

Can they be won to a vision, not simply a programme, of the future? Here there is something to learn from Thatcherism, after all. Paradoxically, she does raise hearts and minds an inch or two because, vile, corrupt, awful as her vision of the future is, we *know* what it is. We can imagine what life according to the gospel of free enterprise, patriarchal respectability and authoritarian order would be like. We know how we would be expected to bring up our children, make them manage their pocket money; how women should live; who should have babies and under what circumstances; how teachers in our classrooms should dress and what lessons are to be read in the religious education hour – as well as what the Public Sector Borrowing Requirement should be. It is an 'alternative future'. It is a philosophy of life.

The one thing nobody knows is what Labour conceives to

No image of future

be an 'alternative way of life'. It currently possesses no image of the future. It provides no picture of life under socialism. It has failed so far to construct an alternative 'philosophy' of socialism for modern times. In its profound empiricism, it has mistaken adaptation to the present as progress towards the future. In fact, realistically, Labour can never adapt enough to become the 'natural inheritor' of capitalism. It has no alternative but to renew itself and its vision or to go out of business. Whether it is capable of that renewal or not remains an open question now – which is why the 'crisis of labourism' is not quite so exaggerated as it may at first have seemed.

Part 2
The Price of Failure

3

Bitter Harvest

DAVID EDGAR

It was Enoch Powell who first sowed the seeds whose harvest Margaret Thatcher reaped last Thursday. What is now called Thatcherism was originally known as Powellism: bitter-tasting market economics sweetened and rendered palatable to the popular taste by great creamy dollops of nationalistic custard. In his case immigration control was the custard and it was a bit too rich for any but the strongest digestions. She was lucky to have the Falklands campaign handed to her on a plate, which did the same job much more effectively, turning far fewer stomachs.

But the original formula was Enoch's and to his great voice should credit go for shattering the Butskellite glacis, the dissolution of which led to the avalanche.

Peregrine Worsthorne, *Sunday Telegraph*, 12 June 1983

Worsthorne is right, and in a number of ways. He is right to note that Thatcherism is a twin-headed beast, and to recognize on one side the cold and calculating face of economic logic, and on the other the equally harsh but more emotive face of nationalism and social authority. He is also right to imply that there is a potential contradiction between the two sides of the coin – Thatcherism's desire to roll back the state in the economic field, and its policies (or at least its rhetoric) on the social questions of policing, education, censorship, defence and immigration.

And he is right, further, to see the nationalism unleashed by the Falklands war as an externalized form of what Stuart Hall has called 'authoritarian populism', and to acknowledge that zapping the enemy without on the beach-heads of the South Atlantic was an effective and timely corollary to confronting the 'enemy within' on the streets of London, Toxteth and Moss Side.

Finally, he is right to locate the roots of Thatcherism in the late 1960s, and in the pressure groups on the conservative right thrown up by Enoch Powell's decisive challenge to the post-war social-democratic consensus. The meteorologists of the quality press have spent much time analysing the relative moisture of the so-called wets and dries on economic questions: they have devoted less time to divining the actual and/or potential divisions on the Tory right itself, between the hard-line economic liberals on the one hand, and the social authoritarians on the other. And he is correct to hint that, in that final conflict, it is the authoritarians who will win.

Pressure groups of the right

Although the post-war debate between economic liberalism and social authoritarianism within the conservative movement was never as pronounced in Britain as it was, say, in the United States, the pressure groups of the conservative right have always fallen, quite distinctly, on one side of the line or the other.

On the one hand, there are economic-liberal groups like Aims of Industry (founded in 1942), the Institute of Economic Affairs (1957) and Sir Keith Joseph's Centre for Policy Studies (1974), which have, by and large, conducted their free-market propaganda through learned papers, pamphlets, seminars and occasionally newspaper advertisements. On the other hand, there have been 'social issue' groups which have tended to concentrate on a more populist campaigning approach. Such groups have included anti-sexual organizations like Mrs Mary Whitehouse's Viewers and Listeners Association, the Society for the Protection of the Unborn Child and the Festival of Light; educational campaigns arising out of the Black Paper critique of progressive schooling and university expansion; and nationalist groups like the self-explanatory League of Empire Loyalists and the Monday Club.

The Monday Club is perhaps the paradigm of the social groups. Set up in 1960 in mourning for the African Empire – Harold Macmillan's famous 'wind of change' speech on African decolonization was delivered on a Monday – the Club has always pursued its aims through fairly lurid periodicals, backed up with public meetings, rallies and demonstrations. It is also typical in that it combined conventionally right perspectives on social questions with a deep suspicion of free-market economics: its journal, *Monday World*, once called for worker participation in running industry and berated 'classic liberals' in the Conservative Party for promoting a heartless and pecuniary capitalism, operating within 'a social and moral vacuum'.

Enoch Powell's 'rivers of blood' speech (delivered, quite coincidentally, on the anniversary of Hitler's birth, 20 April 1968), gave a considerable fillip to those right groups, like the Monday Club, who were obsessed with immigration as a mocking reminder of the death of the Empire. Paradoxically, however, the issue of race was to open the door to the hegemony of the economic liberals over Tory grass-roots activists in the mid- to late-seventies.

In 1972–3, in the wake of the Heath Government's admittance of 30,000 British Asians from Uganda – perceived by the right as a cynical sell-out of manifesto commitments – the Monday Club became heavily involved with, and infiltrated by, open Nazis. In September 1972, what was in effect a joint NF/Club anti-immigration rally was held at Central Hall, Westminster. In January the following year, the Essex branch of the Club was expelled for inviting the NF Chairman to address a meeting. There were some spectacular defections. Finally, the battle for the Monday Club's soul was joined in a bruising chairmanship election fight between Jonathan Guinness and the overtly racialist merchant banker (and former MI6 functionary) George Kennedy Young. Guinness won, but the victory was pyrrhic and the Club faded from view.

The messy collapse of the Monday Club had a considerable, salutary effect on the other Conservative fringe groups, and particularly on a group of right-wingers – including Robert Moss and Norris McWhirter – who set up the National Association for Freedom in late 1975.[2]

The NAFF was in effect a coalition of various tendencies on the conservative right: McWhirter himself had been involved in pro-censorship campaigns; Moss (and Brian Crozier) represented the growing 'counter-insurgency' school of new cold-war ideologues; the free-market pro-pagandists included Ralph Harris (Institute of Economic Affairs) and Michael Ivens (Aims of Industry). Industrialists on the NAFF's council included Sir Frank Taylor (of Taylor Woodrow), and there were a number of MPs, including Jill Knight, Winston Churchill, Rhodes Boyson and Nicholas Ridley.

Despite the catholicity of its leadership, the NAFF resolved from the start to heed the lessons of the Monday Club, and virtually exclude the social issues (apart from militant anti-communism) from its propaganda. The NAFF 'Charter of Rights and Liberties' concentrated on various economic freedoms, such as those of engaging in private enterprise, owning and conveying private property, purchasing private medical and educational facilities, and not belonging to a trade union (the charter also promoted the right to *belong* to a trade union, but this right tended to be defended with rather less energy). The NAFF's paper *Free Nation*, concentrated its efforts on opposing 'collectivism' and exposing 'abuses' of trade union power. And despite its 'high regard for Walter Walker', the NAFF rejected moves towards a merger with General Walker's Civil Assistance organization – widely regarded as a prototype anti-strike private army – although it welcomed 'individual members to join us and encourage local co-operation'.[3]

The association also went to great lengths to distance itself from racism and the National Front. Identifying the NF as fascist, NAFF insisted that the basic divide was not between 'right' and 'left' but between 'individualism' and 'collectiv-ism'. Asserting that 'the Nazis were, and are, socialists', *Free Nation* constantly hammered the idea that both communism and fascism were on one side of the political spectrum, and free-market liberalism on the other.

Under the banner of individual liberty, the NAFF quickly rose to considerable public prominence and was able to claim 50,000 supporters by early 1978. Part of its appeal lay in its talent for spectacular political and litigious stunts, like taking the postal workers to court for boycotting letters to South Africa, and organising a mass mail-in of completed Grunwick photographic prints. But the growth in NAFF's support was also a consequence of the propitiousness of the times. In particular, it was able to draw on the energies of the 'middle-class backlash' which was a feature of the mid-1970s disillusion both with state socialism and the 'corporatism' of the Edward Heath administration. There was a veritable explosion of organized middle-class pressure groups in 1974–5, including the National Federation of the Self-Employed, the Association of Self-Employed People, the National Association of Ratepayers' Action Groups and the Middle Class Association. Together, they claimed a membership of nearly half a million in 1975.

The NAFF's libertarian ideology did not, however, just appeal to the small trader, battered by regulation, harassed by local government and terrorized by the VAT inspectorate. It also appealed to Margaret Thatcher herself, who attended a NAFF subscription dinner in 1977 and employed NAFF director Robert Moss as a speechwriter. Part of the reason for that appeal doubtless lay in the intellectual coherence of the writings of the newly fashionable gurus of free enterprise, whose ideas were so effectively popularized in the columns of the *Free Nation*. For both F A Hayek and Milton Friedman the market was not just an effective engine of wealth-creation, but an essential *and sufficient* foundation of the free and therefore good society.

Armed with such rhetoric, the Conservatives went to the country in 1979 on the promise not to increase but to roll back the advances of the state. But it was clear at the time – and became clearer as the economy foundered in 1980 and 1981 – that economic liberalism had not yet won over all of the Conservative Party; in addition to unreconstructed Heathites, there was a growing body of opinion on the right of the party which distrusted the new course from quite a different perspective.

In 1977, a group of Conservative academics, commentators and politicians, most of whom had present or past connections with Peterhouse College, Cambridge, set up a society to promote traditional conservatism. They called it the Salisbury Group – in memory of the Third Marquis of Salisbury, whose first major political act was to resign from the government in 1866 in protest against the Reform Act, which enfranchised the male working class.

In 1978, the Group produced a collection of *Conservative Essays*, whose keynote statement (written by Maurice Cowling, Fellow of Peterhouse), was a sustained attack on those Conservatives who promote 'the idea that in some exclusive way "freedom" is the ultimate value'. In particular, Cowling berated the notorious Gould Report on 'Marxist infiltration' of the universities, on the grounds that the report was predicated on the assumptions of value-free education. In fact, he wrote, 'society ought to have opinions . . . in relation to which it is not the business of universities to adopt a liberalizing or questioning attitude', and it was indeed 'a matter for gloom and regret' that Professor Gould 'should consecrate the unthought-out pluralism in which we live'. Cowling went on: 'It is not freedom that Conservatives want: what they want is the sort of freedom that will maintain existing inequalities or restore lost ones.'

The spirit of the entire collection was summed up by Peregrine Worsthorne (graduate of Peterhouse) in a long passage in which he urged the Conservative leadership to listen to its own supporters, for whom the real problem was opposite to that posited by the anti-statists.

> The spectre haunting most ordinary people is neither that of a totalitarian state nor of Big Brother, but of other ordinary people being allowed to run wild. What they are worried about is crime, violence, disorder in the schools, promiscuity, idleness, pornography, football hooliganism, vandalism and urban terrorism . . . If one were to probe into the hearts of many potential and actual Tory supporters – and others besides – one might well discover that what worries them most about contemporary Britain was not so much the lack of

freedom as its excessive abundance; not so much the threat of
dictatorship as the reality of something unpleasantly close to
chaos . . . and for Mrs Thatcher to tell a party indignant at the
collapse of all forms of authority, and longing for the smack
of firm government, that the country is suffering from a lack
of liberty makes her seem out of touch with reality . . . The
urgent need today is for the state to regain control over 'the
people', to reassert its authority, and it is useless to imagine
that this will be helped by some libertarian mishmash drawn
from the writings of Adam Smith, John Stuart Mill, and the
warmed up milk of 19th century liberalism.

Worsthorne, therefore, wanted the by-word of the next
government, to be 'authority', not 'freedom'. And if that
meant that businessmen should not be allowed to 'pursue
profit regardless of . . . the possible social repercussions' of
their activities, then so be it.

But perhaps the most interesting figure in the Salisbury
Group, and now editor of its journal, is Roger Scruton,
sometime Fellow of Peterhouse and author of *The Meaning of
Conservatism* (published by Penguin in 1980), whose basic
argument was that 'the Conservative Party has often acted in
a way with which a conservative may find little sympathy',
particularly when, as at present, 'it has begun to see itself as
the defender of individual freedom against the encroachments of the state'. The result of this heresy was

> the wholesale adoption of the philosophy which I shall
> characterize in this book as the principal enemy of conserva-
> tism, the philosophy of liberalism, with all its attendant
> trappings of individual autonomy and the 'natural' rights of
> man . . . [By contrast] the conservative attitude seeks above
> all for government, and regards no citizen as possessed of a
> natural right that transcends his obligation to be ruled. Even
> democracy – which corresponds neither to the natural nor to
> the supernatural yearnings of the normal citizen – can be
> discarded without detriment to the civil well-being as the
> conservative conceives it.

The Peterhouse school and its authoritarian ideas are not
just restricted to the groves of academe. Since 1975, Scruton

and another Cambridge don, John Casey, have been organizing meetings of a dinner-club called the Conservative Philosophy Group, which has more recently attracted a veritable galaxy of right-wingers (including Enoch Powell, Peter Bauer, Lord Dacre, Paul Johnson, Julian Amery and the Prime Minister herself) to discuss socio-political questions. The title of an article detailing the Group's activities – published in *The Times* on 31 January 1983 – was 'Who Thinks For Mrs Thatcher?'

The American connection

Although thereby of great significance, the Peterhouse school is not the only anti-liberal grouping to have identifiable purchase on the intellectual course of Thatcherism. There are, in addition, two important transatlantic influences.

The first is the 'neo-conservative' group of (largely) New York Jewish intellectuals,[4] who provided much of the ideological muscle for the Reagan victory of 1980. Jeane Kirkpatrick, Reagan's United Nations Ambassador (and noted Argentinian partygoer), is a fully paid-up neo-con; while at the centre of the neo-conservative network – and typical of it – is Irving Kristol, a member of Reagan's campaign Policy Council and editor of the quarterly *Public Interest*.

A Trotskyist in the late 1930s, Kristol has been, on his own admission, moving steadily to the right since 1942, and to his credit (and that of his fellows) must go the development of a number of key constructs that have been more than useful to conservatives on both sides of the Atlantic. These notions include that of the 'new class' (the idea that public administrators, in alliance with liberal intellectuals, have a 'hidden agenda' for the destruction of private capitalism), and the convenient distinction between 'totalitarian' and 'authoritarian' dictatorships, which allows neo-conservatives to condemn repression in the Soviet Union while turning a blind, if not benign, eye on the domestic politics of, say, Chile, El Salvador and Argentina.

But most interesting of all is Kristol's specific critique of the free-market philosophies of F A Hayek and Milton Friedman, and his argument that the free market alone is an insufficient weapon against what he has described as 'the self-destructive nihilism' that was, for him, the enduring legacy of the new left radicalism in the 1960s. Indeed, the free market, if unfettered by tradition and authority, can aid and succour the forces of social indiscipline: capitalism, he writes, has degenerated into 'a system for the impersonal liberation and satisfaction of appetites' and thus 'self government, the basic principle of the republic, is inexorably being eroded in favour of self-seeking, self-indulgence and just plain selfishness'. The views of F A Hayek are, indeed, 'ultimately subversive of the social order', because they deny the need for 'the moral authority of tradition, and some public support for this authority'.[5]

The neo-conservatives are not only important because British Conservatives read their journals; the Brits have recently taken to writing them too. Policy Review is a quarterly journal which forms a kind of bridge between the neo-conservatives and the more fundamentalist and aggressive American new right, and its columns (and editorial board) have hosted (among others) John O'Sullivan, T E Utley and Robert Moss of the Daily Telegraph, Ronald Butt of The Times, Julian Amery and Winston Churchill MPs, Kingsley Amis and social democrat Stephen Haseler. Between them, they have spent much time disseminating neo-conservative ideas in Britain, including the 'new class' notion (a favourite of Ronald Butt), the authoritarian/totalitarian distinction (propagated by Robert Moss in his book The Collapse of Democracy and elsewhere) and, particularly, the argument of T E Utley's article in the Daily Telegraph (10 January 1977), titled 'A Free Market Is Not Enough'; in which Utley asked:

Why then, do the ancestral voices of Toryism persistently warn me against Dr Hayek? In a nutshell, because his rigid ideology, which rests firmly on the view that the market is a panacea for nearly all politically curable ills, exaggerates one of the great truths about politics at the cost of neglecting the other. In its concern for liberty, it disparages the importance of social cohesion.

The third major new influence on Conservative thought is rather more tangential, but may prove, over time, to be the most important of all. The doctrine of sociobiology – and particularly the work of E O Wilson (*Sociobiology: The New Synthesis*) and R Dawkins (*The Selfish Gene*) – elevates to the status of science two 'common-sense', right-wing theories of human nature: first, that human beings are essentially acquisitive and selfish and, second, that tribalism and thereby nationalism are the natural and inevitable consequence of human evolution.

Hilary and Steven Rose have pointed out how this new biological determinism 'neatly parallels the growth of the new right's social ideology' by claiming 'to explain such social phenomena as the arms race, altruistic self-sacrifice, male domination and homosexuality as the inevitable features of a society shaped by the biological imperatives of human evolution derived from a remote hunter-gatherer past'.[6]

The Roses emphasize, in particular, the way in which sociobiology 'naturalizes' partriarchy, and provides valuable ammunition for anti-feminism. In his book *The New Racism*,[7] Martin Barker points out that sociobiology also 'offers a highly sophisticated account of racism', turning 'localised worries' about black people into 'an evolutionary trait bred into us over millions of years because of its genetic advantage'.

Taken together, the new authoritarian right presents a comprehensive package. From Cambridge comes a traditional defence of the interventionist state, of order and obligation against freedom and right. From America proceeds a specific critique of the way in which the counter-culture of the 1960s, whether in the form of political radicalism or individual hedonism, has undermined the social constraints and disciplines which alone can prevent a modern society (whether a free or mixed economy) from degenerating into anarchy. And in science, or at least pseudo-science, conservatives find their prejudices confirmed: the pursuit of profit, the maintenance of social and sexual hierarchy, and the instincts of tribalism and xenophobia are all locked, not only into our institutions and our history, but into our very genes.

The climate was right for the authoritarians to assault the commanding heights of the political economy. The opportunity came in the spring and summer of 1981. On 7 July, on the very morrow of Toxteth, George Gale (Peterhouse graduate), in the *Daily Express*, laid the blame for the Liverpool riots fairly and squarely:

> The politicians, teachers, pundits, sowed the permissive wind; and now we are reaping the whirlwind . . . How many more weekends like the last is this civilised country to suffer before authority asserts itself?

Five days later, in the *Sunday Telegraph*, the ubiquitous Worsthorne charged the free-market faction with partial responsibility for the uprisings:

> So obsessed has it been with the rhetoric of economic freedom, which required the rolling back of the state on the industrial front, that it blinded itself to the need for strengthening the state on other – law and order – fronts.

In the same paper, a week later, Edward Norman (Dean of Peterhouse) argued that

> the young people on the streets – black and white – have been nurtured in a society which offered them seemingly endless expectations of personal and social satisfaction. They were brought up to dwell on their rights . . . Robbed by secular liberalism of the experience of authentic spirituality, with its self-denying criteria, their perception of an external dimension to their lives relates entirely to the shoddy morality of 'social concern' (mostly interpreted as a matter of assailing the better-off in society for their supposed failure to help the needy) . . . Supposing that a transformation of human nature

is unlikely, the expected outcome ought to be social disloca-
tion, increased personal indiscipline, crime and a sort of
national *anomie*. That seems to be exactly what is coming to
pass.

And in early August, *Daily Telegraph* (and *Spectator*),
columnist Colin Welch – also a Peterhouse graduate –
returned to the theme of the over-nurtured young, quoting
liberally from a *Sunday Times* interview with the two teenage
sons of a middle-class family, and concluding: (*Daily Telegraph*, 3 August 1981)

> What means all this boastful and pathetic rodomontade save
> that these pitiable dupes reject not only this society and
> authority but every conceivable society and authority; reject
> all real responsibility alike for others and themselves; reject as
> 'definition by others' that long process of disciplined learning
> and discovery, in or out of school, which is education and
> through which alone we can 'define ourselves'; reject all
> fruitful and rewarding work – 'proper jobs'. They will
> indeed, it seems, make their own music, write their own
> songs for their own band. But who will pay to hear them?
> Who but those in proper jobs, or, more likely, those who
> have gained power over their own lives by looting or by
> spongeing on the fruits of the proper jobs of others?

For the authoritarian right, then, the message of the riots
was clear: the underlying cause was the social revolution of
the post-war period, and particularly the removal of what
Dr Norman called the 'traditional symbols of deference and
authority'. And the implication was clear too: the free
market, which was after all the *purveyor* of all the personal
stereos and video recorders and space invader machines, the
very detritus of the *problem*, was pathetically inadequate to
furnish a solution.

The controversy opened up by the disturbances received a
kind of second wind in March 1982, when the Metropolitan
Police issued their notorious 'racial' crime statistics, in a
pretty transparent attempt to undermine the recommendations of the Scarman Report. The ensuing fortnight of Tory
outrage – there was a vote on hanging, calls for deportation,

and much baying for Willie Whitelaw's head on a platter – culminated in a speech made on 27 March by Mrs Thatcher herself, which echoed closely the arguments of Norman and Gale the summer before:

> We are reaping what was sown in the sixties. The fashionable theories and permissive clap-trap set the scene for a society in which the old virtues of discipline and self-restraint were denigrated . . . Children need, respond to, and too often lack clear rules. Only in this way will they grow up in a framework of certainty and learn the self-control necessary to cope with the problems of life.

Five days later, in a regrettable display of juvenile indiscipline, the Argentinian armed forces invaded the Falkland Islands.

Protection of Kith and Kin

It is legitimate to speculate what would have happened to British domestic politics had General Galtieri shown greater self-control. What is certain is that the new authoritarians seized on the Falklands conflict to promote two ideas: first, that the popularity of the war demonstrated 'the continuing strength of blood ties', 'truths about the nation which can only be expressed by brave deeds' and, indeed, the necessity 'to heed ancestral voices summoning us to be true to the nation's past'. Second, the war raised one or two uncomfortable questions, such as whether popular feeling would have been the same had the Falkland Islanders been 'British citizens with black or brown skins, spoke with strange accents or worshipped different Gods'. And the same commentator (it is Worsthorne once again) went on to draw the obvious conclusion: 'Although Britain is a multi-racial society, it is still very far from being a multi-racial nation. Its heart does not beat as one. Only in war does a nation discover what truly "turns it on". Protection of kith and kin evokes the spirit of supreme sacrifice to a degree that nothing else can.'[8]

The same point was made, several times, in the first edition of the Salisbury Group's *Salisbury Review*, (co-editor, Roger Scruton) published in the autumn of 1982. Both Enoch Powell, in an article titled 'Our Loss of Sovereignty', and Scruton himself in his editorial expressed hope that the spirit of the South Atlantic would not be 'a mere flash in the pan' (Powell), and that the reassertion of 'sentiments of sovereignty and national honour' would be reflected in domestic policy, such as that relating to immigration and capital punishment (Scruton).

The logic of this argument was taken much further in the same issue by John Casey, co-founder (with Scruton) of the Conservative Philosophy Group. In a reprint of a speech delivered to the CPG, Casey bemoaned the fact that the Conservative Party's commitment to 'a version of classical laissez-faire liberalism' had caused it to forget 'how to use the language of state and nation' until, that is, 'recent happy events altered things for the moment' – these happy events being, of course, those of Bomb Alley and Bluff Cove.

For Casey, as for Worsthorne, the war was nothing to do with abstract principles, still less United Nations resolutions. It was about the fact that 'the Falklanders were *British* . . . by language, custom and race,' more British indeed than so-called 'Black Englishmen' living on British soil. The West Indian population, he went on, possesses 'an extraordinary resentment towards authority' and is involved 'in a vastly disproportionate amount of violent crime'; and while the Asian community consisted of 'intelligent, industrious, peace-able people', their 'profound difference of culture' prevented them from identifying instinctively with the British state, thus calling 'the actual constitution into question'.

Casey's conclusion was, as he put it, 'generally considered unthinkable in polite society'. Having rejected the notion of voluntary repatriation ('because it would be voluntary the whole process might be out of political control'), he pro-posed that the legal status of Britain's immigrant community be altered retrospectively, 'so that its members became guest-workers . . . who would eventually, over a period of years, return to their countries of origin'.

In other words, John Casey, a Cambridge don, sitting (as

he admits) 'in a civilised drawing room', is advocating a polity hitherto only countenanced by the National Front and points rightward: the compulsory deportation of Britain's immigrant community. His conclusion is simple: 'The state of nationhood is the true state of man.'

Such ideas, though not expressed quite so baldly, have become increasingly current since riot and war rewrote the Thatcherite agenda. The Monday Club has undergone something of a revival, and Harvey Proctor MP, in particular, has used the Club as a platform for promoting repatriation. The *Daily Mail* political commentator, Andrew Alexander, began his 9 November 1981 column with the stark statement: 'The time has come to make a stand in favour of racialism.' While Professor John Vincent of Bristol, himself yet another graduate of a certain Cambridge college, has been sounding off in *The Times* and *The Sun* in favour of the 'assisted exit' of a proportion of Britain's black community, and against the Scarman Report, which has 'left crime doing very nicely, thank you'. For Vincent, indeed, 'the fear felt by the white population is the heart of the race relations problem today.'[9] Finally, even the bastions of the free market have not escaped infection. In January this year, the *Free Nation* announced that it was no longer 'primarily concerned with the analysis and exposure of the political forces currently threatening our freedom', but rather with 'rising crime, sexual permissiveness and family breakdown', quoting the quintessential Tory patriarch, Edmund Burke, in support.

So by early 1983 the authoritarian right seemed to have achieved a kind of hegemony over the Conservative Party, and to have elbowed the pure free-marketeers to one side. All of that said, it is right to question how much it matters. Conflicts of principle which might appear fundamental to the ideologues might not appear so apocalyptic from the perspective of the conference floor or even the cabinet committee. A grass-roots Tory, for example, would see little conflict between getting the state out of the boardroom but back into the bedroom; and would happily advocate, possibly in the same sentence, the privatization of both the National Health Service and the female sex.

Similarly, a government minister might not consider it a matter of great import whether his weekend speech castigated the trade unions as the forces of brute monopoly power, or harbingers of anarchy, or both. And even hardline economic liberals like the recently knighted Sir Alfred Sherman have not found it hard, in the past, to extol the virtues of free trade in things, while objecting violently to free trade in peoples, religions, values and ideas. 'The imposition of mass immigration from backward, alien cultures,' he wrote in 1976, 'is just one symptom of this self-destructive urge, reflected in the assault on patriotism, the family – both as a conjugal and economic unit – the Christian religion in public life and schools, traditional morality in matters of sex, honesty, public display and respect for the law, on educational values, thrift, hard work and other values denigrated as "middle class", in short, all that is English and wholesome.'[10]

Furthermore, it is of course true, as Stuart Hall and Andrew Gamble have both argued,[11] that in many ways a free market implies both the reassertion of the family (to provide previously public services in the home), and a state strong enough to impose its discipline on those unwilling to accept the brisk logic of unfettered capitalism.

But there are at least four things that could happen (one of which *is* happening) which might well not have happened had the economic liberals still been in the position they were in 1979. The first is that the very atmosphere of the times gives permission to judges, policemen, prison governors, head teachers, social security officials and immigration officers to ply their various trades in a more aggressively authoritarian way (as Sarah Tisdall and the miners' flying pickets discovered). The second is that anti-libertarian legislation – whether the Police Bill or measures to rewrite the immigration rules yet again – will achieve greater priority in the government's programme, and be much less open to liberal amendment. The third is that the fiscal and other measures proposed in the leaked documents of the Family Policy Group – proposals designed among other things to return women to the home and to discourage sexual activity among the poor – may well find legislative expression.

There is, however, another social policy which, if implemented, would have profound effects on the life of the country. It would reduce unemployment at a stroke, and allow the government to encourage directly those very values of discipline and obedience it finds so sadly lacking in the young today. It is a policy, however, which would strike at the very heart of free-market, anti-statist ideology, involving as it does the most direct and obvious interference by the state in the economic and social liberties of the citizen. It is, of course, conscription.

Under the headline 'Give Teenage Jobless Spell in the Army', the *Sunday Times* first announced on 6 March 1983 that 'a plan to revive national service, in a voluntary form, is being considered by the Ministry of Defence. It would involve attaching unemployed school-leavers to the army, navy or airforce as part of the Government's new Youth Training Scheme.'

In being voluntary, the Government's scheme differs from that advocated in the second edition of the *Salisbury Review*, which advocated that 'a Conservative government should not dismiss as impolitic the idea of conscription,' which, although 'a form of temporary slavery', nonetheless 'relieves young people of the immediate anxiety of unemployment, while fitting them better for action than the pity-sodden ethos of the welfare state.' And by the same token, Colin Welch told *Spectator* readers (28 January 1984) that he had changed his mind about conscription: 'Better the obscene bellowing of the colour sergeant than that of the Rolling Stones;' he wrote, 'better drill than the disco.'

On 23 May 1983, at the height of the election campaign, *The Times* published an editorial which coupled its call for the revival of military conscription with the Falklands, the mystic 'will' of the people, and the instinctive bonds of nationhood:

The Falklands were rescued by a combination of military prowess and a demonstration of political will which had previously been lacking . . . National will is an essential political precondition of any convincing military posture of deterrence . . . Without a sure sense of self-preservation, nourished as the root of all his instincts, an individual will bend to every whim. So it is with societies and nations. The will to survive has to be cherished and replenished in a dangerous and unpredictable world.

Things have come a long way from the rhetoric, dominant even three years ago, of the doughty, rugged individualist, resentful of any interference in his liberties and demanding release from the suffocating and compulsory embraces of the nanny state.

In its first term of office, the Thatcher administration set out with a will to dismantle the economic infrastructure of the post-war consensus: the public industries, the commitment to full employment and the welfare state. In its second term it will continue this task.

It may also seek to undertake an even greater project – the destruction of those social and political assumptions, from egalitarianism and social compassion to sexual tolerance and an openness to cultural diversity, on which that consensus was based. If it does so, the credit must in part go to those social pressure groups – the Monday Clubs and SPUCs and VALAs – which first sowed the seed; to the academics who tended and nurtured the growing crops; and to the commentators and pundits who are now demanding they be harvested.

Notes

[1] *Monday World* (Summer 1973).

[2] For a detailed history of the NAFF see R. King and N. Nugent, *Respectable Rebels* (Hodder and Stoughton, 1979).

[3] Letter from NAFF Director John Gouriet quoted in *New Statesman*, 15 July 1977.

[4] For a detailed analysis of neo-conservatism see my 'Reagan's Hidden Agenda', *Race and Class* (Winter 1981) and 'The Neo-Conservatives', *Searchlight*, (September 1980).

[5] Irving Kristol, *Two Cheers for Capitalism*, (Basic Books, 1978) and *On the Democratic Idea in America* (Harper & Row, 1972).

[6] Hilary Rose and Steven Rose, 'Moving Right Out of Welfare', *Critical Social Policy*, Vol. 2, No. 1.

[7] Martin Barker, *The New Racism* (Junction Books, 1981).

[8] *Sunday Telegraph*, 28 May and 27 June 1982.

[9] *Times*, 10 November 1982; *Sun*, 30 March 1983.

[10] *Daily Telegraph*, 9 September 1976.

[11] In *The Politics of Thatcherism* (Lawrence and Wishart, 1983) and elsewhere.

4

The Rise of the Authoritarian State

COLIN LEYS

In the early phase of Thatcherism many commentators speculated that its abrasive, divisive policies would heighten social tensions to a level that could only be contained by authoritarian means. Now a series of events have raised the issue in an immediate and practical form. The persecution of Sarah Tisdall; the enforced banning of trade union membership at GCHQ Cheltenham; rate capping, the final abrogation of the financial autonomy of local government, deportations of immigrants whose marriages break up; official suppression of information (over cuts at Queen Charlotte's Hospital) and falsification of records (at Sellafield); the denial of freedom of movement to miners, and police harassment of their pickets. Other events, stretching back for some years, now seem to take on fresh significance: phone tapping, mail opening, jury vetting, the deportation of citizens from Britain to Northern Ireland, the extension of police powers under the Prevention of Terrorism Act and still more widely under the new Police and Criminal Evidence Bill; prison beatings and allegations of torture; the expansion of social security spying and over-publicized and provocative police actions against social security fraud; increased arming of the police: the list is virtually endless, and seems to suggest strongly that the British state has undergone a marked shift in an authoritarian direction. The SDP's David Marquand thinks so, calling for an SDP–Liberal–Labour alliance to reverse the trend; and the left in general need no persuading. Is this the most reactionary government in modern British history, with a massive majority, deliberately aggravating the economic and social crisis and then responding by an increasing reliance on mere power? Such a hypothesis makes sense, and as will be argued below, there is some truth in it. But it is important, especially for socialists, to approach this question critically.

First of all, the evidence is fragmentary. There are (even today) some apparent counter-tendencies – such as the European Court of Human Rights rulings denying schools the right to impose corporal punishment, denying the government the right to restrict prisoners' mail, and – in prospect – requiring the government to introduce adequate controls over phone tapping; or the impending introduction of a form of independent supervision of investigations of complaints against the police. Stuart Hall and his colleagues showed how the so-called 'mugging' epidemic of the seventies was in effect invented, as part of an effort to rationalize the campaign for 'law-and-order'.[1] Could the 'rise of authoritarianism' be a similar phenomenon? This is not to deny that authoritarian attitudes exist among government ministers, civil servants, policemen, judges, prison wardens, editors, headmasters and headmistresses – not to mention ordinary people, such as the 66 per cent who think the police should be able to stop and search anyone they think is suspicious, or the 80-plus per cent who favour restoring capital punishment for a wide range of murders. The question is whether such attitudes, and the behaviour they encourage on the part of the state, are on the increase; and if they are, whether they form part of a single pattern or syndrome.

It is easy to assume that because the Conservative Party has always emphasized respect for authority, and now has some MPs who are openly somewhat authoritarian, there is a new, Conservative-instigated, generalized authoritarian tendency in government. But this overlooks some obvious difficulties. First, some of the tendencies are not new at all. Martin Kettle made this point very effectively in a well-known article written in 1980.[2] He pointed out that virtually every element in the so-called 'drift to law and order' under Thatcher in 1979 and 1980 stemmed from decisions already sanctioned under Labour before the 1979 election – decisions which in most cases flowed from a bureaucratic momentum: habitual Home Office responses to long-term structural changes affecting policing, prisons, and so on. The Sarah Tisdall affair is perhaps a good recent example of the same thing. Section II of the Official Secrets Act, under which she was convicted, has consistently been used (under Labour as well as Conservative governments) to intimidate potential whistle-blowers in the civil service, especially when the issue they may blow the whistle on is a sensitive one for the Americans. If anything was new in the Tisdall case it was the breadth of the spectrum of opinion that seemed upset by the sentence, and by the government's *failure* to prosecute the equally 'culpable' *Guardian*, which it no doubt would have been politically more costly to do. In fact it is a fair bet that if the next Labour government abolishes Section II – which if Kinnock's remarks on the case are seriously meant, it surely must – it will have rather widespread support.

Another weakness in the thesis on the growth of Thatcher-ite authoritarianism is that some similar trends are observable elsewhere, in countries with very different governments. For instance US and French police methods have long been more authoritarian, in some respects, than those of the British police even today. US and Canadian prisons are equally overcrowded, with a far higher percentage of their respective populations in jail, than British ones. 'Social democratic' Denmark has long had its social security fraud spies (the 'duvet-lifters'); and so on. Some instances of an apparent authoritarian trend – arming the police, for example – are matters on which Britain is now coming into line with practices that are common, if not universal, elsewhere. This doesn't make what is happening in Britain acceptable. Arming the police can be provocative and dangerous, as the Stephen Waldorf case showed. Police pressure for arms, while officially denied from time to time, has been a factor, and should be resisted (advice, yes; pressure, no). There are probably more occasions today than 30 years ago in which armed policemen are required. What is wrong is not that the police are trained in and issued with arms but the apparently excessive scale of the arming (on average 20 times a day in 1982), the apparently arbitrary pattern of it, and the lack of any form of democratic regulation of it.

Finally, it seems important to be clear what we mean by 'authoritarianism'. Andreski defined the psychology of authoritarianism as 'a disposition to zealous obedience to an hierarchic superior, obsequiousness and sycophancy towards the stronger in general, with overbearing and scornful demeanour towards those who are under one's power'; and authoritarian administration as 'reliance on apodictic orders and threats of punishment, and aversion to employing either consultation or persuasion'.[3] A Pole, or even a West German – let alone a Chilean – would probably be hard pressed to characterize the British state in 1984 as seriously authoritarian in this sense. This doesn't mean that authoritarianism does not exist in Britain, or that it is not increasing. It is just that it is still relatively limited in scope (notably by being strongly directed towards minorities such as young black people, and geographically concentrated, as in Northern Ireland); by and large mild (by world standards); still officially disapproved (though with some unsavoury equivocation, for instance in regard to police treatment of the miners' pickets); and still strongly contested, at least by an active minority.

Also, it is important to distinguish authoritarianism from class-biased legislation or administrative actions. For instance the Tebbit-King trade union bill, forcing the unions to ballot on strikes and weakening their links with the Labour Party, is class legislation aimed at the strength of working class organization, but it is not in itself authoritarian. Or to take a more controversial case, what *was* authoritarian about the GCHQ affair was that the de-unionization of GCHQ was imposed by fiat, when a non-strike deal of some sort could almost certainly have been obtained by negotiation. (It is clear that GCHQ is really a military operation manned by civilians and once the principle that such activities should be conducted at all is conceded, there is obviously room for legitimate disagreement about how far they are compatible with union membership and union rights.) The government's action displayed more of a colonial mentality (towards the Americans) than an authoritarian one, though there was certainly an element of this too.

Yet when all necessary qualifications have been made,

something has been happening – or rather, at least five separate, though mutually reinforcing, tendencies seem to be evident:

(1)   a struggle by the state apparatus to preserve itself from democratization and to eliminate certain democratic residues 'accidentally' established in the past;

(2)   bureaucratization, reinforced by computer technology, which has greatly enlarged the 'reach' (and no doubt the grasp) of the state, and diminished its dependence on and interest in civic cooperation;

(3)   the contradictions of capitalism in general since the late 1960s, and those of British capitalism in particular, which have intensified class and other conflicts, tempting the state to rely more on orders and threats and the mere exercise of power;

(4)   Thatcherism, itself a specific product of (3);

(5)   the cumulative cultural effect of all this, reinforcing an already 'corporative-subordinate', rather than a 'hegemonic-republican', popular political culture.

De-democratization

It is still not widely enough appreciated how peculiarly undemocratic the British state is. Britain was one of the first representative states. As Tom Nairn pointed out, the distinctive historical circumstances that prevailed in Britain led to the rapidly expanding new classes of capital being socially and politically assimilated to, and increasingly fused with, the old landed class. This permitted much of the old pre-capitalist state structure to survive – there was no revolutionary break or radical reconstruction, only a prolonged process of organic reform. The old structure was one in which the ruling class largely *constituted* the state – as its policy-makers, army commanders and officers, its judges and magistrates, and its ideologists.[4] As the new 'middle classes' were absorbed, the structure was adapted to represent their interests (the key step being the 1832 property franchise) and, at the local level, to entrust them with administrative responsibilty (via local boards and commissions elected by ratepayers). The state became more accurately *representative* (of property), but not *democratic*.

The extension of the vote to the *demos* after 1867 called this in question. The House of Commons became subject to popular control via elections, but was then itself subordinated to the executive via the discipline of the new party organizations. (This process was assisted by the government's arrogation of control over the parliamentary timetable, power of 'guillotine', etc. which was in turn legitimated by the desire of both the major parties to neutralize the power of the Irish Nationalist MPs after 1886 – not the last time in which this legacy of colonial misrule would lead to a loss of democratic rights on the mainland.) The thrust of democracy was thus deflected exclusively into elections for the lower House of Parliament. The executive was made more and more immune to popular control, except by the irregular and blunt instrument of elections. The state apparatus expanded and steps were taken to ensure that its policy-making levels remained in upper middle-class hands by establishing a 'class system' inside the enlarged civil service, and by bringing it under new rules of discipline. The cult of secrecy dates from this time, culminating in Section II of the Official Secrets Act of 1911, which drastically reduces the ability of anyone outside the cabinet (and sometimes even Cabinet ministers) to know what the government is doing, and so be able to criticize it.[5]

Meanwhile the House of Lords, the judiciary and the magistracy all remained, in effect, within the patronage system; and as the state expanded, the principle of patronage – i.e. appointment by secret processes of private citizens to public offices – was extended to almost every new branch of the state apparatus for which the illusion of 'representativeness' was judged desirable, but where it was desired *not* to represent, let alone give power to, ordinary people, e.g. the Health Authorities, the governing bodies of the BBC, the ITA, the public corporations, the Arts Council, the Science Research Council, etc. Effective principles of popular control or accountability, such as the vetting of potential judges by their peers, as in the USA, or their recruitment and training as a public profession, as elsewhere in Europe, were not even indirectly introduced and there was certainly no provision for any right of referendum, or other form of popular initiative or accountability.

There were none the less some limited but important qualifications to this general picture, and it is significant that all of them have been the focus of recent struggles: elected local government (and, before 1934, elected Poor Law Guardians, i.e. unemployment relief administrators); the Watch Committees of local authorities, in charge of policing policy; and the jury system. In each case popular control was introduced in institutions that could be relied on to respect and protect property rights so long as they were monopolized by the middle classes – urban local authorities and Poor Law Guardians from the turn of the century onwards, and juries between 1950 and 1974 (with the rapid lowering and eventual abolition of the property qualifications for jury service).

Labour-controlled councils gradually found their feet and established pockets of strong local 'social-democratic' hegemony. This began to provoke a counter-attack in the interwar years, when Poplar Borough Council's successful fight for equality of burden in paying for unemployment relief led to the abolition in 1934 of elected boards of Guardians to administer it. In the same spirit, local government reforms since 1963 have all tended to reduce the influence of working-class voters by enlarging boundaries (diluting the urban electorates); by bureaucratizing local authority administration (establishing, in effect, increasingly powerful local government executives, in place of direct administration by the committees of councillors); and finally by successively tightening central control of local council finances, culminating in the current establishment of complete Whitehall control by 'rate capping'.

In the same way the 1964 Police Act redefined the powers of the local Police Committees (the old 'Watch' Committees) to make them merely advisory, instead of controlling; and the 1967 Criminal Justice Act abolished the unanimity principle for juries, while the independence of juries was increasingly undermined by the practice of 'jury vetting' – i.e. secretly giving the prosecution police reports on the personal backgrounds of prospective jurors, allowing the prosecution to use its unlimited right to veto particular jurors so as to try to produce juries less sympathetic to the accused. And the record shows that these changes did not just happen accidentally. The class interests represented by urban councils, and by juries that really represented the population as a whole, were seen as 'necessitating' these changes.[6]

The process of de-democratization is, then, one trend towards authoritarianism that has been at work for some time, however much the contemporary crisis and Thatcherism may have brought it to a head. In the same category should also be placed a variety of defensive struggles by the state and party leaders against democratic demands arising from the mobilization of new social forces during the boom years: for instance the state apparatus's successful struggle *against* the introduction of 'freedom of information' legislation, *against* effective 'data protection' legislation, *against* effective popular participation in planning decisions, *against* the introduction of effective machinery to redress grievances (the emasculation of the office of the Parliamentary Commissioner is a classic example).

Bureaucratization and technology

An undemocratic state is necessarily bureaucratic and a good deal of contemporary authoritarianism stems from the 'natural' logic of bureaucracy, immensely strengthened by computers, and legitimized by appeals to 'efficiency' and economy, and to various alleged threats to law and order and 'security' (more and more loosely defined). Under this heading belong the enlargement of local government areas; the introduction of 'cash limits' and other instruments to enhance central control of local spending, and hence policy making; the development of 'pre-emptive' policing (from the introduction of 'panda cars' to 'saturation policing' and 'fishnet' operations); the establishment of the Police National Computer, the CID computer, and the computers of – by now – most of the 43 individual police forces, all of which are not barred from including unsubstantiated and often false information and exchanging it freely within and even outside the state information networks (as the ABC trial of John Crispin Aubrey, John Berry and Duncan Campbell and other episodes have shown); the issue of social security identity cards and the centralization of such things as driving licence administration, with its consequences for automatic police recording of individuals' changes of address, etc.

The effect of all this is to increase enormously the ability of officials to control the ordinary public. Power passes to people effectively immune to democratic supervision and accountability who can use increasingly comprehensive information about individuals to make decisions, on grounds not revealed to them, which affect their lives and even their rights (e.g. their right to serve on a jury, for a start). Anyone who has been stopped by the police while driving, and has waited while a policeman reads the data from his or her driving licence into the computer terminal in the police car, to see what the computer may suggest – perhaps quite falsely – that he or she might be worth investigating for, knows what is involved. The development of phone tapping and bugging technology has meantime reached the point where the already feeble and wholly undemocratic mechanisms for regulating these methods of official surveillance are less and less relevant.[7] In effect there are no barriers to official prying into any activity 'the authorities' please to call 'subversive', including more or less any form of radical political or trade union activity. There is now a vast gap between what people think is their private life, and what the state may (and often does) secretly enquire into and record.

The contradictions of British capitalism

The growth of the state's capacity to keep tabs on the public has been justified, and in some cases directly occasioned, by social conflict caused by the chronic crisis of British capitalism which began in the early 1960s. The wage militancy that followed the Wilson deflation of 1964–9; the Northern Ireland conflict that flowed from a similar contradiction between raised expectations (on the part of Catholics) and the reality of Protestant power in a period of deepening economic decline; the marginalization, repression and scapegoating of black people; the revival of the peace movement in face of the new arms race: each of these contributed to the organization, technology and ideology of social control.

The Northern Ireland débâcle has resulted in the Prevention of Terrorism Act, which among other things abolished the right to freedom of movement of selected citizens who happen to reside in Northern Ireland; the training of virtually the whole army as an instrument for political repression; the establishment in Ulster of the precedent of criminal courts without juries (the 'Diplock' courts); the sanctioning (unofficially-officially) of army, police and prison brutality in Northern Ireland (which has been curbed there only to surface, apparently, in various police headquarters and prisons in England). To the development of racism in the 1970s we can trace the use of police 'Special Patrol Groups'; and to the flying pickets of the 1970s, the development of police 'Support Groups', which since 1981 have been controlled from a national centre in Scotland Yard – the embryo of a single national police force, trained and equipped for 'riot control'?

Thatcherism

Itself a product of the crisis, Thatcherism's capture of the Conservative Party has inflected the crisis in at least four specific ways. It has aggravated the rate of unemployment, and aggravated inequality through budgets that have cut real incomes of the poor and increased those of the better-off, creating resentment and disaffection. It has campaigned on an appeal to 'law-and-order', blaming the victims, scapegoating minorities, those on welfare, and the trade unions. It has introduced explicit appeals to authority ('the smack of firm government') and it has fostered chauvinism and militarism over the Falklands and in relation to the nuclear arms race. Thatcherism can be specifically credited with the expansion of social security spying and agent provocateur exercises such as the 1982 'Operation Major' in Oxford, where the police set up a bogus social security office and then arrested its clients. Thatcherism also has to its credit some notable examples of official disinformation efforts, though it is doubtful if the hands of previous administrations were much cleaner in this respect.

Perhaps Thatcherism's most serious contribution to authoritarianism has been in accepting the permanence of acute social differences and giving official endorsement to a 'police view' of the consequences, which sees active opposition as misguided and ultimately seditious; and in making such an absolute commitment to the cold war and to the acceptance of Cruise missiles and all that they imply. (E. P. Thompson's remark that 'civil liberties and 250 Cruise missiles cannot co-exist in this island together' is surely true.)

Habituation to abuse of power

The mutually reinforcing nature of these different trends has had a cumulative effect on the way people think about authority. One of the reasons Thompson's essays on the abuse of power make such an impact is that he consistently questions everything. Take, for example, the word 'guideline'. 'Guidelines' were (secretly) issued to the police by the Attorney General in 1974 concerning jury-vetting. Thompson asked him: 'What *is* a guideline? Is it a rule of law or is it a nudge-nudge be-careful-how-you-go? What officers have you appointed to see that these "guidelines" are observed? What sanctions have you imposed against transgression?'[8] Good questions. Yet we have gradually got used to 'guidelines', so that 'the authorities' more often than not issue them without much difficulty, and expect people to follow them, and even manage to punish them when they don't. Under the 1980 Employment Act, for example, the Employment Secretary took it on himself to 'lay down' guidelines (called a 'code of practice') on picketing, including the guideline that no picket should number more than six. What could be the point of such a guideline, since it explicitly enjoyed no legal force? Well, it might be 'taken into account' in proceedings in any court. How? Well, for example, by a magistrate dealing with the Yorkshire miner on his way to join hundreds of others at a picket in Nottinghamshire. In other words, the extra-legal *wishes* of a particular politician surreptitiously become part of the *operative law* as it affects the rights of strikers. Continuous efforts to erode rights and blur the edges of administrative authority have a cumulative weakening effect on public resistance.

Another example: in an article on the use of 'supergrass' evidence in Northern Ireland's 'Diplock' courts a *Sunday Times* journalist wrote that the police were finding it 'increasingly difficult to get confessions from suspected terrorists. Closed-circuit television monitors introduced in interview rooms in 1980 to increase safeguards for suspects have shattered *the intimate intensity that induced confessions*' (italics added).[9] But wait a minute. What exactly does this mean? Could it have anything to do with the allegations of *torture* that eventually led to the installation of TV monitors (i.e. when a committee of inquiry found that suspects had sustained injuries, while in custody, that *could not* have been *self*-inflicted, as the state had claimed)? Perhaps the phrase was meant to be ironical, but it seems more likely that the author was trying to avoid offending 'the authorities' by implying that they had, in fact, been responsible for torturing 'suspected terrorists' (another weasel-expression, incidentally). An inability to call things by their names – enforced by 'the authorities' via 'contempt of court', 'crown privilege', and so on – is one of the symptoms of a culture succumbing to authoritarianism.

Thompson remarks that eighteenth-century gentlemen who clashed with the crown were apt to have themselves arrested while reading Magna Carta to their sons. This remark was brought uncomfortably to mind by a report on the GCHQ affair, which quoted an engineer at GCHQ as saying: 'As a body we have strength, but I don't know. With a wife and family, who can afford principles?'[10] True, eighteenth-century gentlemen had advantages that twentieth-century government employees lack, but an important point is involved in this contrast all the same. The corporative culture of labourism ('as a body we have strength') is essentially defensive of a specific range of labour rights. It does not embrace an assertive, comprehensive, 'republican' claim to rights of all kinds. Such a claim implies an active, 'hegemonic' conception of what the state is and should be – the principles on which it should rest, its proper limits and conventions. Some people on the left may believe that the bourgeois state is 'essentially' repressive (so that it is pointless to try to assert civil rights against it), and that the socialist state will merely 'administer things' produced by perfectly cooperating 'associated producers'; but anyone who rejects this as utopian must accept the obligation to work out a socialist conception of civil rights and concrete programmes for achieving it. We have to establish the principles that a man with a wife and family cannot afford to do without, both now and in a socialist future.

This means a significant shift of perspective on the part of the left. It was a Labour (now SDP) Home Secretary who abolished the unanimity rule in jury trials, and who later gave secret sanction to jury vetting, and a Labour government which failed to redeem its election pledge to establish freedom of information about state activities. Out of office the party's leaders have rediscovered the iniquity of the Official Secrets Act, the dangers of Chief Constables and police forces responsible to no one but themselves, the class bias of the higher judiciary and the establishment-dominated magistracy, and so on. The question is whether this rediscovery will translate into a solid commitment to radical and comprehensive action when next returned to office, beginning – first and foremost – with a complete *reversal* of the present position on official secrecy, i.e. the establishment of a public (not just individual) 'right to know', enforced with real sanctions by a new agency openly staffed and responsible not to the executive but the public itself (e.g. through a committee of backbenchers) – at all events an uncompromising opening of the official record on everything of a non-security nature (strictly defined). This must be stressed because real democratization ultimately depends on ending official secrecy; but it remains only the first step, however essential. An obvious and urgent next step is to establish democratic control over the police, including the secret police. Another is to reform the entire system of appointments to public bodies to make it open and accountable. The independence of local government and of juries must be restored, and so on.

It should at least be clear that civil liberties are essential to the struggle for socialism. The enemies of socialism know this and it is one of the reasons why they try to erode them. Civil liberties are also necessary to socialism itself; and the Labour Party meantime has a great opportunity to make allies of all those who in one way or another see their rights being infringed. Civil liberties are certainly too important to be left to the Liberals.

In adopting this position the party will reap some other advantages. The fact that the trend to authoritarianism is an amalgam of mutually supporting tendencies means that a gain on one front tends to strengthen the chances of making gains on others. For instance the experiment of taping police interrogations in Scotland has put paid to the specious argument, which was earlier advanced by the Home Office, that it would cost too much, and has also shown how much the police tend to rely on breaking the rules, by the fact that they have been avoiding conducting their interrogations in the tape-equipped rooms.[11] Adequate protection for 'suspects' will go on being resisted but it can eventually be achieved and the process will enhance the case for reforming other aspects of police practice, and so on. The struggle for civil liberties is pre-eminently a war of many local actions, not one big push, and well suited to the resources of socialist movement. Energy, persistence and imagination are more important than cash.

But the fact remains that a substantial democratization of the state is also essential, which means some major political reforms. The permanent threat to civil liberties comes from secret, centralized bureaucracy, sheltered by effectively non-accountable cabinets; and from equally non-accountable and secretly selected judges, commissioners of police, prison governors, and so on. Laws to restore civil liberties will not work unless they are implemented by sympathetic, or at least accountable, officials. For example, the US 'freedom of information' legislation makes the courts the final arbiters of whether the government is entitled not to disclose an item of information, and over the years they have established some reasonably effective limits to the government's claims. No one who has considered the record of British judges on secrecy issues could believe for a moment that a similar approach could work in Britain. Either a different kind of agency, differently chosen and properly accountable, would be needed, or the way judges are trained and selected would have to be radically changed (preferably both).

Two points are worth bearing in mind here. First, the state is a complex terrain of struggle, and democratization is not a one-dimensional matter. There are many options – many different possible ways of recruiting, training, promoting, organizing, circulating, advising, monitoring, publicizing, reviewing, checking, disciplining and replacing public officials. Elections are only one device, and not necessarily the most useful (and not necessarily always even desirable). There are numerous working models in other countries to consider, as David Held and John Keane argue correctly in this volume. Socialists need to examine this kind of detail.

Second, democratization must be pursued with attention to the specific popular traditions and practices that will have to sustain it. The left's thinking about democratization has sometimes assumed a sort of Jacobin passion for participation on the part of 'the masses' which as far as public life goes is foreign to British experience. Much more democratic participation is needed, but if people felt that they must choose between putting up with some bureaucratic officiousness, and giving up their leisure to continuous meetings with their fellow-workers, neighbours, fellow school-parents, and so on – a sort of perpetual Paris in May 1968 – they might well be tempted to settle for officiousness. Oscar Wilde declared that socialism was impossible because it would mean too many committees; he has to be proved wrong. Popular political participation is needed, but it cannot be a panacea, and more thought needs to be given to such things as *socialist* systems of checks and balances, means to secure *genuine* pluralism in the media, devices to make administration more likely to check its own authoritarian tendencies, etc. Of course anyone who believes that with the expropriation of the means of production from private hands all social conflict will gradually cease, and policemen will become superfluous, will not find these questions very interesting, but a serious anti-authoritarian socialism must find answers to them.

Notes

[1] Stuart Hall and others, *Policing the Crisis* (Macmillan, 1978).

[2] Martin Kettle, 'The Drift to Law and Order', *Marxism Today* (Oct. 1980).

[3] In *A Dictionary of the Social Sciences* (Free Press, 1964).

[4] Tom Nairn, *The Break-Up of Britain* (New Left Books, 1977, Ch. 1).

[5] David Leigh, *The Frontiers of Secrecy* (Junction Books, 1980, pp. 35–39).

[6] See John Dearlove, *The Reorganisation of British Local Government* (Cambridge University Press, 1979).

[7] Duncan Campbell, *Phonetappers and the Security State* (New Statesman Report No. 2, 1981, Ch. 4).

[8] E. P. Thompson, *Writing By Candlelight* (Merlin, 1980, p. 106).

[9] Chris Ryder, *Sunday Times*, 30 Oct. 1983.

[10] *Sunday Times*, 5 Feb. 1984.

[11] Martin Kettle, *Sunday Times*, 18 Dec. 1983.

Part 3
Responding to Social Change

5

The Once and Future Class

JOHN WESTERGAARD

The class debate of the 1980s oddly echoes an old one.[1] The differences between the two debates are odd, as well. Then, in the 1950s, the conventional wisdom came from the political centre and right, and to its own question, *Must Labour Lose?*,[2] it answered 'yes'. Affluence was turning the working class middle class and had thus brought about *The End of Ideology*.[3] This argument evaporated in the 1960s, discredited not just by events but also by accumulated evidence which firmly refuted its underlying diagnosis of the way class relations were developing.

Now a new version of it has been revived, as much from the left as from anywhere else. This seems to tell us that socialism's defeat in the late 1970s and early 1980s (*The Forward March of Labour Halted?*)[4] comes from working-class 'embourgeoisement' – conversion to middle-class ways of life and outlook – in the depths of a recession. Of course, to go by the left-wing versions, there may be hope yet. But, as in the 1950s, the argument now has it that basic shifts in class structure set formidable obstacles to radical mobilization, and that those basic shifts are re-casting society in a middle-class mould.

There is an undeniable case for reappraisal on the left. The need is all too painfully evident from the clash between past prognosis and present reality. A prospect of socialist radicalism spurred by economic crisis has been eclipsed by the triumphant radicalism of the right. Steeply rising unemployment has been coupled with political polarization, true enough. But few people would have predicted the way that polarization has gone – to spawn a thriving mongrel offspring of market liberalism and social authoritarianism. How has this paradox come about?

The echoes of the old discredited thesis to be heard in the new debate should sound a note of caution before we jump to the notion of class-structural shifts as a way of explaining the paradox – the more so because the two share similarities of style as well as content. Like the old theory of 'embourgeoisement in affluence', the new one of 'embourgeoisement in recession' tends to rediscover long-standing trends as if they were startling new events; makes sweeping generalizations from slender or ambiguous facts helped along with a generous dollop of guesswork; slides over glaring socio-economic realities if they do not fit in with the argument; and substitutes rash assertiveness for reasoned uncertainty about the drift of social relations and political consciousness in a world messy with contradictions.

So the first thing is to keep a level head. And the second may be to take cautious note of an element of the 'new revisionism' which seems to characterize its method. It sees the economic structure of class (or that part of it on which the argument focuses in order to claim that significant shifts have occurred) as in some sort of neat correspondence with socio-political consciousness. If the former changes, so in a matching way must the latter; and if the latter changes, there must be an underlying change in the former to explain it.

The distinction between 'structure' and 'consciousness' is certainly important. Marx – among others – made it when he drew a line between 'class in itself' and 'class for itself'. By 'in itself', he meant class as a matter of the divisions *inherent* in an unequal organization of economic relations. By 'for itself', he meant class as a matter of socio-political *responses* to those divisions, by way of consciousness, mobilization and collective action.

The distinction implies a sensible sequence of analysis: 'look at structure first, popular response only afterwards – or you don't know what it is that people are responding to.' But the distinction also implies that there may be no logical pattern of 'response' which can readily be deduced from a particular pattern of 'structure'.

Not only have history and research combined to prove this

is so; but also, of course, if there can be said to have been a 'typical' response by organized labour to its dependent role within capitalism, it has been towards some form of compromise – and not towards the revolution which traditional Marxism has read into the tea-leaves of economic class structure.

So labour's forward march has not been very obviously directed to a socialist reconstruction of society. And whatever its direction at this time or that, it has not been noticeably singleminded. For all the difficulties of inferring 'response' from 'structure', the contradictory nature of inequality in a market economy is likely to produce disunity within labour when it comes to organizing its opposition.

Over and above the primary inequality between capital and labour, labour markets and consumer markets add a clutch of secondary inequalities – each one liable to breed its own pressure groups. And just as reformism has held back radicalism, so sectional conflicts of interest have long been prone to take steam away from central class conflict. This is all old hat, but one might not think so from the myth-spinning which comes with the new revisionism.

What *is* new, against the background of the past three or four decades, is a set of disquieting twists to an otherwise familiar story: the loss of popular support for labour's old organizations and a mood – which extends well into the manual working class – of acquiescence in a sustained right-wing challenge to the class compromise made in the 1940s in the names of Keynes and Beveridge. Does this ominous shift of opinion reflect some significant change in the underlying class structure?

Inequality: alive and well

There is little evidence of it. For a start it must be made clear that over the last 30 years the economic inequalities between different groups of the population – and the gulf in circumstances those inequalities produce – have neither diminished nor shifted more than fractionally.

The range of inequality in disposable income, for example,

has barely altered since the modest advances that came with war-time mobilization and post-war social reconstruction. Some differentials in employment earnings have changed, but these shifts have made no overall impact on the class structure. They have scarcely dented economic privilege at the top while, at the other end, unemployment and enforced early retirement have actually increased the risk of relative poverty.

Two further points are crucial. First, since the post-war settlement, there has been no notable stepping up of state provision to moderate the income inequalities generated by property and markets. Such state provision is, in any case, heavily circumscribed, not least because taxation – supposedly progressive – is shown when an account is taken of all forms of tax, to be nothing of the kind. That says quite a lot about the nature of the 'welfare state'. And it may go quite a way to explaining why resentment of taxation and suspicion of public provision have spread beyond the rich and the 'middle classes'.

Second, the pyramid of income inequality is capped by a peak of privilege concentrated in few hands: the richest one per cent have about as much income at their effective disposal as the poorest 15 or 20 per cent. The nonsensical notion (favoured by politicians, and probably widely believed) that further redistribution to reduce poverty can draw only on 'middle incomes' – because there is too little wealth at the top to 'soak' – would, if it were true, set average wage-earners at loggerheads with the poor. But it is not. Moreover, very much of that privileged minority's income comes from ownership or control of business, and this in turn is just one manifestation of the dominant part which capital continues to play in shaping economy and society.

New revisionists on the left deny none of this, of course. But to take it for granted, and pass it over in silence in order to focus on shifts in class structure well below the peak of power and privilege, makes for an oddly lopsided view. It gets the balance wrong between continuity and whatever change there may be. It also leaves a vacuum in radical strategy. For if ever a common socialist front is to be mobilized across the spectrum of circumstances and outlooks which tend to divide popular interests, it can be only through shared opposition to that power-house of control and wealth at the top.

What's happened to the working class?

But all right, what *has* been going on further down in the class structure? Labour, we are told, has always drawn its strength from the manual working class, and manual workers are dwindling in number. True enough. But that does not explain a key feature of the Conservative victories in 1979 and 1983: the drop in support for Labour *among* manual workers. Yet this occurred both times round, first with a sharp boost for the Tories, then with fresh defections to the Alliance (especially marked among the skilled, but sizeable also among the non-skilled).

Besides, although it has only just been rediscovered, the shift in occupational composition of the working population is a trend of long standing. As a matter of fact, it was a good deal less dramatic in the 1970s – the decade of stagnation and recession leading to Labour's recent electoral catastrophes – than it was in the 1960s, when there was still economic growth and Labour replaced the Tories in office for six years.

The General Household Survey shows that manual workers are still a large majority among 'economically active' men. And in 1981 they made up the same proportion of the total – 63 per cent – as they did 10 years earlier. Among women, though the proportion of 'white-blouse' workers continued to rise between 1971 and 1981, this increase was fairly modest – from over 54 per cent to just under 59 per cent.

True, these figures are likely to conceal some real changes of economic structure associated with the mounting crisis of the 1970s. The unemployed count as 'economically active', and their large numbers in the early 1980s will include many from manual jobs who may never return to work of that, or perhaps of any, kind. What's more, the label 'manual' extends to workers on their 'own account' outside professional work – a small minority but maybe a growing one, as more people try to scrape a living through petty enterprise on their own once the regular job market collapses around them.

Even so, the change from boom to slump in the 1970s could well be expected to slow the long-standing shift of occupational structure into non-manual work; so for this reason too the drastic defections from Labour in recent years cannot be explained away by the declining number of 'blue-collar' workers in the population.

It is true that, in this country, Labour has failed to attract majority support from the many people in the expanding 'white-collar' and 'white-blouse' groups whose circumstances of life and work are little different from those of manual workers. 'New revisionist' commentary to that effect is right, though the point is a good deal more significant in relation to two other developments.

First, the failure is all the more striking in the light of the high proportion of non-manual workers who earn their livelihood from the public sector. Just what that proportion is, and how it varies from one level to another, is curiously hard to establish; there is a serious gap in the national statistics on this point, but the proportion *is* undoubtedly large. Consider administrators and professionals in government and other public services. They certainly have substantial privileges and authority to defend in common with their private sector counterparts but they must also have some substantial interest in preserving the public sector against the insecurity and erosion of their positions. On that score at least their interests come together with Labour's. But if Labour has failed to drive this point home, its failure to win over majority support from routine-level public employees is, of course, even more glaring.

The second point is more fundamental. Labour's failure to make new headway among non-manual workers in the low-to-middling brackets is only half the story; the other half is its loss of appeal to manual workers. Put the two things together (bearing in mind that patterns of voting and political allegiance are more volatile than they used to be, a trend from which Labour has so far stood to lose most) and there is probably now much less difference in outlook between skilled 'blue-collar' workers and their 'white collar/white blouse' counterparts. Moreover, the non-skilled seem to be *disillus. with party* hot on the heels of their skilled mates in creeping disillusion-ment with their old party. If this is so, there is at least a sort of 'structural' sense to the coming together of 'white- and blue-collar' outlooks – if not to the direction this has taken in distrust of Labour.

Redefining workers

The fact is that (for reasons only partly related to real change) the old distinction between 'manual' and 'non-manual' is now of fairly limited help. Leaving aside the small minority with concentrated power, property and privilege, we can get to grips with class better if we distinguish between two broad groups of people whose different 'life-cycle' expectations and experience mark them off from one another.

The larger group are those whose lives are confined within *Jobs* the resources and horizons of routine *jobs*. This is work which, even if skilled, involves neither autonomy nor authority on the job; allows little discretion or variety; carries with it no increments in pay and few chances of promotion to better things after the early years; leads often to hardship in old age; and is relatively vulnerable to redundancy in recession. *Careers*

The other group are those whose lives centre on *careers*. This is work – now or within realistic prospect – of a significantly different kind: it promises regular increments in pay to take income well above job wage-levels after the early years; offers visible opportunity, though no certainty of promotion beyond that; carries some authority even at subordinate levels, while allowing discretion and variety in the application of skills or experience; demands (and tends to elicit) more commitment than goes with merely working for a wage; offers security in retirement; and, while not immune from the risk of redundancy, is much less exposed to it than routine work and provides better resources to cope with it should it happen.

The distinction is rough. It blurs at the edges and glibly neglects gradations and variations on either side. But it makes a good deal better sense than the old 'manual/non-manual' dichotomy for identifying those crucial differences in circumstances among the bulk of the population which link with material interests and are likely to affect socio-political outlook. And if the 'working-class' are defined as those people whose lives and expectations are circumscribed by dependence on 'jobs', they certainly remain a majority: the majority among women, men and households.

It is hard to say how big exactly this 'working-class' is. Adding routine office work to the bulk of manual work gives only a preliminary, rather inflated indication. Deductions have to be made for young workers who stand to gain promotion from one side of the dividing line to the other, and for households with members on either side of the line who will benefit from the better-off partner. But with this in mind, it is reasonable to guess that the 'job' class makes up some 60 per cent of the population.

The continuing shift from manual to non-manual work, moreover, carries no prediction that the 'jobs-dependent' majority must inexorably shrink in the future. True, it has contracted at times in the recent past when the trends towards white collar and white blouse occupations favoured a real growth of administrative and professional, as well as merely routine, non-manual work.

This was so during the post-war boom until the 1970s. It brought with it a distinct increase in 'upward social mobility', and probably a more widespread rise in ordinary people's hopes for themselves or their children – despite the fact that the old inequalities of opportunity between those setting off in life from different starting points stayed remarkably static. But recession seems, as might be expected, to have slowed down the occupational changes and, even if some recovery does come, its effects are quite uncertain.

Changes in economic organization and technology – the latter not least in application to non-manual work – can be expected to put some new skills at a premium. But the same processes will probably centralize control still further and reduce the scope for older skills at several levels – not excluding management. High production and its distribution could, in the not-so-very-long-run, be achieved with much less labour for supervision as well as processing.

But with the pace and incidence of change inevitably uneven, and if market profit continues to be the driving force, the likely consequences will be increased insecurity of employment and livelihood among the many people dependent on routine jobs, and more uncertainty and diversity of prospects for those with careers. The only way of avoiding these risks – of replacing them with a future in which the benefits of technological advance could be equally distributed work reorganized away from monotonous routine and entitlement to a steady income detached from the obligation to spend one's life working for others – would require either some form of full-blown socialism or, at the very least, a radical reversal of today's trend towards privatization of the economy. There is no reason to assume that, if people balance the likely gains and losses offered by these alternatives, most of them would inevitably choose *laissez faire.*

Pursuit of limited sectional advantage may stand in the way of moving towards a common popular interest in radical change – among vulnerable groups in the 'careers class' as well as among the bulk of the 'jobs class'. Workers with a patch of real privilege to protect, however small it is, may use collective muscle to restrict access into their jobs in the face of threats of deskilling and redundancy. But although they have always been there, it is not at all clear that the conditions making for sectionalism are so much on the increase to explain neo-Toryism's recent triumphs, or predict a permanently bleak political future.

In some important respects, long-term trends have favoured more rather than less similarity of condition among routine (and for that matter not-quite-routine) employees. First, the decline of private domestic service and then both the contraction of unskilled casual labour and a growth of affinity in the style of work between skilled and semi-skilled productive labour, have brought the 'traditional' working class closer together in their circumstances and work-place relations. Recent and prospective changes in the organization of routine-grade non-manual work point in the same direction; and for employees at most levels, 'blue-' or 'white-

collar', terms of employment have become more standard-
ized through union and government activity alike.

To note these tendencies is not to maintain a thesis of
relentless 'proletarian homogenization'. Some of the changes
have set up their own counter-processes: worker-resistance
to deskilling; new job monopolies in place of old ones;
dogged defence of differentials and managerial adoption of
alternative tactics for control of production and labour. But
the balance of trends and counter-trends is a fine one, now as
in the past: it does not lend itself to glib summary, least of all
in favour of new revisionist assumptions.

Those assumptions can, however, find support from
changes in two other respects. One concerns conditions of
life outside work. Promoted by the more or less enthusiastic
policies of successive governments, owner occupation of
housing has so spread – unlike ownership of business capital
– that by 1981 well over half of all households 'headed' by
skilled manual or junior non-manual workers owned or were
buying their homes, as were more than a third of all semi-
skilled households and about a quarter of unskilled households. Of course, some of these houses are market liabilities
rather than assets, and quite a number of mortgages are
budget liabilities (especially in recession). But the broad
effect has been to produce a new dividing line among people
dependent on 'jobs': home ownership brings some real
economic advantage.

While a total reversal of policy in this field is inconceivable,
it should not be too late for new initiatives – for example a
policy aimed towards occupancy of both private and council
housing on long leaseholds with freehold reversion to public
hands, in order to ensure common benefit from rising land
values as well as social equity in housing provision.

Another real change concerns not the divisions of economic structure in themselves, but the nature of the interest-
group support they generate. Labour (party and union
movement) can no longer rely on the loyalties of wage-
earners rooted in communal class sentiment. Commitments
to Labour simply 'because we're working class and Labour
stands for the working class' are not dead yet. But they are on

the way out in their old form, in the north as well as the south, and for good reasons.

The post-war boom, especially, raised individual expectations and reduced the influence of work-relations on shaping social horizons. While economic inequalities persisted, the opportunities for ordinary people to create some 'private space' in their lives increased. Popular deference slid away – deference not just to 'social betters' but to authority and the status quo, and Labour's own organizations and activities were subject to the pragmatic scepticism which grew in its place.

Labour's rational alternative

Little new emerged from Labour to hold back that line of scepticism. Hindsight shows that the 1940s settlement of full employment plus welfare had instability built into it of a kind which 'consensus politics' could not resolve. Economic growth and the promises implied by post-war social reconstruction made wage-earners assertive. Successive government efforts to contain their demands through tripartite 'corporatist' negotiation tended to founder. Union collaboration was always liable to be withdrawn when offers of reward by redistribution came to nothing. Employers' collaboration proved similarly tenuous when the curbs on indiscipline and demands by the workforce failed. Recurrent resumption of a market free-for-all would then underline labour sectionalism.

This in turn went to encourage pragmatic support for each union or union section from its own constituency, combined with more general distrust of labour at large. Other unions were seen as competitors. The labour movement and Labour Party were judged to be colluding in a state of affairs prone to conflict and dominance by remote bureaucracies'. Active political campaigning for progressive social change had apparently gone out the window.

If this breathless summary is correct, support has fallen away from Labour not because the economic structure of class has been shifting significantly but because the move-ment has seemed to provide little for supporters who were increasingly inclined to evaluate what politics had to offer in the real world.

Labour has kept up a loose rhetoric of socialist aspiration, but lack of socialist performance has undermined both its credibility and the goal itself. The actualities of party policy and union activity, maintaining rearguard defence of the 1940s settlement, have also shown evidence of an inability to achieve even short-term pragmatic gains.

Recession has certainly not reversed Labour's failure to be convincing in either role; nor has it reversed the new utilitarianism in popular attitudes to politics – despite the fact that those attitudes were originally triggered by the boom. Not only did unemployment begin to grow visibly with Labour already in office – a point that escaped the electorate no more than it escaped the Tories. But also, as unemploy-ment has spread, it has weakened unions even as sectional pressure groups, and brought with it its own kind of 'privatization' – when people lose their jobs, income and self-confidence they also get cut-off from each other. Recession therefore deprives the labour movement of vital resources: morale; market bargaining power, organization and funds.

Although communal class sentiment no longer provides a solid base for socialist politics, there is potential gain to be had from this as well as current loss. 'Traditional' working-class solidarity was parochial in its sources and parochial in character. Its roots were in partially closed communities – locality, workshop, craft and trade – which made for shopfloor strength. But it also produced as much labour sectionalism as commitment to the wider aspirations of socialism.

A labour movement dedicated to radical and constructive opposition to inequality can no longer hope to swing a majority behind it by appealing to intuitive class loyalties. But if that change helps to free the movement from the parochial allegiances which have characterized it hitherto, Labour *can* hope to demonstrate that socialists aims fit in with majority interests – with the rational interests of a jobs-dependent majority that increasingly judges political claims in practical terms.

The Social Democrats in Sweden seem to have done just that, when they fought their election in 1982 on a programme for wage-earner funds to ease economic power out of private hands – and *won*, despite signs of a creeping erosion of traditional class allegiance. Maybe their progress will not last; their base for making it was in any case firmer than Labour's in Britain. Yet there is hope for socialism here, too, though the haul will be a long one. First, the persistent inequities and inefficiencies of current economic organization gives the majority a logical interest in leftward change. Second, the hard-nosed, practical sense now common in the electorate can work to make the majority recognize that interest.

Utilitarian self-interest of this sort need not be at odds with the concern for social justice which must inspire socialism. Popular concern with social justice is not dead, despite Thatcherism. The results of sensitive contemporary opinion-probing point this up when they show some striking ostensible contradictions to the public mood.

Acquiescence in today's economic order, and support for harsher discipline to keep it going, mixes in with widespread awareness of unjust exploitation and common acceptance of the need for public provision of welfare. It is not yet beyond the wit of socialist argument to guide the latter against the former – popular social criticism against pragmatic acquiescence. But there is a corollary. Socialists must demonstrate that their way is *competent* to take away the inefficiencies of markets and property, as well as their inequities.

[handwritten marginalia: Radical + Constructive opposition]

Notes

[1] The point is well made by Richard Hyman in his contribution to this volume.

[2] M. Abrams and R. Rose, *Must Labour Lose?* (Penguin, 1960).

[3] Daniel Bell, *The End of Ideology* (Glencoe Free Press, 1960).

[4] Eric Hobsbawm and others, *The Forward March of Labour Halted?* (Verso, 1981).

6

Wooing the Working Class

RICHARD HYMAN

In the post mortem on Labour's successive election defeats during the fifties, it was argued that the party's social base among the manual working class was shrinking, and that the effect of 'affluence' was to erode former electoral loyalties. The political conclusion of this argument was that Labour should no longer adopt the role of a working-class party but should revise its socialist commitments, as symbolized by clause four of the constitution, in favour of a Continental-style social democracy. (Many of the survivors of this 1960s tendency have, of course, decamped to form the SDP.) When Labour went on to win four out of five general elections, the debate seemed to have petered out. But the recovery gave little cause for complacency. Labour was elected in 1964 with fewer votes than when it was defeated in 1959; and the higher total in 1966 was still almost a million less than in 1951. Even before the 1979 election, Eric Hobsbawm had pointed to the continuous post-1966 decline in Labour voting as evidence of dissolution of the 'political expression of class consciousness'.[1]

The size of Thatcher's victory in 1979 (when ironically the Labour vote was fractionally up on October 1974) prompted Ivor Crewe to call for 'a return to the issues raised 20 years earlier'.[2] His analysis of voting patterns and opinions in June 1983 has re-emphasized the point: 'the class basis of party choice has steadily weakened over the last quarter century . . . True, the Labour vote remains largely working-class; but the working class has ceased to be largely Labour.'[3]

From the evidence of a diminishing link between social class and electoral behaviour, the political conclusions are less straightforward than appeared to Crosland and his supporters in the 1960s. In practice, the revisionist case was embraced by Labour in government during the past two decades even if it was rejected by the party conference. And dwindling electoral popularity has owed much to disillusionment with the actual results of Labour orthodoxy in the sixties and seventies, and scepticism at promises of greater success in the eighties.

While challenging left-wing assumptions that a radical programme would prove more popular, Crewe doubts whether the policies of the Labour right are any closer to the voters' mood: 'the nub of the problem lies in the sheer gulf that separates the policies and principles *of all wings* of the Labour Party from what the public says it wants.'[4] To some degree, all options being canvassed within the party accept that rather than merely adapting to voters' expressed opinions, it is necessary to *change* them.

The same is true of contributors to *The Forward March of Labour Halted?*, a symposium behind which lurks the hidden agenda of the 'broad democratic alliance'. Exponents of this notion insist that the declining size, or political militancy, of the traditional working class obliges socialists to seek a wider (at times almost infinitely elastic) basis of support. But within the many variants of this Eurocommunist strategy there is no clear and convincing indication of the way in which people's current attitudes and experiences could be addressed.

The distribution of employment among industries and occupations has been constantly shifting since the rise of capitalism. The changing balance between 'manual' and 'white collar' workers (the categories are themselves largely arbitrary and conventional) has been a feature for several decades. The largest number of manual workers in Britain (over 14 million) was recorded in 1931 – not the best year for those seeking a simple link between occupation and electoral behaviour! In the subsequent half century the total fell below 12 million, and has now been overtaken by white-collar employment, which in 1931 was only 4.5 million. Table 6.1 shows how the occupational and industrial shifts since the war have been substantial, and have been reflected in the composition of British trade unionism. Thirty years ago, the

**Table 6.1   Employment and union membership
(thousands), 1948 and 1979**

	1948		1979	
	Emp.	TU	Emp.	TU
Textiles	862	476	474	283
Coal	800	691	307	298
Railways	535	475	209	204
Metal & engineering	3514	1914	3809	3034
Construction	1326	611	1415	520
Local govt. & education	1241	861	2880	2232
Health	522	221	1318	971
Banking & insurance	352	137	721	395
Distribution	2089	326	2872	428
Misc. services	2001	106	3576	262
Public sector	4637	3278	6297	5190
Manufacturing	7290	3720	8286	4138
Private services	4578	665	7284	1215
Manual	14027	7056	12035	7577
White collar	6243	2062	11652	5125
Male	13485	7468	13979	8866
Female	6785	1650	9708	3836
Total	**20270**	**9118**	**23687**	**12702**

Source: George Sayers Bain and Robert Price, 'Union growth:
dimensions, determinants and destiny' in Bain, (ed.) *Industrial
Relations in Britain*, Basil Blackwell 1983.

typical union member was a male manual worker in one of
the traditional sectors of British industry. Today, she or he is
more likely to work in an office, hospital, shop or school.
There has been an interconnected increase in the employment
of women, of non-manual workers, and in the hetero-
geneous service sector and, moreover, the rate of unionization in these categories has advanced considerably.[5]

Most of the largest unions today recruit principally among
white-collar workers, in the public sector services, or both.
This changing structure of the movement underlies the
contentious decision in the TUC to alter the constitution of

its general council. And though many unions in the main growth sectors are not affiliated to the Labour Party, those that are – such as ASTMS and NUPE – have enlarged their influence considerably.

In the early 1960s, much of the 'revisionist' case rested on the assumption of a causal chain: white-collar employment conferred middle-class status and led to a rejection of the collectivist traditions of the labour movement. The subsequent expansion of white-collar unionism, and the evidence of significant (even if minority) Labour support, reduced the credibility of this simple proposition. But the interpretation persisted in a new guise. While non-manual workers might unionize, the character of their collective organization was distinctive. In place of the principled solidarity of manual unionism their combination had an ulterior motive of self interest –'white collar workers join unions not because they reject their middle class aspirations, but because they see unionism as a better way of obtaining them.'[6]

Behind such contrasts lie a mythical stereotype of traditional working-class solidarity. In fact, pragmatism has always characterized trade union action. Organization among manual as among white-collar workers has invariably involved the defence and advancement of the interests of the occupational and industrial groups within the membership. Sectionalism – the pursuit of these interests in isolation from (and often in opposition to) those of other workers – has been a recurrent feature of British unionism, frequently belying the rhetoric of a common movement. Political principles, social ideals and a broader class orientation were never spontaneous. They became interwoven with more limited and exclusive concerns only to the extent that their relevance to individual experience could be demonstrated. The connections between particular and general, industrial and political, have throughout the history of the labour movement been established only against resistance and through debate and struggle.

The openness of any occupational group – whether cooks, clerks or coalminers – to appeals of socialism or solidarity can be assessed only through a sensitive analysis of its role within social production, and the constellations of interests which stem from this. (Such analysis would almost certainly demonstrate the inadequacy of lumping together secretaries, shopworkers, technicians, nurses, professors and bank managers under the common label 'white collar'.)

Even more complexities underlie the relationship between occupational identity and electoral behaviour. Political allegiance cannot be taken for granted simply from a worker's occupation. Electoral choice is ultimately determined by 'all those various and complementary processes that contribute to "class formation" and that constitute the structures of everyday life for working men and women: personal relations with family, neighbours and friends; patterns of courtship, marriage and childrearing; leisure habits, cultural symbols and rituals'.[7] Against such complexities, current attempts to interpret the 1983 election in terms of a dichotomy between 'old' and 'new' working classes are particularly crude. What underlies the contrast between north and south? Does home ownership encourage Tory voting through a general inculcation of individualistic values, or simply because Labour is considered hostile to home ownership? How can lasting shifts in political commitment be disentangled from short-term reactions (the Falklands factor, Labour disarray, the novelty of the Alliance)? Psephologists may provide some relevant evidence, but they tell us nothing of the pattern of social relations which lie behind the survey responses.

The changing composition of the working class is related to the decline in Labour support only through a series of complex and contradictory links – including the nature of the political choices which are available. How far has the meaning of Labour politics itself been altering? As a political organization, the Labour Party is an oddity. Its very name – a choice which explicitly rejects a socialist identity – reflects its origins as a political pressure group for the unions. In its formative years, those committed to a socialist transformation of society were far outnumbered by those concerned solely with the representation of labour as an interest within existing society. Labour voting was a derivative of trade union loyalty and identity, buttressed by the relative cultural homogeneity of the communities in which workers constituted 'a class apart'. Like trade union membership itself, Labour support was thus traditionally an expression of defensive solidarity. Even in these limited terms, it was an uphill struggle to win workers' support for Labour as an expression of common social interests. Occupational and industrial sectionalism obstructed class identity; nineteenth-century political affiliations proved persistent. But for the 1914–18 war and the break-up of the Liberals, the Labour Party itself might not have survived. The electoral advances of the 1920s came to a halt in the following decade; Labour gained less votes in 1935 than in 1929, despite the experience of mass unemployment. The intense working-class allegiance registered in 1945–51 was itself historically exceptional, and reflected specific influences.

In this sense, then, the 'old working class' did not automatically cling to Labour. What is true, however, is that with occupational and industrial change the ever-present fragmentation has become more overt, and has eroded the credibility of Labourism as a reflection of workers' common interest. Ironically, this erosion reflects in part the growing confidence and aspirations of workers and their organizations in recent decades. While trade union action traditionally centred on the defence of customary standards, since the war it has been concerned far more with the struggle for advances. In this process, the concern with comparisons – the struggle to do at least as well as other groups – have proved divisive. So has the altered context of trade union struggle.

The elaborate modern division of labour has accentuated the interdependence of disparate activities, while social production, traditionally performed in the community or the household, is now the object of large-scale commodity production or state provision. Hence strikes are more overtly disruptive, and those affected as consumers are encouraged to react by blaming the strikers. Strikes are thus a major source of the unpopularity of the unions – and, by association, of the Labour Party itself.

A further cause of Labour's decline is the increasing detachment between the organizational apparatus of unions and party, and the workers they claim to represent. Today's giant unions all too readily appear as spectres of unwieldy bureaucracy and though most of them sustain a vigorous internal political life, more often than not this engages no more than a small minority of activists. The distancing of 'the union' from most ordinary members has been reinforced by the rapid spread of the closed shop during the 1970s – usually an administrative arrangement between company and union officials rather than the result of pressure from below.

The rise in the number of unionists in the seventies *despite* mounting unemployment, reflects not a sudden expansion of trade union consciousness but the artificial accretion of paper membership. That so many of these paper unionists do not feel themselves to be 'part of the union' constitutes a genuine problem of union democracy – a problem that the Tories have effectively exploited.

Thus the 1983 election is further evidence of a declining sense within the working class – 'old' *and* 'new' – of a common interest as *workers* which unions and the party naturally represent. Does this mean that the politics of class should be abandoned – or else subsumed within a 'broad democratic alliance'? I would argue that the defensive and constricted basis of Labour's traditional class appeal has been undermined. A renewal of the party's appeal requires the reconstruction of a persuasive vision of workers' common interest in the creation of a *new* social order.

It is a curious fact that Labour was established as an avowedly *non*-socialist party; is commonly referred to as the 'socialist party' by its enemies rather than its supporters; yet since the adoption of the 1918 constitution has declared socialism to be its ultimate goal.

But Labour's socialism has always carried a distinctive meaning. One feature is the rejection of class struggle in favour of a diffuse ethical nationalism: 'socialism marks the growth of society, not the uprising of a class. The consciousness which it seeks to quicken is not one of economic class solidarity, but one of social unity.'[8] MacDonald's sentiments helped inform the anti-strike posture of the early Labour governments, and were perpetuated in those of the last two decades. The language of socialism as national unity, inspiring attacks on union 'irresponsibility' and 'mindless militancy', has surely played an important part in weakening the ideological identification of workers with the labour movement.

A second feature – common to traditional Fabians and the orthodox left alike – has been the unquestioned identification of socialism with state ownership and control. The debates of the 1890s, the Webbian constitution of 1918, the great programme of 1945–51, all reflected a bureaucratic model of socialism. On the left, 'public enterprise' and the 'welfare state' are typically regarded with pride and without question as signals of socialist advance; arguments to the contrary are normally the hallmark of right-wing social democrats. Yet the whole tenor of labour-movement thought is out of touch with popular opinion; for most members of the working class the welfare state is not *their* welfare state. State ownership and state provision are fatally conditioned by the capitalist environment of their operation. The benefits of nationalization are rarely self-evident either to employees or to consumers. Clients of state services tend to find them inadequate, subject to explicable delays, delivered in a grudging and humiliating fashion. The whole apparatus of state activity is widely viewed as an unnecessary burden on the incomes of ordinary workers.

Of course there is a mythology of state bureaucracy, assiduously fanned by political misinformation and media hostility. But the stereotypes are potent because they resonate with real experience. In deploying the rhetoric of individual choice and personal freedom, the Tories have shown a perverted but effective capacity to benefit from such sentiments. By contrast, Labour programmes which centre around more nationalization and more state direction reveal a failure to comprehend working–class experience and aspirations. The lesson is not that socialism should be repudiated, but that the traditional equation of socialism with state control should be transcended. The traditional programme of state socialism repels more than it attracts, and for reasons which socialists should consider legitimate.

If Labour is to recover its appeal, three tasks are fundamental: to identify persuasively those areas of social activity where collective control is necessary; to devise new *forms* of collective organization which foster democratic involvement; and to facilitate individual and grassroots autonomy in areas of social life where broader collective direction is unnecessary. It is essential to recapture the appeal to freedom so cynically exploited by the right, while sustaining the traditional socialist principles of collective economic planning to meet society's needs.[9]

If the labour movement needs to rekindle a socialist vision which can speak to today's working class, it must also revitalize its ossified institutional structures. Union officers and activists must re-learn how to communicate with their members (who for the most part rejected Labour), in a two-way process of political education. Union democracy – the active mobilization of collective interests through processes which the members themselves feel that they control – must be a priority in the coming years, if Tebbit is not to irrevocably impose his own malign definition.

The working class *has* changed; but more importantly, so has the environment of a century-old style and structure of Labour politics. British socialism has become modest and banal in its long-term vision, despite the superficial radicalism of its short-term programme. What is needed now is not an opportunist bid for popularity which will merely reinforce popular cynicism, but a patient and self-critical effort to reconstruct the links between the working class, the labour movement and a credible conception of humanistic socialism. Without socialist imagination, accelerating decline seems unavoidable.

Notes

[1] Eric Hobsbawm and others, *The Forward March of Labour Halted?* (Verso, 1981), p. 16.

[2] Ivor Crewe, 'The Labour Party and the Electorate' in Dennis Kavanagh, (ed.) *The Politics of the Labour Party* (Allen & Unwin, 1982), p. 10.

[3] 'The Disturbing Truth Behind Labour's Rout', *The Guardian,* 13 June 1983.

[4] Crewe, 'Labour Party and the Electorate', p. 42; emphasis in original.

[5] Though if private sector services are considered separately, unionization has barely risen above its traditional low level.

6 George Strauss, quoted in Richard Hyman and Robert Price, *The New Working Class?* (Macmillan, 1983), p. 163.
7 James E Cronin, 'Politics, Class Structure and the Enduring Weakness of British Social Democracy', *Journal of Social History*, (1983), pp. 132–3.
8 Bernard Barker, *Ramsay MacDonald's Political Writings* (Allen Lane, 1972, p. 93).
9 I have developed these arguments at greater length in 'André Gorz and his Disappearing Proletariat' in Ralph Miliband and John Saville, (eds.) *Socialist Register 1983* (Merlin Press, 1983).

7

Losing the generation game

PHILIP COHEN

Since Labour's 1983 election defeat there has been considerable discussion inside and outside the Labour Party on the
question, Whatever happened to the youth vote? The evidence, on the face of it, seems pretty clear cut; the swing
away from Labour was more marked amongst first-time
voters than amongst other age-groups. Even more alarm-
ingly, data from the school mock elections organized by the
BBC showed a similar pattern of disaffection amongst those
who will be first-voters at the next election. Concerned to
demonstrate that a 'new generation' has come to power
inside the Labour Party, the new leadership has since made
strenuous efforts to appeal to young people, as part of a
wider strategy to rejuvenate the movement (or at least its
public image). And this seems to have paid off. Recent
opinion polls show that the upward trend in Labour's
electoral fortunes is much more marked amongst the 18–25
year olds than any other group. But unfortunately for the
optimists who have pinned their faith purely on electoral
strategy, the apparent gains on these swings hide a continuing loss on the more roundabout movements of political
ideology.

Only two things can be said with any degree of certainty
about the contemporary youth vote. First, it is highly
volatile; as an age group, first-voters' allegiances are less
fixed than ever before within the ideological frameworks of
customary political discourse. Second, it is not a bloc vote –
and never has been. Class, gender and ethnicity all play a part
in ensuring that there is no single experience of 'youth', no
single social or cultural category. Though that is not to say

'youth' as a whole is not subject to common experiences or the target of common attacks.

It is becoming clear that the most volatile element in the first-time electorate is to be found amongst the new middle class. This group, largely comprised of students in higher education, showed a large swing towards the Alliance in 1983, but an equally large swing back to Labour in 1984. The radicalism of this stratum has always had an instrumental, or frankly opportunist, aspect to it – in part bound up with the search for a political vehicle which would turn its cultural capital into more effective power. It is certainly important in electoral terms that the Labour Party recaptures this base of support, and there are already encouraging signs that it is capable of doing so. But there is also a great danger that success on this front may blind the party to disturbing evidence of a persistent trend in the opposite direction amongst young working-class voters.

A large and growing number of young workers, trainees, unemployed young people and early school leavers who will be voting for the first time in the next election, are consistently refusing even to consider voting Labour. Most of them say they will abstain altogether rather than support any kind of alternative politics, yet there is little comfort in that. This particular haemorrhage in the body politic of Labourism will not be healed by hiring a few media whizz-kids to liven up the party image, or by inviting Neil Kinnock on to a few teen-TV rock shows. The problem is structural. It concerns the disintegration of a whole political culture which once transmitted a version of socialism as a legacy of common sense and customary belief from one working-class generation to the next. And it concerns the failure of the Labour Party, or any other progressive movement, to construct a popular form of youth politics to fill the vacuum. The problem is either ignored in the hope that it will somehow go away, or rationalized in terms of a hedonistic 'apolitical phase' in the lifestyle of all working-class 'kids' – they'll rejoin the Labour fold once they settle down. But they don't and won't, largely because of the assumptions that lie behind this piece of wishful thinking.

Certainly, if their views are anything to go by (and I think they are) the young people I have interviewed give us few grounds for optimism, still less for complacency. I talked to a sample of early school leavers, who were either unemployed or on youth training schemes in London. One group came from Labour-voting families, the others did not. Yet despite the differences in emphasis in what they had to say, both groups were united in their hostility to Thatcherism *and* in their belief that the Labour Party had little or nothing to offer their generation. I was left with an overwhelming impression of cynicism about politicians of every kind and a general disbelief in the solutions to the crisis put forward by socialists.

These young people, did, however, have some specific demands. They wanted decent, preferably skilled, jobs with proper trade training and a living wage. They wanted cheap public housing for single young people so that they could afford some privacy and independence. They wanted better cultural and educational facilities for the unemployed. And they wanted democratically run organizations which would represent their views and give them some real bargaining power. These are modest enough aspirations which ought to be supported by all sections of the labour movement – and are indeed written into the party's manifesto for youth. Yet they were voiced hesitantly, almost apologetically, as if I would think them unrealistic, asking for the moon. Above all, they were not connected to any existing form of youth politics.

In the present mood, people will probably start calling for a new socialist youth movement. But a look at the history of such movements shows that initiatives in that direction are unlikely to regenerate socialism. The story of the various youth wings sprouted by the Labour Party, the ILP, the Communist Party and organizations of the far left, makes fascinating, if depressing, reading. It is a tale of chronic feuds, sectarian rivalries and battles with the parent bodies. The details are not important here. What matters is why it happened like this, and how it militated against any of these groups breaking through to achieve solid, popular support.

I suggested (in articles in *New Socialist*, January/February

1982 and November/December 1983) that, until recently, growing up working class has meant being apprenticed to a special kind of 'inheritance'. In this, destinies were fixed to origins through an *active* mastery of shared techniques and conditions of labour. As a child you were both 'set on' to tasks related to a future function on the shop or kitchen floor, and thereby aquired a sense of being 'born and bred' into your class place.

This code operated through, and linked, the cultures of family, work-place and community. Within it, boys were placed in a subordinate position *vis-à-vis* male elders; while girls were trained in passive support for the lads' counter-assertion of manhood and maturity. These same forms governed customary practices of initiation into working-class politics. The young novitiate was first taken on as a fetcher and carrier of the political message, a skivvy-cum-errand boy, then graduated to the position of 'time server' and finally 'improver' when the craft of running the party or trade union machine had been mastered. Political apprentice-ships into the labour movement thus mirrored the occupa-tional form, but often took considerably longer. 'Young' socialists were expected to reach political maturity only in early middle age. Through this system socialist ideas were entailed in a legacy of struggle. Political knowledge, like trade skills and even jobs, was to be held in trust by one generation for the next. But it was only by accepting the tutelage of elders who 'knew better' that youth could legitimately come into possession of this patrimony.

> In my shop, the older men were always talking politics and arguing with each other. Half the time I didn't understand a word they were on about, but gradually bits and pieces I heard began to fit together. Of course I didn't dare interrupt them, or ask questions – I'd only get shown up as an ignorant kid. But I think that just eavesdropping, as it were, was what first awakened my interest in socialism. (Engineering Apprentice, 1920s)

Socialism could be transmitted as an oral tradition within entire communities as well. In some working-class districts, nine-and ten-year olds might get a political education from one of the 'speakers' corners'. One East Ender had this memory of the 1930s:

> Becton Road corner used to be called the East End's university. The Labour League of Youth, the ILP, the Communist Party, they all used to put up speakers regular, Wednesdays of an evening and Sunday afternoon. I used to go up there with my mates to bunk off Sunday School. We used to go to hear Will Thorne he was an old man then, but still a fine speaker. These places, stumping grounds we called them, they were traditional, passed on from generation to generation and the law knew well enough not to interfere.

The transmission did not then depend on family influences, as this Jewish girl, also from the East End, made clear:

> My father regarded himself as working class and a socialist even though he never took an active part in politics. But I didn't get my ideas from him. The ideas were there, all around us, as we were growing up. It was simply regarded as the correct thing for Jewish immigrants, as well as Irish dockers, to vote Labour.

If socialism was constructed as a patrimony, then it might also be appropriated as a birthright, something you felt you had 'in your bones'. It was then no longer a legacy dependent on the power of elders. This could lead to some remarkable examples of what we would now regard as political precocity, as in this story from Liverpool:

> I came rather late to politics – when I was 13. I knew kids of 11 who were more politically advanced than me. We used to organize public meetings in the streets, by ourselves, without any adults at all. We would get up and talk about unemployment and injustice and the threat of fascism. We used to get quite a crowd around us. There were lots of arguments and hecklers. Some grown-ups would come to take the piss, but sometimes they stayed to listen. I think they were impressed that we knew what we were talking about, even if we didn't

win them over. Yes, we were only 12 or 13 then, still at school. It seems ever so young by today's standards, but in those days it wasn't.

This kind of political culture only ever socialized small numbers of young people for socialism. They were drawn overwhelmingly from the ranks of the labour aristocracy, or from the Jewish and Irish communities. In both cases, though for different reasons, the codes of apprenticeship and inheritance were strong, locking into a mesh of political loyalties rooted in everyday life. The youth wings of the Labour and Communist Parties were largely recruited from these social bases, and in their official policies and practices did little to challenge the patriarchal assumptions of such codes. The notion of politics as patrimony corresponded to the idea that youth organizations should be handmaidens to their parent bodies. They were granted autonomy partly to *minimize* their bargaining power. Young socialists were excluded effectively from adult policy-making and often found themselves confined to purely social and recreational activities, or routine tasks of propaganda.

There is a pattern common to the history of Labour and Communist youth movements, despite (or rather because of) their intense rivalry. Whenever trusteeship of the party's ideological inheritance is under threat, its elder statesmen move to tighten up the system of political apprenticeship to ensure that youth toes the correct line. In the case of the CP this has been bound up with a particular view of the working class as almost congenitally destined to overthrow capitalism – a destiny inscribed in a historical master plan unfolding in stages according to iron laws of development. Consequently any practice which does not conform to these laws becomes defined as adventurist. Adventurism is then identified as the besetting sin of youth. Underlying this view is a curious kind of political Darwinism. Different class fractions or social groups are ranked on an evolutionary scale of 'consciousness'. Adherence to party discipline or programme is seen as a sign of advanced development equated with maturity; resistance to the dictates of party elders thus becomes a sign of chronic backwardness. Ironically the most politically precocious young people, those who claimed socialism as a birthright rather than a legacy, and who therefore refused to take the handmaiden role lying down, found themselves diagnosed as suffering from Lenin's famous infantile disorder, and were often booted out.

The Labour Party's policy towards its youth wing has been no less oppressive in periods when it has been dominated by the great fear of being infiltrated from the left. Yet the problem has been managed in such a way as virtually to guarantee that this would happen. Far left groups have operated with a very different model of youth organization in class politics. What were youthful vices for the other parties became political virtues for groups with a more voluntarist reading of history, where spontaneous forms of direct action or rank and file struggle are seen as the key to proletarian advance. The so-called adventurism of youth is here hailed as a sign that young people are ready to be promoted into the front line, a strategy which often has disastrous results. Yet at least it puts these youth vanguards in a strong position to exploit the discontent generated by the handmaiden models of the other parties. Thereupon the party hierarchy moves to impose even tighter controls over its 'handmaidens', which in turn drives the youth wing yet further into the arms of the 'opposition'.

Labour's youth and the YCL have frequently sprouted Trotskyist or libertarian wings which have flapped about and made a good deal of noise, but never got off the ground in terms of popular membership or influence. The immediate reason is that they have remained locked in chronic conflict with each other and their parent bodies in a way which has alienated large numbers of potential working-class recruits. The real victims in all this have been young socialists themselves, beleaguered by entryists, belaboured by party elders, bewildered by factional in-fights. The very stuff of politics for some, who graduate to positions of adult responsibility having mastered the required techniques of impression management. But the drop-out rate has always been high. For all too many, what began as a political birthright ends in a legacy of disillusionment and personal defeat.

The labour movement has, however, developed some defence mechanisms to deal with the problem. Youthful militancy, including militancy of the far left, can be treated as a kind of rite of passage – a way of sowing political wild oats before settling down into an adult career as a party or trade union official. The biographies of labour leaders provide countless examples of this. Usually the cycle is rationalized in terms of the idealism of youth 'naturally' giving way to the wisdom (or realpolitik) of maturity. In fact it has more to do with the way generations replace themselves inside relatively inert political organizations. New issues, social forces and tactics are continually being thrown up from the grass roots of the movement, but these are only belatedly given official status and representation within the Labour Party apparatus, usually after a long struggle. Thus each generation tends to see the policies and practices it pioneered fall back to the point where they come into conflict with the priorities and persuasions of the next wave of new socialists. A recent example of this was the way some Labour leaders tried to apply strategies for campaigning against unemployment and fascism in the 1930s to the very different conditions of racism and recession today.

Of course, the current crisis of the Labour Party and the disenchantment of young people cannot be put down to these institutional factors or to some simple generation gap. They are bound up with profound changes in working-class culture, politics, and the position of youth. If I have talked about socialist youth movements in the past tense it is because they have proved incapable of adapting to these changes, despite the often heroic attempts of their members to do so. Instead they have preyed upon new forms of youth politics which have developed outside the old class-and-party lines. What has been gained, and what lost, in the process?

The Clash with Keir Hardie

Since the Second World War the culture of work-place and community, which relayed the socialist message most effectively from one generation to another, has had its back broken. The restructuring of labour in the interests of capital, policies of urban renewal and industrial relocation, de-skilling and new technologies all had their cumulative effect. At the same time the spectacular gearing of the 'consciousness industries' such as television or the music and fashion businesses around the manufacture of whole new ranges of consumer demand, served to privatize or make redundant many of the practices hitherto organized through a distinctively proletarian public realm. The stumping ground and the workshop stove gave way to the TV panel and studio audience as centres of political debate. A political culture which had rested on oral tradition began to wither. The chains of association between family, work place and community weakened too. Here is an experience of growing up in the East End in the late 1950s:

> It was just everybody working at the Penal Colony down the road, coming home, up the pub for a quick pint, and then home to watch the telly. Trade unionism and politics were never talked about. It was the 60-year-olds, the grandparents, who used to try and talk socialism to us. So I grew up with the idea that socialism was just a lot of old people going on about the past. It had nothing to do with us youngsters.

Where socialist ideas were still bequeathed in the old way, their transmission tended to be confined to individual families. The political patrimony thus became more easily embroiled in emotional conflicts between parents and adolescent children. Even if the legacy of elders was not rejected outright, its reception tended to be complicated, often in mutually unproductive ways.

In the early 1960s, Ray Gosling was one of the first socialists to sound the alarm bells about what was happening. In an early issue of *New Left Review* he wrote: 'In general, the youth clubs, the Church of England, the Labour Party, the trade unions, are talking a language that doesn't make contact with the new world that has arisen, the new conditions, the new codes of behaviour and living which have grown up amongst this younger generation of workers.' The new codes belonged to the mods and rockers, teds, skinheads and the rest. Each in their own way explored lines of continuity and rupture between the old and new working class. But on the terrain mapped out by these youth cultures, ways of 'showing class' were dramatically dislocated from real divisions of labour.

The youth service tried to learn the new language and modernize its image. Not so the labour movement. Here it seemed that all the youth demands that had been fought for and enshrined in the welfare state – comprehensive schooling, raising the school-leaving age (ROSLA), further education – were being rejected by this new generation in favour of rock'n'roll. One Clydesdale shop steward, in his forties, echoed the complaints of many socialists during the so-called youth revolution of the 1960s:

> Most of the lads in the yard have grown their hair long; they are more interested in drugs and discos than going to college. They've lost interest in any ideas of self improvement that even some of their parents had. The labour movement fought for 50 years to ensure lads like these got a decent education. Now it looks as if they'll be fighting for another 50 to get out of it.

State schooling had never been popular. But the tradition of self improvement and rational recreation could simply not compete against the glittering array of youth cultures. The painful fact was that they attracted not only the unskilled, the unorganized, and the unemployed, but young people who would previously have grown up socialists. With the arrival of hard times the appeal has persisted. Today youth cultures offer an even more dazzling mirror image of the fragmentation of class identities.

There have been two main responses to these developments on the left. On one side are the Jeremiahs who wring their hands over what went wrong, and conclude that labour has sold its socialist soul for a mess of capitalist potage – higher wages, home ownership, holidays in the Costa Brava and ever higher fi. Seen in this light youth cultures are Machiavellian devices designed to seduce the working class away from its historic mission to build the New Jerusalem.

The appeal to the labour movement is to return its authentic roots, located in some golden age of uncorrupted consciousness before the consumerist Fall. This myth addresses itself to an imaginary subject, an idealized vision of the 'old' working class. The truth is that the mutual aid of the labouring poor was always tempered by large doses of penny capitalism; the militancy of the skilled worker shot through with petty bourgeois aspirations of 'being your own boss'. Working-class youth cultures have resisted these 'seductions' neither more nor less than the old forms.

There are, however, strategic objections to be raised against the attempt to outdo Thatcherism: a return to our own version of Victorian values is neither possible nor desirable. In my *New Socialist* articles, I tried to show how the inheritance of socialist ideology was realized through certain patriarchal forms of 'apprenticeship', but that whole system of political patrimony is in irreversible decline: it is not a question of keeping the good bits, and getting rid of the bad. Those who wish to restore this old political culture end up by tacitly endorsing all those practices which confined women and young people to subordinate positions within it. As for those who wax lyrical about growing up with socialism in their bones, perhaps we should remind them that this sense of political ancestry not only included the image of the freeborn English*man* but all too often that of an inherently superior Anglo-Saxon race.

The weakening of traditional allegiances has helped open the field to hitherto disenfranchised groups. They are not, by definition, based on class or party ideology; indeed they may explicitly reject the old codes in favour of personal politics which give priority to issues of gender, age and race. The response from some sections of the left has been to endorse these new developments uncritically and then, in some cases, to try and co-opt them. Will these new movements succeed in mobilizing mass resistance to Thatcherism where Labour has so obviously failed?

The most successful attempt so far to politicize youth culture was organized by the Anti-Nazi League. The ANL tried to bring white and black youth together around two-tone music, to build a progressive anti-racist movement with its roots on the streets of the working-class city. But the ANL failed to hold together the volatile constituencies it had mobilized so brilliantly, not just because it lacked the organizational structure but because to have succeeded would have deprived youth culture of its *raison d'être*.

Youth cultures work by scrambling fixed signs of identity into more fluid and imaginary configurations of differences based on style. They thrive on what Freud called the narcissism of minor differences, already powerfully installed in adolescence and now vastly amplified by the fashion and music industries. But if they can only operate in an arena of stylistic oppositions and rival codes, they cannot be unified under any single political banner. They remain inherently unstable forms, resisting anchorage to any political ideology or movement.

It is doubtful, too, whether rock groups, however committed their lyrics, can ever be effective political educators while for the majority of their followers the medium is the only message that counts. Moreover the ambiguity of the populist message which most rock ideologues purvey can all too easily allow the music to dissociate itself from the politics. Perhaps it is no coincidence that The Clash's 'White Riot' was a hit with both the racist and anti-racist youth movements. Certainly the skinheads I worked with saw no contradiction between going along to ANL rallies because they liked the music, and continuing to attack black people on the street. If numbers of potential recruits were persuaded that the NF was No Fun it was not, in my experience, because they had rocked against racism. Rather they had learnt that involvement in racialist politics might mean being subjected to counter attack by the black community, or even, occasionally, getting into trouble with the police. Only the hard core fanatics felt it was worth getting your head kicked in for your beliefs. Not that the majority were converted to an anti-racist position; they simply became rather more circumspect about how they expressed their prejudice. Finally, if the National Front were No Fun it was for much the same reason as any other political party. Active membership involved more than going on marches and hurling abuse or broken bottles at the enemy; it meant attending meetings, addressing envelopes, delivering leaflets and all the other humdrum tasks attractive only to the committed few.

None of these points should be taken to imply that the ANL or Rock Against Racism was a waste of time. They succeeded in dramatizing the issue of racism in a way that the labour movement never even tried to do. And they opened opportunities for a whole new generation of middle-class youth, who then went on to become active in the peace movement and feminist or left-wing politics. Unfortunately the impact on white working-class youth was far more problematic.

The history of the schools movement during the 1970s confirms this picture. The shift from a politics of class to one of subjectivity is encapsulated in the movement's two key moments. The strike of 1971 was led by the Schools Action Union armed with a 'Marxist-Leninist' analysis and the slogan 'smash the dictatorship of the Head'. Its paper *Vanguard* was filled with dense Maoist rhetoric about the need for revolutionary discipline and the correct proletarian line. In contrast, the National Union of School Students went through a reformist phase and then discovered sexual politics. Its magazine *Blot* carried articles championing the cause of masturbation, feminism, gay rights, paedophilia, not to mention drugs and rock'n'roll. This version of the cultural revolution could not have been further from the clenched-fist puritanism of the SAU, and would have had the poor Chairman turning in his grave. But through all these ideological swings and roundabouts the movement remained the preserve of a small rebel sixth-form elite who had a material stake in the education system as well as a privileged awareness of its contradictions. Working-class pupils had neither, and their cultures of resistance to schooling obstinately refused to be connected to *either* kind of ideology. Plagued by sectarian rivalries and lacking organized support from teachers, the schools movement eventually collapsed.

To understand why neither the old political culture, nor the new cultural politics cuts much ice with a generation of school leavers headed for youth training schemes or the dole, it is necessary to look both at how the links between growing up, working and class have changed, and at how these hubs of identity have become disconnected from each other, and from the transmission belts of organized ideology. Quite simply, as the codes of inheritance and apprenticeship have weakened, they have increasingly pulled apart into separate, cultural forms. When inheritance is only to and for itself, its frame of reference contracts to the immediate confines of kith and kin. Family relations become the epicentre of a war of fixed position waged between genders and generations, stalemated in the old patriarchal binds. Growing up no longer means striving to take control of one's own destiny, but simply going through the motions of a more or less pre-ordained fate.

Amongst the unemployed young people I interviewed this was certainly one clear pattern. Colin, for example, came from a strong socialist and trade union background. His father, once a YCL militant, had had an accident at work which had left him disabled; he was now a somewhat embittered armchair critic of politics. Colin said of him:

> My dad's a Communist. It's all he ever talks about. He makes me sick. He sits in front of the telly all day and argues with them. But he never does anything about it. He just sits there. Everyone I know, it's just as if they've been sitting all their lives. Then I realized why. There was no reason to try and stand. There was no point. Life makes you like that, my mate says.

Instead of the father's injury evoking a sense of anger and injustice in the son, his physical immobility becomes a metaphor for Colin's own passivity – which is then justified in terms of a more general sense of class defeat. Instead of renewing a family tradition of militancy, Colin has inherited a fatalism which makes the struggle to grow up or stand up seem simply irrelevant.

In contrast, where apprenticeships turn in on themselves, youth is promoted to the centre stage where it busily constructs a world in its own image, proclaiming its freedom from the legacies of class. The political connections are often hard to make. Consider this encounter from a TV debate between Joan Lestor, representing the old code, and The Clash, thoughtful and committed exponents of the new:

> *The Clash:* Politics is just so remote from young people. You don't feel part of it, that you can change it or affect it in any way. You learnt in school how it's supposed to work. It was just boring. The problem is politics works in terms of what's going to happen in ten years, amounts of time like that. You say ten years to a young person and you might as well say eternity. You're thinking about what you're going to do tonight, what you're going to wear tomorrow. You're thinking in terms of half an hour, not ten years. Politics is just a big mess and you just feel like 'well, I don't want to have anything to do with it, I'll go and hear a good record instead'.
>
> *Joan Lestor:* But it's not only young people who want to see things happen quickly. Most people do. People who have been waiting years to get rehoused. People a lot older than you probably share your disillusionment. We have certainly got problems in this country, with the recession, which are not of our own making – and certain things have to take priority and certain things have to wait. What would you put forward in place of the system we've got at the present time?

A lot of people would like the answer to be socialism! Clearly we are going to have to wait some time for that. Meanwhile we have not even begun to articulate the terms in which a real dialogue between these two attitudes could take place. Joan Lestor's views are widespread in all sections and tendencies within the Labour Party. The essential message is 'young people must learn to wait' – until, presumably, they are old enough to join the silent majority who vote against Labour!

Enfranchising young people

From this perspective, the fact that young working–class people are already at the back of the queue for housing and jobs is either ignored, taken for granted or even held to be a good thing. Yet their consequent dependence on continued family support pushes these school leavers to seek autonomy in a 'body politic' whose pleasure principles, as indicated by The Clash quote, distance them even further from organized struggles. The whole process is a self-fulfilling prophecy, and one for which the labour movement bears considerable responsibility, not least for the way in which it has disenfranchised youth within its own ranks.

None of this will be changed by writing a new Youth Charter, with yet another shopping list of reforms. The first-time electorate may not have much of a memory for broken promises, but it does not go by party manifestos or policy statements. The Labour Party will be judged by its performance in practice. And here it is all too clear that for the majority of Labour administrations, both locally and nationally, the youth question has a very low priority. Where it is tackled, the approach has been either unpopular (ROSLA) or cosmetic (youth service provision), or both (youth opportunity schemes).

There are, of course, notable exceptions to this rule. The Greater London Council has consistently supported progressive youth movements, campaigns and projects. Wolverhampton Council recently appointed a senior youth policy advisor to cut through the red tape and produce a comprehensive programme aimed at the basic material and social needs of school leavers, young workers and unemployed young people. At present such initiatives are few and far between. The success of Youth Aid as a campaigning agency in the field of provision for 16–19 year-olds, and the growth of a national network of radical professionals around the magazine *Youth and Policy* are encouraging signs of a more co-ordinated response.

The problem with all these developments is that by definition they are not originated by young people themselves; they are designed to implement changes in state policy and provision which may hopefully benefit specific categories of youth, but in which youth itself has little or no say or stake. The real test of a youth policy, especially one that claims to be socialist, must be the extent to which it creates the conditions for the emergence of genuinely popular and democratic forms of progressive youth politics. Such politics could only be based on places where young people are already concentrated in large numbers – schools, training schemes, work-places and housing estates – and whatever forms of self-organization and collective representation were constructed would also have to break down existing patterns of exclusion and discrimination based on gender or race. Are there any new developments in political education and youth work which point in this direction?

Bernard Crick, in association with the Hansard Society, recently launched a programme to radicalize the teaching of 'civics' in schools. This started from the correct view that re-enfranchising the young involves more than lowering the voting age or the age of consent. In Crick's view, it is conditional on young people acquiring 'political literacy'. Essentially, this involves mastering the skills and protocol of democratic procedure and public debate as established within the framework of the parliamentary tradition. Crick's approach has been rather more successful in the context of youth and community work than in schools themselves; it is particularly geared to raising issues of civil liberties affecting groups of young people who are more than usually deprived of them. Some very interesting work has been done with young people in care on this basis; the move to establish youth councils as politically representative bodies for local youth organizations is inspired by similar principles. But the problem with this approach is that in challenging existing monopolies over due political process, it also rules out of order as politically illiterate, undemocratic or immature many of the key practices of popular struggle within the working-class community. In particular it reinforces the 'great moral divide' between respectable sheep, who join youth clubs, sit on committees and so on and the rough goats, whose main idea of collective bargaining is to riot. This in turn echoes a fatal split in socialist conceptions of youth politics – between the Labourists who recognize only bureaucratically organized youth activities, and libertarians who romanticize youth's more spectacular subcultural manifestations. Needless to say, the majority of working-class boys and girls, black and white, do not fall into either of these camps!

A rather more promising approach to political education –

one, I believe, that at least tries to avoid these crude prescriptive classifications – derives from the Marxist tradition of cultural studies. Originally inspired by the work of Raymond Williams, and increasingly influenced by the feminist and oral history movements, this approach sets out to enable school students to locate their own contemporary practices within the social history of youth labour and cultural forms in Britain over the last hundred years. The aim is both to challenge dominant constructs of class, gender and ethnicity, and to equip young people with the skills they need to gain more effective control over the production of their own cultures. At its best, this approach makes continual cross-reference between the personal and the political, between what is historical and what is unconscious, between the constraining realities of schooling and unemployment and the pleasures which can still be set against them. This strategy is a long way from the techniques of inculcation advocated by the traditional left. Its success is not to be measured in terms of propaganda/recruitment but by the extent to which it shifts the ground of common sense towards a more open discourse, where socialist or femininst ideas can be tried and tested for their realism and their relevance to a new generation.

However it has to be admitted that no programme of political education will make a decisive impact if it is confined to institutional sites and captive audiences. Indeed if the socialist, feminist, or anti-racist message is only relayed through the medium of teachers, youth workers and other professionals, the majority of working-class girls and boys will continue to turn a deaf ear. For example, despite the important gains being made by feminists at the level of youth policy and provision, and the growth and popularity of girls' projects, working-class girls remain a tiny minority within the women's liberation movement and continue to leave the initiative to their middle-class sisters when it comes to fighting sexism in schools. This is primarily a result of the deep subordination of girls within working-class culture, and the intensity of their sexual harassment by boys. Far from moving them towards active political engagement, such pressures force them back into the arms of the women's magazines and their own versions of the peer-group romance. With obstacles like these to overcome, feminism would undoubtedly have to take a militantly separatist line if it were eventually to capture the hearts and minds of working-class girls – a line hostile to any attempt to connect it with socialism.

This is already the pattern amongst the new wave of youth organizations emerging from sexual and ethnic minorities. Gay teenagers' groups, The Black Sisters, The Southall Youth Movement – there are many encouraging signs that in dealing with specific sites of oppression new kinds of political apprenticeship are being constructed. Yet by the same token a cultural politics of separatism makes alliances harder, not easier, to sustain and alienates these groups even further from the Labour Party and its traditional working-class base.

The difficulties of mobilizing a sizeable youth vote thus mirror the wider problems facing the Labour Party. But there is also a special problem of credibility on this front, concerning the issue of youth unemployment. All sections of young people agree in identifying this as the number one political issue. Yet it is also the issue about which they are the most fatalistic, believing that no political party or policy can make much difference. And it is an issue on which the labour movement and the left are deeply divided.

The optimists believe that a reflationary economic policy will do the trick and restore something like full employment for all 16–19 year-olds who want to work rather than continue in some form of education or training. The alternative optimists take the completely opposite view and argue that new technology is ushering us towards the New Jerusalem of the leisure society, and that young people will not miss full-time paid employment, since they have never known it and so are in the best position to experiment with new lifestyles and alternative kinds of work. The pessimist tendency, of which I confess to being a fully unpaid-up member, believes that both kinds of dream ticket offer a one-way ride to cloud-cuckoo-land. If a British economic miracle were to happen tomorrow, the displacement of youth labour as a result of the automation of its servicing functions or the elimination of its more unproductive forms, would more than counterbalance the rate of absorption from the growth. Moreover, to train the reserve army of youth for employment as low-grade people-minders within an expanded welfare state is no more a socialist solution than to encourage them to find 'alternative work' in the hidden economy, or in do-it-yourself forms of small business enterprise – which is what the other optimists seem to have in mind.

It is also becoming clear that structural unemployment is having an increasingly regressive effect on both girls' and boys' cultures of transition from school. Working-class girls have customarily been trapped in a position of chronic maturity – as little wives and mothers apprenticed to housework, child care and other 'labours of love' while still at school. Waged work may have echoed many of the features of their domestic servitude, but it also offered them a brief interlude of economic independence before marriage and this is now being drastically threatened. Unemployed daughters are under enormous pressure to go on 'making themselves useful about the house' in return for their continued upkeep. For many girls, the only way out of this impasse lies in early motherhood – though not necessarily marriage. Getting pregnant and becoming a single parent may not be a calculated choice, but it's a way of qualifying for council housing. As one girl put it to me, it may be out of the frying pan into the fire – but at least it's your own hearth! Naturally, such a course of action does not predispose these girls towards challenging central aspects of their subordination.

Unemployed boys are subjected to the opposite pressure – of feeling that unless they earn money to pay their way at home they are not entitled to be there, or be accorded adult status. They may even begin to feel guilty about treating their mums and sisters like skivvies! Some respond by acting the hard man, others by taking to their beds; but either way the increased sense of powerlessness tends to addict them to cultural activities which support the more infantile modes of male omnipotence. Walk round almost any inner-city housing estate and you will see how easily patterns of boredom and drug use interact to turn these lads into imaginary kings of castles in the air, while locking them into the most vicious kinds of territorial rivalry.

If structural youth unemployment is here to stay, and if it is armouring working-class girls and boys against feminist or socialist politics, it seems that all we are left with is a counsel of despair – concentrate on student, ethnic and sexual minority youth and ignore the rest. Certainly, given the Labour Party's scarce resources it might seem sensible to concentrate them where they are likely to reap the most immediate electoral benefit. In my view this would be a short-sighted policy; and it would mean a massive abstention amongst potential first-time Labour voters at the next election – something that need not happen. For there *is* an alternative.

It is necessary to conceive of a long-term strategy for building the material and ideological conditions of a new kind of autonomy for working-class youth – one that is no longer conditional on being paid a wage or on continued parental support, still less on regressive cultural practices or the kind of 'mobile privatization' sponsored by consumer capitalism. The central *material* condition for this is the provision of cheap public housing available to all 16–19 year-olds not in full-time education, as part of a massive pro-gramme of rehousing in the inner cities. To recognize this group as a priority for housing may seem unrealistic, but in terms of the likely saving on health and on social services it certainly makes welfare sense. It would also, of course, ease transitions for young working-class people. Boys would be more strongly motivated to 'grow up', learn how to look after themselves and do the housework; girls would be able to set up their own independent households without having to have a baby to 'legitimate' the move. The combination of sexual privacy with forms of collective self-management and sharing would provide at least a framework within which a more desirable form of autonomy could be developed than that offered either by the market-place or the work-place. Finally, a youth housing programme would not only attract widespread support from existing youth organizations, it would give feminists and socialists who are working with ordinary 'apolitical' young people in working-class areas a chance to introduce a material stake around which ideological issues could be anchored.

I have few illusions that this suggestion will be discussed seriously within the labour movement, let alone acted upon. Yet if we look at the solutions which school leavers and unemployed young people are themselves improvising to weather the crisis, we can see the starkly opposed directions in which the search for a sense of their own place leads. One way points towards a restless individualism anchored by various kinds of territorial chauvinism and petty delinquency; the other towards a more open and equal relationship between the domestic and the communal, and between the masculine and feminine spheres. Out of this a popular and democratic youth politics might just emerge. Labour may have more to lose than the youth vote if it fails to respond positively to *this* youth question.

Part 4
Learning from the Past

8

Britain Left Out

GÖRAN THERBORN

Intervening in the political debate of a foreign country is one of the easiest ways of making a fool of oneself. A large part of every culture is virtually unspoken, and in these silences are stored some of the most important pieces of knowledge about the culture – and *of* the culture – accessible only to those who are living in it. On the other hand, socialism is not merely a universalistic view of the world, it is also a universalistic goal and aspiration, and internationalism is a general socialist virtue. Yet internationalism is, perhaps, the socialist virtue against which socialists sin most easily and most often. There is, in fact, amazingly and distressingly little communication between socialists of different countries, compared with the constant, smooth dialogue between and within multinational corporations. What I will try to do here is to put the debates of the British left into an international context in matters of class politics, the problems of social democratic reformism and socialist discussion.

The Labour debate

The debate on the British left since the 1983 election seems to have largely centred around Eric Hobsbawm's article 'Labour's Lost Millions', which in turn is a follow-up of another remarkable piece by the same author, the Marx Memorial Lecture for 1978, *The Forward March of Labour Halted?* Before going any further, let me convey my envious congratulation to the British left for having the terms of two of its most central contemporary debates set by one of the world's most distinguished labour historians – perhaps even *the* most distinguished. There is nothing really on a par with this in any advanced capitalist country today.

However, from the other side of the Channel it seems that the terms of the British debate could well do with being put into perspective in the light of developments outside the British Isles. Let us first examine Hobsbawm's famous lecture from an international point of view. Hobsbawm's conclusion was that, 'in the past thirty years this movement seems to have got stuck, except for one trend: the "new" labour aristocracy of white-collar technical and professional workers has become unionised, and the students and intellectuals – from whom it is largely recruited – have also been radicalised to a greater extent than before.'[1] While Hobsbawm's arguments were largely couched in terms of historical changes of British class relations, his final conclusion threw light in another direction: 'If we are to explain the stagnation or crisis, we have to look at the Labour Party and the labour movement itself.'[2]

The same year as Hobsbawm gave his lecture, Theo Pirker, a West German sociologist and historian of the postwar West Germany labour movement, delivered another famous diagnosis, in a lecture tellingly entitled 'On "the End of the Labour Movement" '.[3] The quotation marks in the title are not meant ironically, they simply refer to a West German discussion. Pirker's conclusion is that as a class movement struggling for another kind of society, the labour movement is finished. Though formulated with the academic detachment of an old West Berlin professor of sociology, for those who know Pirker's work and background – a socialist social democrat of the classical Central European kind – his conclusion clearly comes as a tragedy.

In Italy, it was the time of the 'crisis of Marxism', masochistically proclaimed in December 1977 by Althusser in his intervention at the *Manifesto* symposium on post-revolutionary societies.[4] Behind Althusser's conclusion was not so much anything French or Italian, but the end of the Chinese Cultural Revolution, which could then no longer overshadow disillusion with the Soviet Union. In Italy Althusser's statement had an overwhelming impact, spreading far beyond the perspective of its author who stayed a tough Communist militant – an impact fed by the floundering of the Italian Communist Party in the miasma of Italian politics.

The year 1978 in France was, above all, the year of electoral defeat of the disunited left, which opened up a rift in French left-wing culture. By 1980, the politico-intellectual debate, which with the utmost ecumenical generosity might be called left-wing, had its terms set by two mutually congratulatory books – Alain Touraine's *After Socialism* and André Gorz's *Farewell to the Working Class*. Classical socialism was buried with joy, and by a characteristically Parisian post-empirical logic Gorz argued that the working class had become a privileged minority and heralded as the bearers of the future 'the non-class of non-workers'.[5]

From Northern Europe came the opposite message. In 1978 Routledge and Kegan Paul published *The Working Class in Welfare Capitalism* by Walter Korpi, a Swedish left-wing social democratic sociologist. Korpi wrote from the background of the strengthening and radicalization in the 1970s of the strong Swedish trade unions. In his perspective welfare capitalism was being eroded – in the direction of welfare socialism – by a working class which was growing stronger, more united and more demanding.

So, to summarize, by the end of the 1970s, labour was marching forward in good social democratic order more steadily than for a long time (Korpi); was halted (Hobsbawm); was in theoretical crisis (Althusser); had sadly expired (Pirker); and had fortuitously been transcended (Gorz, Touraine)! As far as I can see, none of these eminent authors is entirely correct. In my humble opinion they are all wrong – at least partly. As befits his intellectual status, Hobsbawm is by far the most cautious and circumspect. But looked at from a broader international context, his analysis seems to me to require a fundamental contextual displacement.

Working-class advance

Put briefly and crudely, the period from the mid-1960s to the early 1980s was a period of *major working-class advance* in the history of developed capitalism. The rate of unionization rose; working-class power at the point of production grew, expressed in terms of collective agreements, industrial legislation, the outcome of major industrial conflicts and the distribution of the pie of production between labour and capital. Another major development also took place in this period which, though inherently ambiguous in the totality of its implications, clearly restricted the immediate power of capital over people's lives: the great expansion of the welfare state.

In most countries these working-class advances also expressed themselves in electoral form. Before 1965, only five countries had ever given labour parties – social democratic, socialist, or communist taken together – more than 50 per cent of the vote: Australia (1914), New Zealand (1938), Czechoslovakia (1946), Norway since 1945, and Sweden since 1936. Since then, six more countries have displayed the same electoral confidence: Austria (1971, 1975, 1979), Finland (1966), France (1981), Greece (1981), Portugal (1976), Spain (1982). Repetitions have occurred in Sweden in 1968, 1970, and 1982, and in Norway in 1969. In Denmark, social democracy and the parties to the left of it scored 49.9 per cent in 1966 and 49.8 per cent in 1979. Other historical electoral records were beaten in West Germany, where, in 1972 the SPD reached its highest point ever, and in Italy, where the total vote for the member parties of the Socialist International, the CP and the far left peaked in the election of 1983. In 1976 the Italian Communist Party alone received 3.4 per cent more votes than the Popular Front of Communists and Socialists together in 1948. Electoral scores second only to a single top year right after the Second World War were reached in Japan (in 1972), and in the Netherlands in 1977.

The first part of this working-class advance holds for Britain, too. Unionization reached a historical record, while among manual workers the closed shop spread widely. The outcome of the miners' strike in 1974 was the opposite of that of the General Strike of 1926. The Trade Union and Labour Relations Act of 1974 and the Employment Protection Act of 1975 codified significant labour advances on the labour market and at the point of production. By the end of the Attlee government public expenditure accounted for 36 per cent of Gross Domestic Product; in 1975 for 49.9 per cent. After three and half years of Thatcherism, by the end of 1982, the figure is 46.1 per cent.

Electorally, however, recent British history charts a series of Labour defeats. What is to be explained here, then, is that Britain is *exceptional*. When almost all the other labour parties of the advanced capitalist world started to grow again, Labour in Britain declined.

The British deviation made its appearance in the latter half of the second Wilson government. In 1968, 'local and by-elections showed an unprecedented record of disaster'.[6] That was the year not only of the French May, but also the year when Swedish social democracy found its widest support ever among the electorate, and a year before the accession of the first SPD Chancellor in West Germany. By 1970, Labour's share of the British vote was 3.7 percentage points below that of the defeat of 1959, and it has declined ever since.[7]

Labour's defeats are not quite unique. They are shared by the labour movement in Belgium. After a series of blows beginning in 1965, the Belgian labour movement polled only 27.4 per cent in the most recent parliamentary election (1981). The fact that this fate is common to the labour movement in the two first industrialized countries of the world is a cause for serious reflection. Both countries were hit early by the current crisis; both have lived through dramatic industrial and regional upheaval – Belgium much more so. Both labour movements have had strong traditions of working-class solidarity capped by far right leaderships, even by social democratic standards. However, the similarities can be taken too far. Britain has no equivalent to the French-Speakers' Front of Brussels, to which the Belgian social democrats lost almost half of their metropolitan electorate in 1965, and no ancient Catholic labour movement entrenched in the now expansive economic region.

General features of the British class structure do not give any major clues to Labour's plight. Let us make two comparisons in this respect. The labour movement has always had its base among manual workers in production and transport. Comparative figures are difficult to come by here, but assuming that the manual/non-manual distribution in advanced capitalist countries is at least roughly equal within branches of economic activity, we may relate the number of employees of all kinds in all sorts of non-agrarian production and in transport to that of employees in commercial services – commerce, hotels and restaurants, banking, insurance and the like (see table 8.1). While contemporary capitalism is clearly not quite following the route envisaged in the *Communist Manifesto*, the preconditions in Britain for what I have called working-class work-place collectivity[8] are the average for comparable countries. Because of the early demise of its peasantry, Britain has traditionally also been the country with the smallest proportion of employers, self-employed and family helpers. Since 1975 the British percentage of employees and workers in the economically active population – 92.3 per cent in 1980 – has been slightly lower than that of the United States. Another important comparative measure is the size of public employment. Theories of the state still have to catch up with this massive phenomenon, which adds a new basis of collectivist politics to the declining class of manual industrial workers. In this respect, the British labour movement stands fairly strong (table 8.2).

One conclusion is clear. There is no direct sociological or

[margin handwritten note: Not following route of Communist Manifesto]

Table 8.1 Employees in commercial services as percentage of employees in mining, manufacturing, construction, transport and communications, 1980

USA	94*
Netherlands	62*
Japan	52*
UK	52
Sweden	52
France	49
Belgium	44
West Germany	34
Italy	29

Note: *1979
Source: Eurostat Review 1971–1980, Luxemburg 1982, pp 125ff.

Table 8.2 Public employees as percentage of total economically active population, 1979

Sweden	37	Finland	23
Denmark	31	West Germany	23
Austria	31	Canada	22
UK	30	Italy	21
Belgium	27.5	Netherlands	19[b]
Australia	26	New Zealand	19[c,d]
Norway	25[a]	USA	18
France	23	Switzerland	10[c]
		Japan	7[c]

Notes: a 1980. *b* In man-years. *c* Excl. public corporations. *d* 1978.
Sources: Nordic countries: *Den offentliga sysselsättningsutveckling-i Norden under 1970-talet,* Oslo 1983, p. 6; France: *La Fonction Publique,* Paris 1982, p. 10; Austria and Belgium public corporations: CEEP, *Die öffentliche Wirtschaft in der Europäischen Gemeinschaft,* Berlin 1981, pp. 47 & 154 for the rest: OECD, *Employment in the Public Sector,* Paris 1982, pp. 12 & 79.

social-historical explanation for the current travail of the British Labour Party. Labour's decline cannot simply be attributed to the contraction of its traditional working-class base. Other comparable parties in Europe have flourished in spite of similar changes in their countries' class structure. So it seems to me that Hobsbawm was right in his conclusion, if not all the way through his chain of arguments, that for explanation of the crisis of the British Labour Party, 'we have to look at the Labour Party and the labour movement itself'.

This conclusion brings us to the next section, but before that a few more words will have to be said about the practice and the theory of the 1970s. If the period from the mid-sixties till about yesterday – which fell on somewhat different dates in different countries – was, on the whole, one of working-class advance, why so many Cassandras on the left? Brief answer: because nowhere did these advances match expectations. Strategies for a move to the left, towards Euro-communism, Latin socialism, or left-wing social democracy never materialized – a bitter lesson which Swedish social democrats and French and Greek socialists are learning now. In this respect, alas, the British defeats constitute no exception. This lagging of theory behind practice poses a challenge to socialist thought which has still to be met.

A view from outside

The British Labour Party is perhaps an oddity, similar only to its imperially connected parallels in Australia and New Zealand. But it is not these days an exception, as Richard Hyman seems to imply in Chapter 6 of this volume, 'Wooing the working class'. Therein it is now in good company throughout the labour movement of Europe. To those of us who happen to have been born and to have lived with social democratically dominated labour movements, the oddities of the British Labour Party lie elsewhere. (I am here using the word social democrat in its classical Central and Northern European sense, not with the Italo-Anglo-Portuguese connotation of right-of-centre parties which have no links whatsoever with the labour movement.)

Three things about Labour leadership in the period immediately prior to the recent defeats are striking to an outside observer. One is its clubby, cultural elitism. Of the Labour cabinets of 1964, 1974 and 1976, about half of the members were educated at the two medieval elite universities of Oxford and Cambridge.[9] In narrowness of socio-cultural experience in contemporary Europe, British Labour governments are rivalled only – British Tory governments apart – by the cabinets of Pompidou and Giscard, up to 30 per cent of which may be graduates from that tiny elite nursery, the National School of Administration.[10]

The second feature is Labour's parliamentarian exclusivity. In virtually all other member parties of the Socialist International, the party leader is of old elected by the party. Even after Labour's modest constitutional reform, the party's devotion to parliamentary decorum is amazing. For instance, in the recent leadership contests Tony Benn was apparently an impossible candidate even to his own followers, because he was not an MP at the time. In Sweden, the Conservatives elected a new leader in 1982 who was not a Member of

Parliament, and who led his party in the election of 1982 without being an MP. In 1983 the Swedish Liberal Party made the same kind of choice. In the Netherlands, a possible successor to Social Democratic Party leader, den Uyl, is the chairman of the Dutch TUC – who is not an MP. *Lack of international authority*

Thirdly, the lack of international authority of Labour leaders is also surprising, given the size of the country and the party. William Beveridge was an international social democratic authority, but he was, of course, no Labourite. Ernest Bevin was an important figure (alas, one might say), when the social democratic cold war alignment was established. But since then, there has been no one. The activated and radicalized Socialist International is run by the West Germans, seconded by the Swedes. Austria's Bruno Kreisky cut an important role for himself, and there is a Latin bloc – now growing in importance because of the Iberian Latin-American connection. Looking at the record of Messrs Gaitskell, Wilson and Callaghan and their entourage, I think this international role in the shadow is well deserved.

In the matter of policies, there appears to have been a striking lack of initiative, imagination and capacity, ever since Bevan set up the National Health Service. From a perspective of reformism, Wilson's blowing of the superannuation scheme in 1970 is a most telling episode. A belated but fairly good reform was on its parliamentary way when Wilson suddenly called an election, during which pensions – turned into a major issue of social democratic realignment in Sweden in the late fifties – remained peripheral. The election was lost and the result is the current motley collection of private schemes, investing abroad in the decline of Britain.

While the policy record of post-1951 Labour governments is most notable for steadfast attempts at and regular failures of an incomes policy, the British welfare state has decayed by international standards. The NHS still stands up well, though infant mortality rates at higher than in the Nordic countries and the Netherlands, and regional inequalities of health and health care greater than in Norway and Sweden.[11] The British health care system is one of the cheapest in the world to administer,[12] but Britain has among the lowest statutory pensions in the developed capitalist world.[13] British sickness benefits are lower and more restricted than in most countries, even when the varying enterprise schemes are taken into account.[14] Income loss through unemployment is also larger in Britain than in comparable countries.[15]

Though the causal processes certainly are entangled and complex, from the combined evidence of the British class structure and the character of Labour Party leadership and policies, it seems reasonable to conclude that what halted the forward march of labour was not so much the demise of the working class as the decomposition of the party. Even at its peak, British Labour was only moderately successful in rallying the manual working class, and since then there has been a dramatic decline. Table 5.3 gives a comparative overview in the early 1950s and around 1970 of the percentage of the manual workers' vote received by member parties of the Socialist International and by parties further to the left.

The British Labour Party owed the success of its electoral mobilization more to the unusual preponderance of the industrial working class in the make-up of the British electorate, than to an embodiment of any particular working-class unity. There may be only one mass working-class party and only one trade union movement in Britain, but this has

Table 8.3   Votes for social democracy and left-wing parties as percentage of manual workers' votes

	Early 1950s	c. 1970
Finland (1958, 1966)	80	80
Austria (– 1971)	—	82
Norway (1957, 1965)	75	76
Sweden (1948, 1968)	74	76
Denmark (1953, 1971)	73	69
Italy (1958 –)	71	—
France (1951, 1973)	67	64
Britain (1951, 1970)	65	51
Belgium (1954, 1968)	63	47
West Germany (1953, 1969)	48	58

Sources: M. Dogan, 'Le vote ouvrier en Europe occidentale', Revue Française de Sociologie (1960) p. 29; J. Raschke, Organisierter in Westeuropäischen Parteien, Opladen 1977, p. 257.

not prevented a bourgeois colonization cutting deeply into the British working class. Over the last decades these bourgeois inroads have been dramatic.

The socialist chance

But the British Labour Party is being noticed abroad not only for its disastrous electoral performance and the political shabbiness of its recent past. Today, Britain is the only advanced capitalist country with a sizeable, militant and spirited socialist left. This is an important asset which is overlooked in Hobsbawm's analysis. And in spite of certain sectarian jarrings – which seem to imply that behind the cool analysis and preoccupation with wooing back a majority of the population sinister forces are at work – the reactions to the defeat of June 1983 among the Labour left (judging, for example, from the pages of *New Socialist*), have been much more healthy, robust and combative than, say, the reactions of the French left to 1978 or of most Italian communists to the recent disillusionment and outmanoeuverings in Italy. If I had been in Stuart Hall's position I would have added another 'message to Neil Kinnock': take good care of this amazing socialist combativeness in the British Labour Party, so different from the demoralized gloom virtually everywhere else. This left promise remains to be fulfilled, however. Let me end by pointing to five major tasks. Two seem to be of particular urgency for Britain.

First of all, Labour's loss of working-class confidence has to be properly analysed and practically overcome. Before that no further advance can be expected. Rather than starting from sociologizing about *the* working class, such analyses should focus on the specificities of British socio-political relations. With regard to political practice, the sensitive question has to be asked and answered, what makes Thatcherism more attractive to many workers than the Labour left and the Labour right? Explanations mainly referring to media image-building should be regarded as an impermissible cop-out (because they beg the question of why media images are accepted).

Secondly, Britain is still confronting a basic national task of modernization – of transforming an ex-empire, a former economic superpower and a country which still has a heavy late-nineteenth century cast of social relations into a modern major country beneath the class of superpowers. The fiascos of old-style Labourism and genteel Toryism in this respect paved the way for the current onslaught of Thatcherism. Whatever its hollow electoral victories, there seems to be little evidence that Thatcher will succeed in modernizing Britain by neo-liberal methods. Here is challenge for a programme of *socialist modernization*.

Socialists everywhere are also facing a number of crucial areas calling for novel reflection analysis and practice. Tables 8.1 and 8.2 identify two such areas. Clearly, the social character of production has taken a new turn. The 'commanding heights' of the economy and the field of class battles look rather different from what we expected, now that McDonald's hamburger chain employs more people than the American steel industry,[16] and employees of commercial services make up between a third (in the UK) and a half (in the US) of capitalist employment. What conclusions should socialists draw from this?

The fourth task of my five-item agenda is the state. The current advanced capitalist state is neither merely an instrument of the ruling class, a 'condensation' of societal class relations, nor an autonomous machine of extraction and violence – to summarize rather crudely Marxist and neo-Weberian wisdom of the 1970s. The state has also affected the structure of class relations, with public employment determining the socio-economic position of between 25 and 40 per cent of the economically active population. This massive fact still has to be digested, let alone clarified in terms of its political implications.

Finally, the challenges to the classical socialist class struggle put by the women's movement and by other forces of human emancipation still have to be met. So far, the debates have largely swung between attempts at clothing feminist analyses in concepts borrowed from Marxist economic and class analysis, and anti-labour movement stances. Neither has been very productive – little in theory, much less in practice. What is required, it seems to me, is a recognition and an elaboration of the *irreducible heterogeneity of several strategies for human emancipation* – the socialist class struggle, the feminist struggle and others – *and the links of interdependence between them*, in terms of structural preconditions and fighting forces in existence. Grasping this set of differences and complex links will also have to entail a capacity to provide a strategic compass to forces and struggles, the movements of which are most likely to remain non-linear, discontinuous, and irreducible to doctrines and strategems. No left seems better equipped for these formidable tasks in terms of political vigour and intellectual capacity than the British left. That is Labour's promise.[17]

Notes

[1] E. Hobsbawm, *The Forward March of Labour Halted?* (London, 1981), p. 17.

[2] Ibid., p. 18.

[3] R. Ebbinghausen & F. Tiemann (eds.) *Das Ende der Arbeiterbewegung in Deutschland?* (Opladen, 1984), pp. 39ff.

[4] In Il Manifesto, *Potere e opposizione nelle societá post-rivoluzionairie* (Rome, 1978).

[5] A. Gorz, *Adieux au Prolétariat* (Paris, 1980), p. 96.

[6] Philip Williams in D. Kavanagh, (ed.) *The Politics of the Labour Party* (London, 1982), p. 59.

[7] Ivor Crewe, in Kavanagh, ibid., p. 13.

[8] G. Therborn, 'Why Some Classes Are More Successful Than Others' *New Left Review*, 138 (March–April 1983).

[9] Dennis Kavanagh in Kavanagh (ed.) *The Politics of the Labour Party*, p. 101.

[10] P. Birnbaum, *La Logique de l'État* (Paris, 1982), p. 73.

[11] P. Townsend & N. Davidson (eds), *Inequalities of Health* (Harmondsworth, 1982), pp. 109–10.

[12] OECD, *Public Expenditure on Health* (Paris, 1977), p. 23. Figures relate to the first half of the 1970s.

[13] OECD, Directorate for Social Affairs – *Old Age Pensions*, mimeographed report (Paris, May 1983), p. 4.

[14] International Society for Labour Law and Social Security, *9th International Congress* (Heidelberg, 1978), vol. II/1–2 pp. 415–727.

[15] OECD, *The Challenge of Unemployment* (Paris, 1982), p. 58.

[16] cf Mike Davies, 'The Political Economy of Late Imperial America', *New Left Review*, 143 (January–February 1984).

[17] For a more elaborate analysis of labour movements and welfare states in the countries of contemporary advanced capitalism, the interested reader is referred to an article of mine in *New Left Review* 145 (May–June 1984).

9

The Failed Consensus

ANTHONY BARNETT

Coalition talk is on the increase. A majority of the population are against Thatcher. But while the opposition is divided she will rule. It is common sense, therefore, to get our act together and put her out of business. There are variations on this theme. One of the most attractive is that the Liberals should be seduced from their alliance with the Social Democrats by the promise of PR. This will recreate on an electoral basis the Parliamentary coalition that kept Callaghan in office. Perhaps even some of the Tory wets will join. But at any rate, a broad alliance is needed to get rid of Thatcherism. What could be more obvious?

The superficial plausibility of these arguments, however, conceals a highly improbable assumption about recent history, perhaps best expressed by Eric Hobsbawm in the initial and as yet most coherent presentation of the call for a 'broad alliance':

> Thatcherism is committed to a radical and reactionary change in British capitalism, and indeed in the British political system. It is pushing ahead with this new, militant and formidable policy of class struggle from above, and the dismantling of the past reformist consensus . . .[1]

Was there such a 'reformist consensus' in the past? If so, if the post-war order was fundamentally a progressive one, then it does indeed follow that socialists must seek to preserve it: that we should gather together the largest possible alliance to push *her* out, in order to ensure that she becomes nothing more than an aberration in the long wave of adaption that is British politics. In short: oust Thatcher and get back to business as usual, perhaps even a little bit better than usual now that it has been tested by her fire.

Thus the argument for a 'broad alliance' rests on a double presumption about British politics: the nature of the post-war consensus and the character of 'Thatcherism'. The first worked, and is now under assault by the second *because* it worked.

The alternative view is that post-war politics in Britain was *not* a successful reforming consensus. Indeed had it been such, and thus – at the very least – an efficient source of modernization, it would have taken more than Margaret Thatcher to have 'dismantled' it. Instead, the consensus proved so conservative that it died on its feet, due most of all to Labour itself, in particular under Harold Wilson. While with Callaghan it was precisely business as usual that delivered Thatcher up to us when the electorate could stand it no longer. Despite all her rhetoric of purpose, this argument goes, and it is the one I wish to pursue here, Thatcher is more the flotsam left behind on the beach by a retreating post-war tide than she is the tide of history itself.

My argument can only be valid if the post-war consensus has indeed disappeared irretrievably into history. Which seems to be the case, if only because so much of what really mattered after 1945 was the publicly unspoken agreement between the overtly contending sides. True, a Party that sought to re-introduce consensus policies might well be returned to office. But today such a government, especially if it were to be Labour or Labour dominated, could not conceivably be operating within a consensus environment. To succeed, therefore, it would *have* to act differently from any previous Labour administration. And almost certainly this means that it will need to promise to act differently before it takes office. Such promises, however, are unlikely to attract what Hobsbawm and others mean by broad, i.e. middle of the road, approval.

How far has this downfall of the consensus been Thatcher's doing? Is she the architect of its destruction or the beneficiary of its collapse? I put it dramatically for the purpose of clarification only, especially as I wish to argue against any exaggeration of Thatcherism. But we do need to clarify the alternative lines of argument. Their importance is that different answers lead to different responses to Thatcherism. Get it wrong and the politics that she personifies may never be defeated.

The 'broad alliance' arguments presume that the post-war consensus was reforming, civilized, effective – for all its faults – and created of course by Labour after 1945. In his recent study Kenneth Morgan notes how at the time people felt combative and militant in their views. But he also concludes:

> No stronger confirmation could have been found of the broad wisdom of the policies pursued by Attlee and his colleagues than in their Conservative successors' respectful affirmation of them.[2]

This is an apt description, because meant as praise of the way Labour in fact mortgaged its policies, domestic as well as foreign, to Tory assent, as Party and Trade Union leaders relied upon ruling-class endorsement rather than popular support. Today we are living with the consequences of such 'wisdom'. Labour proved unable to keep up the interest payments, so the bailiffs tossed it out of the house.

It was easily done. No great plan was needed. Thatcher's own bailiff mentality is proof enough. Hers is a bruiser's posture, rather than a strategy of transformation. In February this year she said that she had no doubt how she wished her governments to be remembered a century hence. She wants to be seen, *above all else*, to have broken 'with a debilitating consensus of a paternalistic government and a dependent people'.[3] In other words, no policies of any specific character whatsoever, nothing apart from the termination of one style of administration and its substitution by another. Better than any critic, Thatcher herself has captured the vacuum of her political programme.

But who can deny that Labour administrations were debilitating and paternalistic rather than dynamic and socialist? Thatcherism is not so much a powerful and coherent counter-attack upon social reform but rather a philistine protest at the failure of post-war change. Hence Thatcherism, more style than substance, can certainly be overturned by a radical counter-assault, provided only that this seeks its popularity by appealing to a future undebilitated by consensus respectability. Amongst the first duties of such a politics, therefore, must be a convincing assessment of 'Thatcherism', which the left has so far over-estimated ideologically and under-estimated economically.

If it is to be given a year, Thatcherism's date of origin was significantly 1968. That was when Enoch Powell made a famous racialist speech prophesying rivers of blood. He was then dismissed from the Heath shadow cabinet. Today, Thatcherism may be described as Powellism in government, while Enoch Powell has paid the price of the pioneer. It was he, not Thatcher, who first broke ranks from the Tory gentry and appealed with some success over the heads of Westminster to the prejudices of the population at large. Powell had been the first to demand disciplined monetary policies from the government. Above all it was Powell who articulated in the terms of the radical right, a protest against the plight of Britain as a nation in its post-imperial epoch.

In what is now seen as a key statement of Thatcherite politics, the eponymous founder herself made a speech in October 1968 in which she called for a life of personal effort and independence from the state. No great intellectual or imaginative leap lay behind these cant phrases. Their importance, it can now be seen, was threefold: first, Thatcher picked up on the libertarian anti-statist theme widespread at that time; second, she expressed in traditional English terms the American spirit that was so much a part of 'the sixties' in Europe, at once a middle-class protest and a demand for consumer opportunities; third, in the specific political context of the United Kingdom, she sought to exploit the tremendous frustration generated by the failure of Wilsonian 'modernization'.[4]

Perhaps this is why Thatcherism, for all its implausible rhetoric, seems so self-assured, and why it has given left theorists so much trouble. Seeking a fascistoid intelligence behind the ruthlessness, and cogent class interest, many of Thatcherism's critics fail to register the primacy of Labour's role. Despite her talk of 'Victorian Values', it is really the

Labour Party that draws directly upon the spirit of the past. In personal terms this was clear in the choice between Foot and Thatcher. As Gareth Stedman Jones has recently argued, the formative 1945–51 Labour administration of Clement Attlee, which created the welfare state and set the direction of politics for the next thirty years, was, 'globally and nationally . . . the most glorious flowering of late Victorian liberal philanthropy'.[5] Michael Foot was the perfect representative of this tradition.

In the aftermath of that post-war administration, Gaitskell and Wilson – both Oxford University liberals – sought to bring the Labour Party 'into the 20th century', from their respective positions on the right and left of the Party. Both failed, and, naturally, the blame was attached to those whom they had tried to 'help', the ungrateful workers – their bovine trade unions and backward practices. Of course the scapegoats were not utterly blameless, after all they had created the Labour Party itself in the first place. But the real source of Labour's frustration, was its fixation on inherited national institutions, the global pretensions and patrician attitudes of the ruling class and the civil service. This crippled its modernizing ambition. Born in war-time coalition, Labour came to embody the established state. A patriotic alliance with traditional elite rule became the lodestar of Labour's commitment to peaceful, parliamentary reform: to rule from above which, precisely, could not be socialist in any democratic sense.

The consequence was immobilism, and it was the rejection of this, not just by the middle classes but also by important sections of industrial capital and of the skilled working class (both of which stood to benefit from an efficient, West German type, social democracy) that gave birth to Thatcherism as a potential alternative. Thatcherism has not struggled to create a new alignment of class forces; she has not raised a *levée en masse* of the petty bourgeoisie. Despite even the Falklands victory, what had anyway been a minority vote for Thatcher's party in 1979 declined in 1983, both in absolute numbers and as a percentage of the poll, from 44 to 42 per cent. Thatcher projects her policies as 'conviction politics'. But this emphasis on 'purpose' is masquerade. In truth she knows hardly at all what she is *for*, because hers is essentially a politics of *rejection*. Hence its long-term weakness.

This is not to say that Thatcherism is empty of effect. Its first crucial obsession is with the repressive apparatus necessary to police a competitive economy in which the strength of unionism has been broken, through perpetually high unemployment aided by legislation. Its second a rhetorical emphasis on the values of domestic consumption and ownership; one of Thatcher's most frequent sources for illustrations of her style. When asked how she managed to stay calm during the Falklands War, she answered: 'It's like when you have a family crisis. Someone has to stay in control and keep going.' When asked for her overall vision of British society, she replied: '. . . what I am desperately trying to do is to create one nation with everyone being a man (*sic*) of property, or having the opportunity to be a man of property.' As Anne Smith put it, she believes in 'The Fortress Family'.[6] Third, there is a genuinely desperate regard for the Empire and British 'greatness', now symbolized by the Falklands.

If the political theory of Thatcherism is sub-zero her economic policies are positive, at least for some. Her monetarism and its associated devastation of British industry have been excessively expensive as well as intellectually derisory. They have benefited, however, from a fortuitous 'rationality', for their advent coincided with the one thing the consensus epoch lacked, a largesse of external funds – from North Sea oil.

The most forceful interpretation along these lines has been that of John Ross.[7] While emphasizing the long-run decline of Conservatism and with it the whole balance of contemporary party politics, he has tried to demonstrate that Thatcherism has worked to the immense advantage of the City and its associated branches of finance and banking capital, the oil companies and the combines retailing consumer goods. In other words non-manufacturing sectors of British capitalism have positively benefited from Thatcherite economics and have endorsed it accordingly. Thatcher herself and many of her cabinet are petty bourgeois in origin and their contempt for aristocratic ways is vocal. Yet they are more completely under the sway of the traditional financial oligarchy than any administration this century.

The relative strength of the pound and continuous, massive investment overseas have allowed a reconstruction of the old imbalance of English capitalism's strength and weakness. Tentacles from the City of London stretch parasitically around the world, while manufacturing and productivity in domestic industry is starved and left relatively uncompetitive. This was a nineteenth-century pattern, the industrial revolution in Britain was dominated from its beginning by banking and landed capital. A hundred years ago, however, the loss of manufacturing competitiveness was relative whereas today it shows signs of becoming absolute. The domestic base of the economy is far weaker, the reliance on international growth with its attendant risks far greater.

Without North Sea oil none of this would have been possible. It has been crucial to the success of Thatcherism. Without the enormous subsidies of the North Sea glut, her financial policies would have led to catastrophe. The Oman deal was a poetic scandal then, for when Prime Minister met Sultan like met like. British oil has rightly been compared to the Spanish gold once drawn from that country's possessions in the Americas. Its revenues allowed the old imperial order and successive generations of state functionaries in Madrid to preserve the wondrous appearance of their rule as the populations of Iberian Spain itself sunk into poverty and desuetude. Today, the Imperial British order at home, which could not be resurrected in the aftermath of the Second World War, has been given the kiss of life by the hydrocarbonated forests of pre-glacial eras. 'Thatcherism' is less the inspiration of this resurrection than its expression: the stale breath emitted by the corpse as it coughs back into life.

How is this possible? How is it that something in its way so apparently archaic as Thatcherism can so effortlessly make Labour look dated? One part of the answer lies in the very institutions of Parliament and the City – twin centres of secrecy and speculation – that Labour declined to confront and which themselves were never comfortable with the domestic task of making British industry competitive. Another part of the answer lies in the Trade Union movement's conservatism and its loyalty to the same received institutions. Elsewhere I have called this patriotic alliance 'Churchillism', for it was forged during the wartime coalition after Labour made Churchill Premier in 1940.[8] This was the birth of the 'reformist consensus' that Hobsbawm seeks to preserve: a formative moment of socially combative popular nationalism. Yet it was born with a fatal defect, aptly demonstrated by the way that Thatcher has used the symbol of Churchill to help bring down 'Churchillism'.

James Callaghan was a splendid example of it, in attitudes and body language. He reckoned that 'the woman' would over-reach herself and through some blunder show herself unsuitable for office, thus conveniently obliging the electorate to return him as Prime Minister in 1979. This was not just a tactical error at the time, it was a gross strategic miscalculation.

It might be said that at least it was better than Labour's suicidal internal strife that followed. Personally, I don't see why it is not at least as honourable to commit *auto-da-fé* by fighting over what is right or wrong, than to submit oneself to death by a thousand cuts in the hope that the executioner might some day hit her own toe and bleed away. Anyway, Thatcher *has* over-reached herself already and will do so again. Possibly, probably even, one of her own blows will indeed prove fatal for her. Her many enemies, perhaps most of all in the Conservative Party itself, will then 'rejoice'.

But what will happen to Labour if Margaret Thatcher is replaced by, say Michael Heseltine? If Labour waits to cash in on the vulnerability and the stylistic defects of Thatcher personally, it may be even less likely to return to office than if The Boss stays. This is the trap of belief in the 'past reformist consensus'. Not only is it a false version of the last 40 years. It induces passivity by blaming Thatcher. It seeks a return in the name of democracy to a politics that resulted in . . . none other than Margaret Thatcher. Its most likely conclusion will be a son of Thatcher.

To spring the trap we should welcome the end of consensus politics. That epoch when reform was accepted to stifle change, when change was projected as wind, to which one bowed with a sly smile without shifting a root.

Consensus politics meant restrictive practices writ large, not reform. Its passing should not be lamented.[9]

The politics of the GLC is surely a pointer in the new direction. For example, after two years of frustrated negotiations, Livingstone's group unilaterally abrogated the long standing County Hall agreement with the Trade Unions. It did not wish to do so, because this would set a precedent for Tories who might wish to cut wages, but to promote women and blacks it had to be done.

The GLC's politics has so far emphasized the variegated and heteroclite composition of 'the labour movement'. Livingstone has spoken out strongly against the British presence in Ireland – a key symbol of all-party consensus politics. He opposed the Falklands War. And despite the vast tonnage of macho fumes that pollutes County Hall from across the Thames, he continues to support women, blacks and gays. In short, he is an 'extremist', which means nothing other than that he has declined to play consensus politics – but from the left.

Yet he is popular! How amazing. Carvel's recent book on him is a fair account, except that he explains Livingstone's political success exclusively in terms of the foolishness of his opponents.[10] The Law Lords, Thatcher's determination to abolish the whole GLC caboodle, these have been 'gifts' that have made Livingstone into an honourable under-dog and the people's Ken, despite his actual policies. Don't you believe it; and not only because most people actually are women, blacks, gay, Irish or otherwise eccentric.,

The GLC experiment shows that Labour never should have sought to become, in Harold Wilson's phrase, 'The natural party of government'. That approach was redolent of the vegetable mentality induced by the desire for respectability. As A. J. P. Taylor has said, 'A Labour Party that aspires to become respectable is a Labour Party doomed to decay.'[11] Thatcherism took root in and grew from the decay. It will be defeated only when it is no longer nourished by the vegetable deposits of post-war consensus politics.

How this should be done remains far from the clear – socialists have a great deal to learn. Egalitarian claims to moral values greater and more humane than property and nation, institutionally embodied, for example, in the National Health Service, are certainly not to be abandoned. During and after the Second World War collective aspirations, such as the right to full employment, were obtained. But they were also incorporated into and expropriated by a ruling order that sought above all else to preserve itself. What it termed 'consensus', as opposed to majority, meant at that time as it still means today, the degree to which we were allowed to agree with them. The popular strength of Thatcherism is perhaps largely drawn from its demagogic hostility to this old ruling order. Which is another reason why Thatcherism is unlikely to be successfully displaced by any appeal for its restoration.

Notes

[1] *Marxism Today*, October 1983.
[2] *Labour in Power, 1945–51*, Oxford, 1984, p. 491.
[3] Speech to Parliamentary Lobby's Centenary Lunch, 18 January, 1984.
[4] The Speech is reproduced in Nicholas Wapshott & George Brock, *Thatcher*, London, 1983.
[5] *Languages of Class*, Cambridge, 1983, p. 246.
[6] *New Statesman,* 17 June 1983.
[7] *Thatcher and Friends*, London, 1983.
[8] *Iron Britannia*, London, 1982.
[9] See Steven Lukes, 'The Future of British Socialism?', in Ben Pimlott, ed., *Fabian Essays in Socialist Thought*, forthcoming.
[10] *Citizen Ken*, London, 1984.
[11] *An Old Man's Diary*, London, 1984, p. 77.

10

From Defeat to Victory

TONY BENN

I believe that the main causes of our defeat were that over the years the parliamentary leadership became separated from the party, and that we have conceded basic arguments which no socialist party can afford to concede and still expect to win. If Labour is to rebuild its strength and its unity for the future, as it must, we owe it to each other to say what we believe has happened and why; and how we think the party should approach its tasks over the next few years. Nothing must be allowed to obscure the political issues and the choices we must make.

Conceding the economic argument

Our starting point must be the economic background against which the election was fought and the political situation it created. After years of relative decline Britain was especially vulnerable to the world recession. Welfare capitalism, which had been created after 1945, ceased to be a viable proposition. A severely weakened market economy could no longer 'afford' to sustain full employment, pay for the necessary public services or 'allow' free trade unionism to practise collective bargaining.

A choice had to be made between the maintenance of unrestricted, international capitalism and a shift towards a more rationally and, where possible, a more internationally responsible system for the greater development of world resources. Within the United Kingdom, the need was for greater equality and more democratic control over our economy. This choice was not forced upon us by extremist pressure from an allegedly revolutionary left, but by the bankers, and in particular by the IMF which virtually blackmailed the 1976 Labour Cabinet into making cuts in public expenditure and clamping down on the trade unions by imposing a rigid policy of wage restraint upon them. The decision to give way to that pressure was justified by Labour's cabinet majority on the grounds that the alternative economic strategy would lead to a siege economy.

Two years later, that government then actually found itself besieged by its own political allies during the so-called 'winter of discontent', which defeated Labour a few months later. The incoming Conservative government, armed with an electoral mandate, then proceeded to implement the bankers' policy with a will. Unemployment was deliberately stimulated because it achieved everything that the new government wanted to do. The dole queues controlled wages, undermined trade union bargaining power, limited imports, made further cuts in the public services seem 'inevitable' and boosted profits. It divided working people – men from women, black from white, the employed from the unemployed – and it created a climate of fear which became the most powerful Tory weapon in the 1983 election campaign. When challenged to justify what was happening, the Tories chose the same argument that Labour had chosen – namely that it was the 'unavoidable' result of the battle against inflation. They were able to point out that when Labour had been in power it had completely rejected the very same alternative strategy that it was now arguing should be implemented.

Fear is a potent political weapon and it certainly played a major part in our defeat; for when people get frightened they become suspicious, cautious and conservative, and vote accordingly. If hope is to replace fear, people have to be able to believe that there is an alternative. Unfortunately for us, the electorate did not believe in Labour's alternative – and wondered whether we all believed in it either.

That is where we have to start – with what we believe, and how that belief differs from the analysis of the Tories and the SDP/Liberal Alliance.

Conceding the defence argument

We conceded many arguments over the years, and in 1983 some of those concessions came back to haunt us. From 1979 the Tories used fear of foreign enemies to win support for their defence policies. The unceasing cold war propaganda to which we have been subjected over the last five years, conducted with the willing co-operation of the BBC, the IBA and Fleet Street, paid rich dividends in terms of electoral gains to the Tories. Without any hard evidence being produced in support of it, many people were persuaded that the Soviet Union was actively planning an attack upon Western Europe, including Britain, and was only held in check by the massive American military presence in this country, and by huge stocks of US and British nuclear weapons.

By falsifying figures of the East-West arms balance, and by ignoring the crushing of human rights within the Western sphere of influence – including Turkey and Latin America – the complexities and dangers of the present international situation were over-simplified to the point of crude distortion. People were presented with a stark choice between 'Capitalism and Freedom' on the one hand and all forms of 'Socialism and Tyranny' on the other. Thus the public were led to believe that Britain was engaged in a holy war which required a permanent crusade and the maintenance of this country on a semi-war footing.

Unfortunately Labour did not offer a serious alternative analysis of world politics. People remembered that the post-war Labour government had originally invited America to establish its bases here without insisting upon a British veto over their use; had built the hydrogen bomb without telling Parliament; and that the Chevaline project had been similarly authorized without even the Labour Cabinet having been fully informed. This record made our manifesto commitments to a non-nuclear defence strategy seem unbelievable.

It must also be said plainly that the support given by the shadow cabinet and a majority of the NEC to the government's decision to send the task force in the spring of 1982, fatally undermined Labour's claim to be the advocate of internationalism and peace, and also hindered Labour's capacity to combat jingoism. We were thus unable to criticize the government effectively for its failure to negotiate with Argentina before the invasion, for its handling of the military operations or for its conduct since. In this context, the attempt to make an election issue of the sinking of the *General Belgrano*, or to call for a new inquiry, lacked credibility. We have to learn these lessons now, in case the same choices have to be made in the future over, say, a crisis in Gilbraltar or Hong Kong. Labour must have a socialist framework of analysis if it is to be able to respond correctly to the world situation and the pressure of events.

Conceding the political argument

A third factor contributing to our defeat, both in 1979 and in 1983, can be traced back to the Tory landslide of 1959. It was at the Blackpool conference following that defeat that the party was explicitly invited to abandon its commitment to socialism. Though the attempt to drop clause four failed in a formal sense, it succeeded in undermining the faith of many people in Labour's socialist vision and purpose. It also devalued the role of ideas in the political process. Elections, thereafter, seemed to rotate around which political leaders and parties could best run an unchanged capitalist system. The controversy over 'In Place of Strife', Labour's 1969 proposal to control the unions by law, succeeded in affixing the main responsibility for Britain's economic weakness upon the trade unions and the working class. This analysis naturally appealed to the Tories, their business allies and the media, and became the accepted explanation for Britain's problems among large sections of the population.

During those revisionist years Labour's share of the popular vote declined steadily, our party membership collapsed, and when capitalism sank into its present crisis – worse even than in the thirties – Labour had to discover its socialism all over again. In short, a revisionist Labour Party evacuated whole areas of analytical, moral, political and social territory, so painfully won over decades of effort.

After the defeat of 1979 this territory was easily overrun by
primitive and dangerous ideas, and values that we had been
told in 1959 had been banished forever and would never
threaten our people again. Perhaps the greatest price we paid
for this tragic episode of revisionism was that we allowed
ourselves to forget that any socialist movement needs moral
values and a sense of history and class solidarity if it is to
mount a successful challenge to injustice, and sustain itself
during the many setbacks which such a long campaign
involves.

The ideology of socialism, properly appreciated, with its
rich and diverse inheritance of experience and analysis, offers
us a basis for understanding and belief. Ideology should not
be confused with sectarianism, the rigid imposition of
particular interpretations of old texts, or the entrenchment of
state or party bureaucracy with its narrow and intolerant
attitude to independent thought.

The split between MPs and the party

Another contributory factor to Labour's successive defeats
derives from the still unresolved problem of the relationship
between the party and its representatives in Parliament,
which has given the impression of disunity. The conference
was strongly behind the manifesto policies; the main centre
of opposition to them was in the PLP. In the last four years,
conference not only consciously decided that it wanted to
change the policies which the last Labour government had
followed, but it also wanted to be sure that its own policies
were carried through. It therefore went on to make constitutional changes – reselection and the electoral college –
designed to make it more likely that the PLP would advocate
and implement those policies. Ironically, many Labour MPs
seemed to see these changes as an attack upon them
personally, whereas the effect would, in many cases, have
been to strengthen their role – especially if the further
proposal had been accepted which would have given MPs the
right to elect cabinets when Labour is in office.

In particular, the shadow cabinet consistently declined to
put forward Labour's conference policies by tabling explicit

opposition motions in support of them. Thus, in the years leading up to the election itself, there was no proper parliamentary advocacy of those policies. The case for a non-nuclear defence strategy; for the closure of US nuclear bases; for British withdrawal from the Common Market; for the full alternative economic strategy, was simply not put in the Commons.

Hence Parliament was never properly used to develop a public understanding of, or support for, these central manifesto items upon which the election was eventually fought. Until the relationship between the party and the PLP is resolved, the party as a whole will continue to be presented as forever divided between Labour at conference and Labour in the Commons. And the electors will not know which to believe.

A warning to the party

These explanations for our defeat will not be accepted by everyone in the party. We shall be told that our policies were unacceptable because they were too 'extreme', and that the main reason for our defeat can be traced back to what has happened within the party since the Tories came to power. It will be implied that if only we had stuck to the policies of 1979 (pro-market, pro-nuclear, pro-wage restraint and so on), and had left the constitution alone; if only the 1981 deputy leadership election had not taken place; if only the expulsions of the left had happened earlier and on a wider scale, the SDP defectors would still be in the party and Labour would have romped home to an electoral victory on a tide of popular revulsion against Tory policies. Such an argument only has to be spelled out for its inherent absurdities to become apparent. It must also be evident that if any attempt were made to carry this strategy of reversal through, it would meet with the opposition of the majority of the party. To argue along these lines is to encourage a grand illusion – a new myth that does not stand up to a moment's serious examination.

First of all, we were beaten in 1979 with the very policies

to which we are now invited to return, and when the SDP were all still with us. Secondly, such an argument assumes that policy commitment must be subordinated to the polls or the election results, without regard to what we believe, or to our capacity to win support for it by sustained public campaigns. Thirdly, the demand for a policy change now is, in the main, coming from those who never supported such policies in the first place. It also overlooks the fact that over the next few years, as the economic, social and political crisis deepens, events will almost certainly confirm the relevance of, and necessity for, what we wrote in the manifesto. Furthermore, no one will ever believe the Labour Party again if we are now ready to drop the very policies which we put forward in the election campaign. Finally, if the situation calls for the further development of our policies, or changes in them, the whole movement is entitled to play its proper part in the decisions through conference.

So this is no time for the British Labour Party, in the depth of a real crisis for British capitalism, to announce to the world that it has decided to abandon its socialism – perhaps in the vain hope that some of its leaders might secure ministerial office in a non-socialist coalition government.

Five tasks for Labour

There is overwhelming grief within the party at Labour's defeat, and a consciousness that millions of people who needed a Labour government in power will be suffering directly as a result of what has happened. But more than 8½ million people stayed with us and we experienced active support in many constituencies on an enormous scale. Many new applications for membership are coming in and we have a strong foundation on which to rebuild. I believe there are five tasks that we should set ourselves now, beginning at conference.

1. Protecting the people

We must do everything we possibly can to protect all our people, including the trade unions and Labour local authorities, by supporting them in their struggles for jobs and homes, for education and good health, dignity in retirement and for peace. We cannot confine our work to the parliamentary arena, nor should we forget that campaigns for social justice have always begun outside Parliament. The present media campaigns against extra-parliamentary activities are devices intended to defuse the pressure for social change.

Vigorous campaigning by the party, at local as well as at national level, may reduce some of the damage caused by government policies, or secure some real gains even while we are in opposition. But their long-term value lies in raising people's hopes and expectations and shifting public opinion towards the need for Labour policies.

2. Rebuilding the party

We should set ourselves a clear target of achieving within a period of one year, a million new members drawn from amongst Labour voters identified through canvass returns. And we must start at once on a campaign to establish workplace branches all over the country. This will feed the experience of those in paid work more directly into the constituencies and encourage more individual trade unionists to affiliate to the party by paying the political levy. In such ways will the links between the unions and the party be strengthened at a time when new anti-union legislation threatens to weaken them.

We must also recognize that a mass party, if it is to win and hold the confidence of the public, has got to listen to and campaign actively on behalf of the people whom it seeks to represent. We must be there when we are needed in the communities where people live and work, to help them in struggles for their rights. Our support must be equally available to assist women who work in the home and lack the protection of a trade union against domestic exploitation, and to support people under pressure because they are black, disabled, old, gay or hold unpopular views.

As socialists, we know that popular rights and social justice cannot be achieved without a major change in the power structure of society, and of its values. Indeed, it is the awareness of that fact that has brought many radical Liberals to see the relevance of socialism, and has brought some of the best of them into the Labour Party.

3. Constructing a progressive alliance

With the growing complexity of an industrialized society, campaigning for social justice has, in recent years, also developed outside the political and trade union structures that Labour has built up. Many single-issue pressure groups have evolved non-party responses to some of the biggest problems in society. They are fighting for the rights of women, for ethnic communities, for justice for the old, for a decent environment, for peace, and represent important intiatives that the Labour Party should be encouraging. Most of these groups are critical of one aspect or another of the values of capitalism. Some have come into being out of frustration at the bureaucracies that have disfigured the welfare state, and because we have not been as active as we should be in putting things right.

As socialists, we should also take an interest in the many socialist groups that have appeared on the scene, often with their own newspapers and campaigns. These schools of thought – some using the language of revolution – are usually highly critical of the Labour Party, and the immediate reaction of some Labour members and party officials is to organize a witch-hunt against them and then expel anyone associated with them. In fact, these sects are an indication of the growing interest in socialist ideas. They should be regarded as ideological pressure groups along with the explicitly non-party community action groups to which I have referred. Though the direct affiliation to the Labour party of such groups or sects would enlarge our own perception and contribute directly to our policy-making, we have to accept that even if they remain autonomous they may have many common interests with us. Joint campaigns with them would provide exactly the sort of progressive alliance that we shall need if our own aspirations to represent the majority of people in this country are to be realized.

The evolution of such an alliance should be a high priority for Labour in the immediate future. Once established, it would be better able to identify a whole new range of social needs, evolve policies to meet them, win public support and raise legitimate expectations that are capable of being realized.

4. *Insisting on collective leadership*

Past experience has shown us time and again how unwise it is for Labour to put too much faith in individuals, or to suppose that personal leadership can be a substitute for the party itself. Our future prospects depend upon our success in building a strong and democratic mass party that allows the rich diversity of radical and socialist traditions within it to grow in such a way as to reinforce each other. This is why we want a leadership that is like a wheel with spokes which may seem to point in different directions but converge to provide stability and strength.

We are also entitled to expect that all those who are privileged to represent the party at every level will conscientiously and consistently put forward the policies that have been democratically decided. That would be the surest way to restore confidence in the party and to win majority public support for it amongst the electorate.

5. *Reasserting socialism*

The Tories, the Liberals, the SDP and the mass media which, being lumped together, are really the voice of the combined British, Atlantic and Common Market establishments, are united in their determination to eliminate socialism from the nation's political agenda. Our objective, by contrast, is to move socialism back into the centre of discussion about the future. The case for socialism must be firmly rooted in daily experience; when people are allowed to learn what socialists are saying, its relevance becomes apparent. Indeed it should be our long-term purpose to persuade all parties, and all groups, that any discussion that leaves the socialist analysis out of account is not likely to lead to a solution. A few years ago, every major political party in Britain was, to a greater or lesser extent, monetarist and accepted the existing institutions of the state uncritically. Our aim should be that, in the future, socialist ideas have as wide a currency and become a normal part of our understanding of all political choices.

I believe that the most interesting and relevant arguments over the future will be the arguments that take place about the many different ways in which democracy and socialism can be applied. If the British Labour party keeps faith with its own long commitment to those ideas we can avoid the mistakes which led to our defeat in 1983. And we shall also stand the best chance of winning a majority Labour government at the next election, which must be an aim we all have in common.

Part 5
New Political Strategies

11

Mobilizing in Defence of Freedom

NEIL KINNOCK

Mr. Kinnock: On this election day, will the Prime Minister tell us whether she is glad or sorry that she, who was going to roll back the state, has actually brought a greater concentration of power to the central state than ever before in British peace-time history?

The Prime Minister: That just is not true. We have abolished controls on prices, incomes, industrial development certificates, office development certificates, and also abolished many other controls, including exchange control. We have reduced the number of civil servants by the greatest number since the war.

Hansard, 3 May 1984

Mrs Thatcher's instinctive answer was a model definition of modern conservatism. The essence of her beliefs is, of course, that liberty for capital is liberty for all and that withdrawing State interventions which impede the conveniences of capital enhances freedom in the land. That is her theory of government.

The facts of her government are that first, their curtailments of state intervention have been directed at those state functions which provide the individual security and individual opportunity of millions of people in this country. Far from extending individual freedom they have eroded it for a whole cross-section of the population. Secondly, any Tory extensions of state power have also been detrimental to individual rights and opportunities because they have started to erode not only the benefits previously produced by political democracy, but the very basis of democracy itself.

They have – amongst other things – taken £8,800 million in Rate support Grant away from local authorities; legislated to deny the right of elected Councils to set rate levels related to local needs; removed the rights of 13 million to vote for the Metropolitan counties and Greater London Councils; the freedom of GCHQ employees to belong to a trade union; promoted an unprecedented extension to the powers which the police can take in anticipating an assumed breach of the peace; contrived a punishment for Sarah Tisdall which grossly exceeded any that could have been merited by her offence; adjusted the rules of benefit so that the most needy have new indignity added to their poverty and insecurity. Any one of these infringements on civil liberties would represent a serious erosion of our country's democracy. Taken together, they demonstrate clearly that the present Prime Minister and her Government have no intention of 'rolling back the state'. Her primary purpose is to encourage the rolling on of the state – over individual civil liberties, local democracy and trade unionism.

Of course, this is not the language employed by the Government. We are told that they are merely 'upholding the law', maintaining order, or – with supreme irony – defending basic freedoms. The phraseology comes as no surprise. Authoritarianism rarely appears on the stage carrying a placard advertising the loss of liberties among its coming attractions. It parades as the stern guardian of stability – usually having created or contributed first to conditions of instability.

Such authoritarianism is a challenge to democracy which must be fought and defeated. Only the Labour movement can do that. Partly because other critics of modern conservatism are worried by its excesses and not by its nature. Partly because labour is entirely dependent upon democracy as the means of action to secure change. Partly because we are the only political force with the breadth of support to provide a convincing alternative to the present system. Those intrinsic strengths are clearly not enough, however, to win the contest by themselves. Our conduct in pursuit of power and the purposes which we specify for the use of power are essential to gaining the support necessary for achieving that power.

Fifty years ago in times that were even more dangerous for democracy and for the Labour Movement R. H. Tawney counselled that

> The only version of socialism which . . . has the smallest chance of winning mass support in Britain is one that accepts the existence of a body of opinion, larger, probably, than in most other countries, which is sensitive on such subjects as personal liberty, freedom of speech and meeting, tolerance, the exclusion of violence from politics, parliamentary government – what, broadly, it regards as fair play and the guarantees for it. Socialism's exponents must realise that the class which is the victim of economic exploitation, instead of merely reading about it, is precisely the class which attaches most importance to these elementary decencies. They must face the fact that if the public, and particularly the working class public, is confronted with the choice between capitalist democracy, with all its nauseous insincerities, and undemocratic socialism, it will choose the former every time. They must make it clear beyond the possibility of doubt that the socialist commonwealth which they preach will be built on democratic foundations.

That is the case for democratic conduct in pursuit of the Labour movements democratic objectives in Britain. It is as valid now as when it was first put. And now – even after the intervening years of development – the circumstances posed by modern conservatism require us to publicly and persistently restate our central conviction that socialism and freedom are absolutely interdependent, that individual liberty is our whole purpose and that democracy is our means. To some that may be so obvious as to be tiresome. But it is vital that we repeatedly draw attention to the democratic credentials of our socialism that have been earned by years of effort against the conservative forces that have so often and so stoutly – dare I say resolutely – resisted economic, social and political emancipation. That reaffirmation is an essential part of the offensive against Toryism and its 'nauseous insincerities'.

Freedom needs to be defined for every generation lest its meaning and its importance be lost in antiquity, weakened by complacency or employed for merely sentimental purposes. That is particularly necessary now. Conservative government is eating into some of the precious, primary liberties of organization, representation and association. Conservative ideologues are trying to steal the garb of radicalism and – in the name of liberty – impose cuts and conditions which reduce the freedoms of employment, opportunity, consumption and self-confidence of millions. Freedom must, above all else, involve the power to choose. And it must not be a matter of abstract choice, nor a nominal power to select, but a genuine power to exercise a true choice between real alternatives. What matters is freedom in fact and practice, not freedom as an embellishment; freedom which brings responsibility with its entitlements but not jeopardy with its exercise.

The freedom – for instance – of working people to organize in free Unions is not a freedom if it means dismissals for those who choose to exercise that course of action or bankruptcy for the Unions supporting them. The right to freedom of movement is hollow if cuts in resources deny it in practice to huge minorities who suffer physical or mental disability. The right to legal representation is neutralized if it can be bought by the rich, but is too costly for the poor. The right to speak can become nominal if access to the broadcasting and publishing media is limited by prohibitive cost or impeded by the interests which own and control those media. The right to take opportunities to learn or to work – and aspire to the status, security and self fulfilment that goes with them – can be made meaningless if access to those opportunities is effectively limited because an individual is female or black or poor. And personal economic poverty – from whatever cause – is in itself a suspension of freedom no matter how libertarian the general political environment appears to be.

These would be commonplace observations in a democracy were it not for the fact that the rhetoric of abstract freedom is so often accepted as the reality of substantial choice. The duplicity is the main stock-in-trade of modern conservatism. It demeans liberty and turns it into a tool of political illusionists, which can be conjured up in crisis as a tribal emotion, but left to casual, generalized chance in less fervid circumstances – that is to say, most of the time. Tidal waves of liberty-touting may stimulate popular enthusiasm, but when they recede they leave cynicism.

The same reaction is provoked when liberty is confined to limited groups. If freedom of access to the essentials of existence – education, health care and protection in sickness, infancy and old age – carries a price tag requiring substantial payment at time of need and use, it ceases to become liberty and becomes purchased privilege. For these are not commodities to be marketed; they are determinants of the whole condition of life, personal security and individual liberty.

When a political policy has as its main purpose the granting of additional freedoms to a minority by the process of diminishing provision for a majority, it is not promoting anything as decent as choice or as virile as liberty, it is fostering privilege for a few at the price of disadvantage for the many. Thus it is ensuring that the expansion of freedom for a minority is achieved by incursion upon the freedom of the majority. The increase of minority privilege and the enhancement of majority liberty are incompatible. The erosion of collectively organized and provided services, far from extending the freedom of individuals, means the imposition of additional individual burdens.

We Socialists are thus asserting also that liberty must be collective. That is not a paradox. It is a matter of historical fact that the liberties most precious to our people have been attained by collective action and are sustained by collective consensus and determination. They did not happen as a result of accident or easy concession. They are the product of conscious decisions, deliberate preferences produced by prolonged battles against economic, social, cultural or political tyrannies. And the effort to overthrow or mitigate those tyrannies had to be collective.

The indelible fact of life is that most of the people, most of the time do not provide surpluses of income in the right amounts on the right occasions to permit them to provide themselves and their dependents with sufficient supply of the personal services of opportunity, learning, care, security and employment. The task of provision must be a shared task and co-operative and collective contribution by the community has been the greatest single source of individual emancipation of our century. It has not diminished vitality, it has increased fitness. It has multiplied not eroded talent. It has not frustrated inventiveness; it has given the inventive the facility for development. It has not subordinated peoples, it has stimulated their self-confidence. And even though the state has been the most dependable source of provision, the result has not been a supine mood of dependency on the state but an increase in critical faculty towards the state.

We know only too well, of course, that conservatism – ancient and modern – does not take that view of the state. In spite of controlling the state and moulding it to their own advantage whenever it suits their purpose, conservatives consider that use of the state to achieve balance of opportunity is malign, but that operations of the market which result in imbalance of opportunity are inevitable and if not actually benign, at least natural and neutral. Thus it is apparently vindictive of us as socialists to wish to impose sanctions on the purchase and inheritance of privileged opportunity, but not vindictive of history, the market, and the vagaries of parental fortune, aspiration or commitment to anonymously and whimsically conspire against the opportunity of the unprivileged majority. And conservatives believe that when an economic and political system imposes disadvantage on the already under-endowed it is not malice, but necessity provoked by mystical market forces beyond mortal control.

Such fatalism can be expected and accepted among primitives who must, in the absence of technical knowledge, attribute all of their fortunes and misfortunes to the supernatural. Fatalism among the sophisticated is less acceptable, for it is not innocent helplessness, but an excuse for deliberate inactivity. That is immoral and unjust for it is the conscious denial of freedom passed off as an uncontrollable accident of nature.

For decades it has been accepted – and not just by socialists – that it is a primary purpose of parliamentary democracy to actively impede such immorality and injustice by subjecting the allocation of resources to a system of social and economic priority and thus providing the means of collectively resisting the oppression of circumstances or of accident. Modern conservatism – Thatcherism – seeks to detach parliamentary democracy from that function. Instead it emphasizes the power of a parliamentary majority to extend controls so that it intensifies rather than ameloriates disadvantage. The resulting deprivation is called 'saving'. The resulting inequality is regarded as a reward for the few winners and a goad to greater effort among the rest, no matter how incapable of effort the economically, socially or physically halt and lame may be. It is that which above all separates our attitude toward the role of the state from that of the Conservatives. To us it is an agency for the extension of individual freedoms by means of collective obligations. To them the state is still mainly an instrument for imposing regulations and curtailing collective provision in order to give maximum protection and benefit to sectional economic interests. The result is that a Conservative government with a fundamentalist conservative philosophy increasingly imposes the state on the backs of the people. We and generations of radicals, libertarians and socialists before us are part of a long struggle to put the state where it should be in a democracy – under the feet of the people. Conservatism has long sought to impede that effort. Today's Conservatives are working to retard it.

The scale upon which that reversal is taking place and the ease with which a government can do it should rouse even the most complacent into understanding that liberties which seemed to be firmly embedded in Britain were, after all, fragile. They depended upon a complacent public and political consensus. In our time that has been uprooted by a political party selling the fantasies that freedom would be increased if taxes and expenditure were cut, that the services of care and opportunity were mainly bureaucratic sinecures, that individual rights would remain intact even though collective provision was demolished, that prosperity would flourish whilst the resources for production were erased.

We can curse the cunning of the 'New Right'. We can rage about the gullibility of people who voted themselves into being victims. Neither activity is productive. Both, in any case, evade the blame that must be shared by the Labour movement. There has been too much dependence on the assumptions that the body of liberties that had been achieved was irreducable, and that the very existence of a governmental and bureaucratic structure for care, opportunity and representation meant that the substance of those rights was guaranteed. That complacency resulted in our failure to promote widespread comprehension of the vital link between collective provision and individual freedom. That's the *most* basic element of our practical political philosophy, but we did not work hard enough to sustain public understanding and support for it. And to compound the error we even gave the impression that the municipal, trade union and governmental agencies of care, opportunity and representation were, for us, ends in themselves instead of mere means to an end of individual emancipation. Some have always recognized and resisted that monumental mistake. But for others, realization is only coming now with the advent of a government that gained and retained power to strip the social and economic welfare state threadbare in the name of freedom and vigour and virtue.

The moral for the Labour movement is obvious. In every policy that we compile, publicize and practise we have to show that our central objective is the development of freedom and that our chosen method for linking need and provision is democracy. This is a return to basics which is necessary in order to give public and private clarity to our purposes after decades in which they have been obscured by day-to-day, year-to-year preoccupations with performing governmental and party and trade union tasks. It is necessary too, in order to demonstrate the contrast between our commitment to individual liberty that is tangible, universal and collective and the Conservative concept of liberty which is in essence decorative, conditional upon payment, selfish and related – naturally – much more to capital interests than to public interests.

The recoil against that system is coming – indeed evidence shows that it is already under way. Such reactions have come before. Twice in this century they were big enough to produce major strides towards a welfare state, but on neither occasion did the resentment against injustice and waste produce a surge of progress by itself. The attitudes had to be given form. General public feelings of ill-being had to be turned into a systematic programme for redress that was coherently offered by political parties which demonstrated that they were capable of providing acceptable alternatives to the system which generated antagonism and showed that they were in tune with public opinion and popular values. We have that task in the Labour movement now. The British people have realized for years that a combination of investment, planned trade, training and positive employment policies were preferable to the costly and cruel operation of Toryisms' strategy of solvency through slump. We have to keep on joining up that public instinct with public understanding of our policies, keep on proving that our mixture of those recovery strategies is not only preferable but feasible. And as we do that we must insist – and by every action show – that the purpose of implementing those policies is freedom. Freedom from idleness and insecurity. Freedom from the disadvantage and lack of opportunity which results from cuts in resources. Freedom from fear and poverty. Freedom from the prejudices and conventions which sustain racism and sexism. Freedom from the loss of civil and personal rights. Freedom from a government that believes that liberty is an adornment, a consumer durable available in superior quantities and qualities for those who can afford to buy. That advance of liberty has long been the cause of our socialism. Again we must demonstrate that it is the course of our socialism.

12

Socialism and the Limits of State Action

DAVID HELD and JOHN KEANE

The remarkable upsurge of debate about the future of socialism and the Labour Party testifies to the continuing vitality of the socialist tradition in British politics. One of the central issues of controversy (evident in the lively debate sparked by Eric Hobsbawm's writings)[1] has concerned the tarnishing of the image of socialism because of its identification with the centralized bureaucratic state. This controversy is clearly of great political significance. None the less, and with very few exceptions, it is currently hampered by three major deficiencies. First, it is marked by excessively vague and imprecise reflections on the principles and corresponding institutional requirements of democratic socialism. Although there is an emerging consensus about the need for what Bernard Crick calls a long-term socialist 'public philosophy' which emphasizes decentralization, less bureaucracy and more democracy, there seems to be an inability to go beyond these general slogans. Second, the controversy about the bureaucratic image of socialism reflects a striking insularity; the important discussions and new socialist policy initiatives already underway in other European countries are barely acknowledged, if at all. And third, socialists who call for less bureaucracy have failed, with few exceptions, to recognize that some positive things can be learned by engaging the new right, which has taken the lead in popularizing the demand for less state action.

In this chapter, we want to address these three weaknesses. Our argument will be that questions about democracy and socialism can only be posed fruitfully by rethinking the relationship between state and 'civil society'; that is, between the apparatus of government (including its military, economic and cultural institutions) and the realm of social (privately owned or voluntarily run) activities.

This relationship must be rethought in a way that recognizes the necessity of drawing strict limits upon the scope of state action, while expanding the sphere of autonomous social life. We are convinced that the state's relationship to civil society is emerging as a central theme within socialist discussions in countries like France, Germany and Sweden and is of great relevance for socialists in Britain. Our contribution is therefore 'European' in perspective, and offers new terms for thinking about how socialism might be productively redefined. A socialism that is viable and worthy of respect must be synonymous with the democratization of society as well as of the state. For us, socialism involves *deepening* the division between the state and society by making state policy more accountable, and by democratically re-ordering non-state activities. Only if the 'democratic road to socialism' is understood as a double-sided process of transformation of this kind can it regain its position as a credible and practical political alternative.

We believe that the relationship of state and civil society is very useful in highlighting the reasons for the dwindling popularity of the Keynesian welfare state, or what we call 'state-administered socialism', of which centrally controlled bureaucratic institutions are typical. Despite its considerable achievements during the post-war years, the programme of state-administered socialism has lost much of its radical appeal because it fails to recognize the desirable form and limits of state action. This is true in at least three related respects.

To begin with, the model of state-administered socialism – nationalized industry, state-provided health services, households regulated on the model of the partriarchal family through social services and so on – assumed that state power could become the caretaker of existence. Intervening in social life by securing capital investment, reducing unemployment and expanding welfare opportunities, the state tended to assume omniscience over questions of needs and wants. The effect was to encourage the passive consumption of state provision and, in so doing, seriously to undermine people's confidence to direct their own lives. This 'passivity' was necessary to the achievement of socialism by gradually extending networks of intrusive state power into civil society. In retrospect, it is hardly surprising that among its unforeseen effects were a profound loss of trust in the apparatus of government, a deep scepticism about expertise and a general decline in the legitimacy of 'socialism'. It became widely assumed that socialism meant bureaucracy, surveillance, red tape, and state control – not only in the rhetoric of Thatcher, but also in the actual experience of those in daily contact with the welfare state.

Secondly, the shortcomings of state-administered socialism are compounded when successive governments progressively fail to 'deliver the goods', as they inevitably do in the deteriorating circumstances of the international economy and British capitalism. This climate of economic crisis undermines the assumption that the state can, at a stroke, secure economic growth, reduce unemployment and expand social welfare. Economic crisis brings sharply into focus the state's incapacity to realize the ideals of welfare socialism, as it dramatizes the bureaucratic, hierarchical, inequitable and often repressive character of many state policies.

However, circumstances of economic crisis are not necessarily the most important stumbling block of state-administered socialism, as many on the left still believe. Governments' inability to 'deliver the goods' and 'keep their promises' has been reinforced by the dramatic expansion of state agencies at national and local level. The growth of the state has proved to be progressively more costly, creating permanent shortages in public finances and leading to pressures for selective (and arbitrary) reductions in policy areas such as education. In order to implement their stated objectives, both Labour and Tory governments had to expand and diversify their bureaucratic structures, thereby increasing the chances of severe conflicts between different departments. Consequently there were once again growing pressures to 'rationalize' policies by privileging some (defence, for example) and downgrading others (such as social welfare).

State effectiveness was also weakened by the attempt to broaden the regulation and control of social life. This made the state more dependent upon, and vulnerable to, the resistance of powerful social groups (above all, City interests, industrial organizations, certain trade unions) – a trend already strongly evident in the years of the Callaghan government. For all these reasons, the 'hand of the state' became more visible while becoming no more capable of progressive and effective reform.

It is, of course, a sadly ironic fact that the difficulties of state-administered socialism have been most successfully popularized by the new right. While the extremely regressive consequences of Thatcherism are not of prime concern to us here, it is important to stress that these difficulties have both played into Thatcher's hands and highlighted the political vulnerability of state-administered socialism. This is true in two decisive respects. First, Thatcherism is preoccupied with the need to redraw the boundaries between the state and civil society, to segregate spheres of life that have become highly interdependent, and to popularize a highly distorted interpretation of social virtues – self-interest, hard work, self-reliance, freedom of choice, private property, the patriarchal family and distrust of state bureaucracy. According to this so-called 'libertarian' ideology, comprehensive state regulation saps both individual initiative and social resources that make self-organization and 'mutual aid' possible. Such claims have enjoyed a considerable measure of success to date precisely because they mobilize that massive body of cynicism, distrust and dissatisfaction with which people had come to regard the interventionist welfare state. In other words, the success of Thatcher and the new right is parasitic upon the profound difficulties faced by an excessively bureaucratic, state-administered socialism. Secondly, the new right tries to capitalize upon the failure of governments to keep many of their promises. It seeks to distance itself from such promises – and discredit their considerable achievements in practice. The rhetoric and political strategy of the new right is founded not only on an aversion to state intervention and control over civil society, but also on the belief that the state has neither the management capability nor the responsibility to oversee the economy and its related social institutions. The new right consequently attempts to increase the effectiveness of state policies by uncoupling the instrumental dimensions of the state (as a provider of goods and services to society) from its role as a powerful, prestigious and enduring representative of social order. This is the new right's strategy for simultaneously restricting the state and increasing its power.

There are many reasons why this strategy of redrawing the boundaries between the state and civil society is likely to fail. Not only are the problems of the British economy – unemployment, flight of capital overseas, the constant erosion of the manufacturing base – deeply structured. Thatcherism is also incapable of realizing the 'libertarian' values it affirms – above all, those of freedom of choice, mutual aid and self-reliance. A capitalist-directed economy, male-dominated households and the strong state – the trump cards in the hands of the new right – directly contradict its professed anti-bureacratic, non-hierarchical principles. In our view, only the socialist tradition – and *not* the new right – can genuinely defend the libertarian ideals of mutual aid, democratic accountability and a restriction on state power.

The left's capacity to rework and publicly articulate the issues of state and civil society, which Thatcherism has helped to make a public problem is, however, a crucial factor in determining whether the new right's grip on the public imagination can be loosened. The new right ideologues have contributed to a discussion about the *limits* of state-administered socialism with which the left must engage now. The rich, if histrionic, vocabulary of these ideologues (freedom of choice, individual rights and so on) can be neither confidently neglected nor left unquestioned. The pseudo-libertarian appeals of the new right are a reminder that controversies over who shall inherit the vocabulary of freedom are long overdue; and they are imperative for the survival of democratic socialism.

Redrawing state boundaries: lessons from Europe

What form, then, ought state action to take, and how should its limits be defined from a socialist perspective? There is growing consensus on the left that for the socialist movement to become once again publicly credible and viable it must re-emphasize the old goals of equality *and* liberty. To put the point schematically: the new right counterposes equality (which it assesses from a wholly negative point of view) against liberty (which it sees as wholly positive), and so concerns itself with minimal state interference in people's existence and the application of 'free' market principles to more and more aspects of life. The 'old' left (Labourism) emphasizes the state's capacity to create equality and down-plays questions of liberty; hence, it has too often been satisfied with the notion of a 'big state' to impose equality on civil society. The question posed by the growing consensus on the left in favour of equality and liberty is how can 'the state' and 'civil society' be combined to promote equality and liberty?

In our view, these goals can be realized only by recognizing the need for reforming and restricting state power and radically transforming civil society. What is civil society? We certainly don't define civil society solely in the terms used by the new right – a non-state sphere dominated by capitalist corporations and patriarchal families. Civil society in this sense is real enough today. But, for us, it has a vital additional meaning: it has the potential to become a non-state sphere comprising a variety of social institutions – productive units, households, voluntary organizations and community-based services – which are legally guaranteed and demo-cratically organized.

Understood in these terms, the democratic road to social-ism would mean attempting to re-define the boundaries between civil society and the state by two interdependent processes: the expansion of social autonomy and the re-structuring and democratizing of state institutions. Two conditions would be necessary for this. First, the power not only of capital but also of patriarchy and the state would have to be curtailed through struggles that would enable citizens to strive for equal power, and so maximize their capacity to play an active part in civil society. Secondly, state institutions would have to become more accountable by having their functions as responsible co-ordinators and regulators of people's lives recast. The democratic road to socialism would consequently avoid the well-known pitfalls of syndicalism and the excessive bureaucratic regulation of state-administered socialism. It would reject the assumption that the state could ever replace civil society or vice versa; and would thereby defend the principle that the separation of the state and civil society must be a permanent feature of any democratic social and political order in which productive property, status and the power to make decisions would no longer be privately appropriated.

Civil society and the state must become the condition for each other's democratization. State institutions ought to be devices for enacting legislation, promulgating new policies, containing inevitable conflicts between particular interests within well-defined legal limits, and for preventing civil society from falling victim to new forms of inequality and tyranny. In this scheme of things, on the other hand, a multiplicity of organizations – whether self-managed enterprises, housing co-operatives, refuges for battered women, independent communications media or health centres – must increase their powers in order to keep their political 'representatives' under control. In short, we argue that without a secure and independent civil society of autonomous public bodies, goals such as freedom and equality, participatory planning and community decision-making will be nothing but empty slogans. But without the protective, redistributive and conflict-mediating functions of the state, struggles to transform civil society will become ghettoized and divided, or will spawn their own, new forms of inequality.

To speak in this way of democratization as a 'two-pronged' strategy is more than simply a plea for clarifying the framework of the present political discussion about the future of British socialism. The limit of desirable state action is also becoming a crucial theme in other European discussions of *practical* socialist policies, a debate which can be illustrated briefly by new socialist initiatives in the areas of investment, employment, trade unions and the reorganization of social welfare provision.

Since 1975, for instance, extensive discussions have occurred on the left in Sweden about the ways in which a gradual extension of social ownership of productive property can be achieved. One thing to emerge from these discussions was the Meidner Plan. Its details are complex, but the thrust of its programme, as interpreted by Korpi and others,[2] is to create the means for increasing the level of socially controlled investment. This would be done by formulating an egalitarian, planned wages policy (keeping wages within limits tolerable to an open economy), and by using increased taxes on profits to create investment funds on a local and regional basis which are *citizen-controlled*. This proposal seeks to avoid the problem whereby wage restraint leads traditionally to an increased rate of private profit without increasing investment, let alone greater social control over productive resources. In the long run, it also aims to break with the conventional view that state economic planning plus nationalization equals socialism.

The emphasis on self-determination is further evident in the West German Green Party strategy for dealing with the growing cleavage between the holders of secure jobs and marginalized groups of the partly employed, the unemployed and the unwaged. The core idea is to redistribute wage labour in such a way as to produce greater time flexibility and a radical reduction in the present level of working hours. According to this programme, the demand for full employment for men and women can only be fulfilled by democratizing and redistributing a variety of equally important and frequently routine forms of wage labour and informal social labour, such as housework. This search for a new framework for the 'right to work' is part of the Greens' strategy of 'social defence' against all those who are powerful and privileged. It is in essence a renewal of the old socialist struggle against wage labour which, in addition, breaks down the conventional patriarchal division between household and market. It is also an alternative strategy for enhancing workers' and citizens' rights. And when linked (for instance) to industrial conversion schemes designed to transform military production into the production of socially useful goods, or to opposition to nuclear power plants, it aims to defend the realm of non-state activities from both the power of capital and the bureaucratic state.

Such considerations have radical implications for trade unions, some of which have been explored since 1978 by the French Democratic Labour Confederation. The CFDT has attempted to create a new non-sectarian social solidarity against employer and state intransigence. This not only means concern about alternative technology and wage rates, but it also addresses the problem of the 'break up of the working class'[3] by agitating for the recognition of the needs of workers with low wages, precarious jobs and no trade union representation. The CFDT's priorities have been increases in the minimum wage, remuneration for the lowest wage groups, an overall reduction of the working week, flexible working hours and greater self-management. The CFDT is concerned to stimulate the independent formulation of broad social demands upon the state. While recognizing the importance of the state in pushing through reforms for all workers (unionized or not), the CFDT strategy is, significantly, opposed to corporatism and blind reliance upon the state. It proposes a strategy not for enhanced trade union powers for their own sake, but for solidarity with the less powerful in civil society.

The final example of new socialist strategy is the Scandinavian proposals to 'lease back' institutions of social policy to the community. These proposals are a democratic response to the evident increase in the post-war period of bureaucratic, hierarchical and non-market state institutions such as hospitals, schools and housing authorities. At the same time, such proposals attempt to counter the socially regressive consequences of the new right strategy of privatization. They suggest that state institutions of social policy can be turned into something more positive and democratic if control of them is reclaimed or leased back to the people who use and service them. Although they would remain publicly funded, their policies would be guided neither by capitalist markets nor by state direction, but by criteria of social need generated by producers' and consumers' decisions. As a consequence, the state would guarantee the resources and facilities for childcare, health clinics or schools, while leaving the government of these organizations to local constituencies. These broad leaseback proposals – which are currently no more than that – were inspired by the success of local education initiatives by Sweden and Denmark. With financial means provided by the state, and within guidelines which specify minimum standards of learning, these initiatives have enabled parents to agree collectively on curricula, forms of assessment, types of discipline and staffing arrangements. Furthermore, should parents be dissatisfied with existing state-run schools, they have the additional option of establishing a new school of their own design. Under this second scheme, parents must provide the school's first year of funds and adhere once again to minimum educational standards. If the school is successful, however, parents are reimbursed and the state assumes responsibility for subsequent funding.

Making the state democratic

In our view, these policy examples are important not because they can be imported directly into Britain, But because they explicitly recognize the urgent need to deal with the undesirable elements of bureaucratic state regulation and surveillance which have grown so enormously since 1945. However, such policies do not automatically secure more decentralized, horizontally structured egalitarian patterns of social life. Vigorous political initiatives, funding and legal recognition are necessary conditions of their survival and expansion. Thus, the second and equally important prong of a new strategy for socialism becomes crucial: the democratization of state policy making and administration. So far in Britain the need to democratize political institutions has mostly been confined to questions of reforming party leadership, union decision-making and electoral rules. This parochial focus leaves out a whole variety of issues which socialists must address if they are to resume leadership in the battle for democratic political rights. Proportional representation and the internal reform of parties are only two of a wide gamut of necessary demands. Others must include public funding of elections for all parties meeting a minimum level of support; genuine access to, and equal distribution of, media time; freedom of information (for example, abolition of the Official Secrets Act and the many rules and regulations concerning secrecy); decentralization of the civil service to the regions; and the defence and enhancement of local authority power against rigid, centralized state decisions.

But none of these strategies for making the polity more democratic will enjoy full success unless a further difficult problem is confronted: can the requirements of democratic public life (openness, controversy, pluralism, universal participation) be reconciled with those domestic and international institutions for maintaining 'law and order' which thrive on secrecy, cunning and the monopoly of the means of violence? This problem can only be confronted, first, by reversing the present drift towards militarism and bringing agencies such as the police back to the community as a leased-back service; and secondly (as Tony Benn correctly emphasizes) by establishing the sovereignty of Parliament over the state to ensure the political control of these and other institutions.

Altogether, we have argued that socialism today must break with its defensive and statist character, and become synonymous with the vitalization of civil society and the democratic reform of state power. Policies based on this general programme could play a decisive part in current ideological debates prompted by the failures of state-administered socialism and the authoritarian initiatives of the new right. In a period in which the spell of state-administered socialism is being broken, such policies could also provide credible socialist alternatives. This strategy of transforming civil society – of creating a *socialist* civil society – and reforming the state indicates that the real question facing socialists in contemporary capitalist countries such as Britain is not the old alternative between reformism or revolution to abolish the state. It is the question of how to enact the 'two-pronged' strategy of creative reform protected by state action, and innovation from below through radical social initiatives.

Notes

[1] See in particular D Massey, L. Segal and H. Wainwright, Chapter 14 in this volume.

[2] W. Korpi, *The Working Class in Welfare Capitalism* (Routledge & Kegan Paul, 1978).

[3] A. Gorz, *Farewell to the Working Class* (Pluto Press, 1982).

13

Socialists and Coalitionists

RAYMOND WILLIAMS

Since the 1983 general election there has been a marked change of political mood in Britain: a recovery of morale by Labour; a series of misfortunes for the Tories. At the same time there has been comparatively little change in the underlying political realities. This contrast between mood and reality can be misleading and even in some respects dangerous. The very hard questions posed by the defeat of last June can be softened or allowed to slip away in the name of necessary resilience or a merely foolish optimism, each strengthened by the passage of time. It is for this reason that we have still to take seriously the questions defined by Eric Hobsbawm, with his usual plainness and lucidity. I disagree strongly with the answers he suggests or implies, but I find myself at an even greater distance from those who think they can dispose of the questions by simple and self-righteous cries against 'coalition', which in this context is often little more than a swearword.

It is true that it has long been the purpose of right-wing and centrist commentators to get rid of the Labour Party as a significant independent political force. This is also the explicit intention of the Alliance parties. Indeed for more than 30 years there has been a sustained attempt to form a left-of-Tory party or grouping in which the socialist component would be minimal or altogether excluded. Moreover it should not be forgotten that elements of this attempt have come from within the Labour Party including, at times, its leadership. It would be a simple matter for the whole of the current discussion to be absorbed by this long and dangerous campaign.

But this would be too easy. The current problem is not so

much in the campaign itself as in the deteriorating political situation to which it is a response. It is a fact that we have a very dangerous right-wing government elected by only 43 per cent of the electorate. Yet appeals against its legitimacy, on this ground, cut little ice against its actual monopoly of state power. It is also a fact that on all recent and current evidence there are now three parties or party groupings each capable of gaining at least 20 per cent of the popular vote. Both Labour and the Alliance believe that they can make the other go away and there are some signs, among the ideologists of each party, that they give higher priority to driving out the left-of-Tory rival than to opposing the main enemy. They rationalize this by the belief that the only way to defeat the Tories is to dispose first of the alternative anti-Tory vote. But it is then reasonable to ask how this displaced emphasis will affect real political opinion, when it is Tory support that has really to be reduced. Reasonable also to ask what will happen if, regardless of the energy devoted to such efforts, it turns out that a three- or four-party system has come to stay. This connects with the alarming central fact that the 'Labour vote' had declined to 28 per cent: a low point only reached in any comparable situation during a period when there were, as now, three contending parties. It is tempting to link this obvious correlation between so low a vote and the existence of three parties to the tactic of giving priority to eliminating or reducing the third party. But this is especially dangerous for the Labour Party because it obscures or postpones the question that has really to be answered: what kind of party is it? Is it a broadly socialist party, or is it (as it became during the generations of Liberal decline) the only realistic left-of-Tory coalition?

For we have in fact been living with one kind of coalition politics for many years, inside and – on both wings – outside the Labour Party. The real question raised by Hobsbawm is whether that kind of coalition – the Labour 'broad church' and its friends – can be successfully continued or revived, or whether some new kind of coalition is now necessary, given the rise of a third party grouping. It seems clear that he would be glad to see either, though with a preference for the first. It is here, especially, that the grounds of the whole argument need to be widened. On the hitherto limited electoral terms no useful resolution of the argument seems to me possible.

The true context of any practical politics is always the general social and economic situation, and only secondarily the party dispositions and shares of the popular vote which follow from this. One obvious weakness of recent electoral analysis, as with the analysis which followed Labour's defeat in 1959, is that it treats current distributions of votes as if they were primary data from which the social and economic situation, or at least the main responses to it, can be inferred. There is a related habit of inventing social entities in the form of 'the Labour vote' or 'Labour voters' and so on. It is true that there are some significant numbers of people who vote consistently for this or that party over a long period, and that relative increases or decreases in these numbers are significant. But these groupings taken together are never anywhere near the sum of the electorate. A pattern of multiple shifts this way and that, even at times appearing to cancel each other out in a relatively unchanged general distribution, has been characteristic of British politics since the 1950s and has increased markedly in recent years. These multiple shifts have been in evidence even since the June 1983 election.

Moreover, although speculative reasons for shifts are often advanced, very little is known about their causes. Some appear to be settled shifts in social affiliation; others are almost certainly short-run impulses. In practice, it is impossible to infer from these, or from relative changes in more sustained groupings, either the true social situation or the requirements of political practice. This is especially the case when there are more than two electorally significant parties. It is instructive that the erstwhile 'Liberal vote' and the more recent 'Alliance vote' have been exceptionally 'unstable' in these terms. This is only one of several reasons why we should not begin a political analysis from 'shares' of votes, but from the more important and more objectively discoverable general situation.

Whether Britain is viewed in isolation or, as should be the case, the uncertainties of 'Britain' are seen in the context of a critical and uneven world politics and world economy the general situation is even more unstable and volatile than any pattern of voting. No realistic policy for, say, the next 10 years of the labour movement can be based on simple projections from the present situation or even the present crisis. Britain, in so far as it is still an autonomous economy, is now a weak and exposed sector in a severe and prolonged world crisis. As far as it is still an independent political nation, it is a junior partner in a system of military alliances, and an uncertain partner in the attempts at a Western European Community which is itself now in crisis.

Within these very broad determinations, all of which indicate continued and dangerous uncertainty and instability, there can be varying assessments of what will happen within the sphere of British electoral politics. The orthodox view from the left assumes a steady, chronic degeneration of the existing social order: a still failing economy, continued mass unemployment, a greatly reduced welfare state, an extending domination of capitalist values. The orthodox view from the right, though it speaks of recovery and regeneration, transposes these damaging changes into the vital reconstitution of a profitable capitalist economy. This is not to be confined to Britain alone, but to be extended by the worldwide deployment of British capital. Continuing mass unemployment, reduced welfare costs, weakened trade unions and the defeat of socialist ideas and organizations are the deliberate conditions of this reconstitution. So also is the pursuit of an aggressive and heavily-armed foreign policy in the struggle for control of key areas of the newly industrializing and dependent poor world.

Another orthodox view from the left goes beyond the usual account of 'Tory mismanagement' and understands current Tory policy as a hard and, in its own terms, rational programme. It then assumes that there must eventually be a gathering of political opposition to its inevitably heavy costs, of a kind that will return the left to power. This is very much better than the older assumption that there will be sufficient opposition to mere 'mismanagement': ground on which Labour, from its recent record in government, is in no strong position to fight. But it may still not be strong enough, for there is a third possible assumption, different both from the hard right and from the orthodox left in either of its versions. What is interpreted from the left as a process of chronic degeneration, and from the right as a process of profitable capitalist reconstitution, is seen from this third perspective as imposing strains on the whole social order which will radically change the terms of British politics. A minority of Marxists believe this will lead eventually to some kind of pre-revolutionary situation in classical terms. But alongside them other Marxists see the danger of a further break to the right, with much harder authoritarian controls to contain the pressures which the capitalist reconstitution must inexorably increase.

This perspective does not often appear directly in current arguments for left coalitions or similar arrangements, but I think it is no coincidence that its kind of response – in effect an updated version of the popular front – is now coming from some eminent Marxists. Nor, in any real historical perspective, should this kind of thinking be dismissed by mere labelling. There are undoubtedly possible circumstances in Britain and in the rest of Western Europe in which the organization of a popular front would indeed be a priority. The historical lessons of the defeat of the left in Italy in the early 1920s and in Germany in the early 1930s cannot be forgotten, and must indeed still be taken seriously. But any such proposal must be assessed in contemporary terms. The historical memories and the futurist projections have to be related to where we are. It still matters very much which of these assumptions of the nature of the next 10 years we adopt, but in any case we have to move on from retrospective accounts of the movements of votes and into this real area of political analysis.

If the Tories had lost . . .

One useful way of testing the arguments about electoral policies and arrangements is to set them in their real or probable political context. Let us suppose, for example, that the 57 per cent of votes against the present Conservative government had not been distorted by an absurd electoral system but had produced a majority of non-Conservative representatives. On what kind of political programme would they have been able to agree? The answer is, I believe, disconcerting to both main sides in the current argument, but at first sight it is most disconcerting of all to those who dismiss the whole discussion with cries against 'coalition'. For it would almost certainly have been possible to form a government with the following main heads of policy: first, deliberate reflation of the economy by extending the public sector borrowing requirement to some figure between the Labour and Alliance proposals; second, cancellation of cuts in the welfare services, education, transport and general infrastructure; and third, refusal – or at least delay – or Cruise missile installation, and introduction of Polaris into general disarmament negotiations. Obviously there would be other areas in which simple agreement would be out of the question – wages policy, trade union legislation, the electoral system itself. But the three areas cited above are of such commanding importance that in practice few people would turn down the chance of realizing them, whatever other disagreements remained. Moreover, such policies would, without question, produce some marked improvements in our present circumstances. They have only to be compared with current Tory policies for that to be evident.

It is from this conclusion, and from seeing the alternative as prolonging current Tory policies while the non-Tory vote remains so divided, that the coalitionists – whether explicit or not – draw their strongest arguments. But of course any such coalition is hypothetical. There are, as Hobsbawm fairly said, substantial objective and subjective obstacles to its practical realization. One of these is the electoral system itself, currently a major difference between the prospective partners. Even where this is modified, as in the 1983 election, by a good deal of tactical voting (which, it should be noted, itself distorts the crude figures of shares of the vote), there is no way of effecting a practical coalition of policies except by negotiations before the election. Yet such bargaining instantly challenges the full national ambitions of the separate parties, and is indignantly rejected.

What then happens is an appeal to balance the political

advantages of some new arrangement – positive advantages, as in the three heads of policy; negative advantages, in that at least the Tories would be out – against what can be seen as merely residual and hidebound party positions. Alternatively, these probable gains are seen to outweigh the likelihood that one of the potential partners, Labour or Alliance, can in the next four years so thoroughly defeat or reduce its anti-Tory rival that it will itself gain majority power to execute both the main heads of policy and its other, more particular, commitments. Put this way, the appeal seems very strong.

The trouble with coalitions

So what's wrong with it? The answer lies in the politics rather than in the electoral calculations. The main objection follows from the fact that, in the present electoral system, such arrangements have to be made in advance. For even if we could agree that current objections to such arrangements are decisively outweighed by their political advantages, the actual effect would be a relative freezing of current policy positions: not only agreement on the main heads of policy, which in real terms would not be difficult in current circumstances, but agreement also that certain other kinds of policy, while they could of course be independently retained, would be relatively played down so as not to threaten any proposed, plausible agreement. Thus there would at least have to be some loose coalition of policies *before* any practical electoral arrangements were possible.

It can, of course, be argued that this is desirable, as a way of achieving at least the major policies. Or it can be said that this kind of advance agreement is very much more desirable than a post-election coalition resulting from a hung parliament, in which broadly similar policies would probably be agreed – but behind closed doors between the leaderships rather than in the open between full parties. In fact we cannot now say which of the two election results relevant to this argument is more likely next time: a Tory government even on a reduced minority vote, or a hung parliament in which some kind of coalition would inevitably occur. Perhaps one of the best reasons for having this argument in the open now is to force us to think not only about the relatively improbable pre-election agreements but also about the much more probable post-election problems in which Labour would be embroiled if it failed to get its own majority.

Everything, in the end, must come back to the real politics, and here there is a more challenging argument. For we have to ask what real differences there are between these proposals for what can be called the Big Coalition – Labour and the Alliance in any of its possible forms – and what has to be called the Smaller Coalition, which is that version of the Labour Party which draws on the same types of argument as the explicit coalitionists – pressing for electoral unity around certain main heads of policy while other differences lie on the table – as a way of maintaining the practical coalition of diverse tendencies which the Labour Party has long been. There is one clear difference between the two kinds of coalition. To the extent that the Labour Party maintains or extends its recently improved democratic structures so that policy decisions are of an openly discussed and contested kind, the implicit coalition of socialists and social democrats within the party will be continuously active, as distinct from manoeuvred coalition agreements between separate leaderships. At the same time we can all imagine circumstances in which the appeal for electoral unity could be made to override this active process, and some of the same arguments as those of the Big Coalitionists would then be deployed: the need to maximize the vote against the real enemy; the subordination of contentious policy decisions to the unifying imperatives of electoral organization.

One version of these arguments is acceptable – at least initially. All of us who have experienced the defeats of Labour and the left not just as analysts or observers but where they really hurt, in the lives of our own people, are understandably determined not to be defeated again. In fact, from this determination a new kind of politics can really begin. But there is another version of what are apparently the same arguments which leads us directly back into the old politics of defeat. The distinction between the versions is not primarily in relation to elections: it is in relation to actual policies. For what has to be said very clearly is that if Labour's major policies are broadly the same as those of the Alliance, it would be very foolish indeed not to seek some mutually beneficial electoral arrangements. (There is an obvious practical limit to how many centre or left-centre parties there can be: even two is already too many in the present electoral system.) Of course it is indignantly denied in both camps that there is any such identity. Minor, marginal or dispensable differences are maximized as a condition of becoming the only true contender for the sensible anti-Tory vote. And if this sensible ground is where majority public opinion now is, but two or three parties are contending to represent it, there are only two reasonable tactics: driving out the rivals or coming to an arrangement with them. Hobsbawm assumes such a ground, and while he would doubtless prefer Labour to drive out the Alliance he is realistic enough to face its great difficulties and to contemplate the alternative.

Yet to be reduced to a choice between these two limited tactics would be the most important defeat which the left could now suffer. The reasons for this are political. They become clear if we look again at the main heads of policy which might now be agreed in some anti-Tory coalition, or which might alternatively be most strongly emphasized in Labour's drive for its own government. None of the policies is in any distinctive sense socialist. Reflation of the economy, in the terms usually proposed, is a continuation of Keynesianism. Restoration of the welfare state is in the broad tradition of the liberal and social-democratic consensus out of which the Labour governments emerged. Limited measures of disarmament are within the broad internationalist and peacemaking consensus of the same tradition at its best. None of these identities proves any of the policies wrong or insufficient. Yet the underlying identity, while it is held at this practical level, indeed makes dividing and splitting votes between parties which broadly adhere to it foolish. What is wrong, from any socialist position, is the definition of such policies as adequate for any sustained recovery or advance. Nor is it enough to add in some of Labour's more distinctive policies, such as opposition to the Common Market, opposition to incomes policies or repeal of anti-union legislation. None of these makes the basic body of policy more realistic or coherent. It is in the main heads of policy themselves that there must be significant and convincing socialist development, if we are to substantiate Labour's claim to be a unique alternative not only to Tory policies but also to the liberal/social-democratic consensus now electorally available in the Alliance.

Some people think that this development can be brought about by a bold announcement of a commitment to socialism. But for many years this has been not the solution but the problem. Nominal socialist commitment has broadly co-existed with actual liberal/social-democratic policies, and this has led to confusion inside the party as well as to justified criticism of it by others as incoherent and unconvincing. What really needs to happen in the next four years is a radical reconstruction of all the main directions of policy in the light of the most open and informed contemporary socialist analysis.

So in the case of the general direction of the economy, it is necessary to move beyond 'one-nation Keynesianism' in each of its component terms. It is clear from the experience of the French socialist government that economies of the size of Britain or France cannot pull away on their own from the main forces of the international capitalist economy. Thus co-ordinated or integrated policies with other left governments are a condition of any sustained success and need to be carefully discussed and agreed in advance, at least in general outline. One obvious route for this is within the EEC; it could mean changing the residual option for negotiated withdrawal to a policy of forcing the pace for a co-ordinated socialist reconstruction of a group of European economies and thereby reforming the EEC itself.

But the simple Keynesianism also needs to be changed. Centralized management of credit and the money supply, as in simple reflation policies, has to be only a part of a much more developed process of democratic economic planning and control, including hard *selective* policies on investment, prices, taxes and incomes. This connects with the need to go beyond a simple welfare state. In the current employment and demographic crisis it is impossible to isolate an area of services and benefits recommended only in their own terms (pensions and compensation for early retirement are only the most obvious examples), without reference to the direction and priorities of the general economy. Opportunism in this area has already been heavily paid for politically, and it is essential to rework the principles and costs of the system as part of a general policy on investment, taxation, employment and benefits. On the third head of policy, in relation to peace and disarmament, it is necessary to transcend the limited holding initiatives which are now being emphasized and re-work from the beginning a coherent and sustainable inter-national policy. This must include realistic relations between the requirements of British security and the problems of membership of either a nuclear or a non-nuclear military alliance. It must also include policies for the reconstruction of economic and political relationships with the Third World – a greatly neglected area. It is here especially that general monetary and economic policies beyond Keynesianism inter-lock as matters of political struggle with policies to change the role of British finance capital in the international econ-omic order.

These are brief examples in relation only to the three main issues previously defined. A whole range of other social policies has to be developed in coherent relationship to them. It is then easy to say that getting even provisional agreement on them by majorities in the Labour Party would be a formidable political task. For it would be particularly impor-tant that the policies be developed well beyond the status of conference resolutions into genuinely practical programmes. There would need to be professional detailed and con-tinuously updated work drawing on the research resources and practical experiences of the whole labour movement.

Yet even this would not be enough. The whole point of this new political direction would be the attempt, by informing and educating each other in the hard realities of the contemporary world, to launch the widest possible public process of reconsidering and (where necessary) changing every popular assumption, habit and attitude. Indeed the

centre of this new politics would be a campaign to shift the
popular ground on which we have in fact been defeated: not
to adapt to it or to manoeuvre around it, but to go out and
try to transform it. As it happens this would also be the best
possible kind of electoral campaign, with the organization of
an electoral machine genuinely powered by an expanding
socialist awareness and conviction. Otherwise, as so often
before, there will be arguments about who is to drive, which
maps will be used, even how best to tune the machine. And
still there will not be enough bloody petrol.

Finding an alternative

This kind of politics is, I am sure, the only immediate and
practical alternative to the politics of overt or covert coalition. I am not saying that the answers to come out would be
the ones known and already advanced by the left of the party.
On the contrary, that assumption – still common on the left –
is merely the way to more divisive factionalism. Until the
work has really been done and has come to include detailed,
convincing answers to the objections already made and acted
upon by the right of the party and beyond it, there is no
ready-made socialist programme to translate into simple
resolutions and majorities.

The long neglect of fundamental research and political
education has produced an uneven but unmistakable mixture
of half-formed policies and half-convincing protests. Much
of the most essential detailed work is being done outside or at
the edges of the party – in the peace movement, in the
women's movement, in the ecology organizations – and all
these bear especially on that politics of the future to which
Labour must now redirect itself from the depths of defeat.
But there is also promising work inside the party itself as well
as great potential within the trade unions and their research
departments for work on the central issues of employment
and investment – an area in which all convincing policies
need to be very specific. Through these various channels and
through the Socialist Society, the Fabian Society and constituency political education officers, the necessary work *can* be

done. The true intellectual resources of the labour movement have never been so rich and diverse, and the political problem is to bring them to bear in general public debate rather than internal dispute.

The campaign must be much more than 'bringing the message' or even 'winning the intellectual argument (though that, too, is necessary). In one linked area after another what we really have to discover – and as far as possible agree on – is what that intellectual argument actually is: the fully contemporary intellectual argument for socialism. This is why coalitions must be opposed. Whether it's the Big or the Smaller version, the advocates of either have in effect abandoned the struggle to transform belief and opinion. In a cold climate, they say, the many but now disparate remnants of decent and sensible opinion must huddle together, pooling their surviving resources against the Tory storm. I can see how easy it is to feel like that or to respond hopefully to a few brave words flung back against the wind. I also know that the kind of campaign for renewal which I have been describing has been proposed before, and has never fully happened. Are these words, too, no more than a cry against the wind?

It is for many of us to answer. If this new kind of politics is too hard for us, if there is too little time or if we already believe that these more radical tactics must fail, there are still answers – indeed now common answers. Ruling the new politics out, or merely paying it lip service without the practical changes which need to go with it, leaves plenty of room for other kinds of political activity: we can sustain the Smaller Coalition without any real work on policies, or reach out for the Larger Coalition, adapting ahead of its formal arrangements by trimming or underplaying those innovative socialist policies which are known to be incompatible with it. But we can then draw a clear line, to our mutual advantage, between socialists and coalitionists. We can begin to see where we really are, and what we have to change.

14

The Politics of the Popular Front?

BEN PIMLOTT

If the mood of the Labour Party has been brighter in the year following the 1983 election defeat than in the months before it, the reasons are not hard to find. Two sentiments have been dominant. One is the sense of relief that we are still alive. The second is a brittle hope that we have learnt our lesson. Both seemed to inspire the new leader's rallying cry at the 1983 party conference in Brighton:

> Just remember how you felt then, and think to yourselves: 'June the ninth 1983; never again will we experience that.' [*Applause*]. Show that we understand it; show that we mean it; show that we know, taught by the hardest school of events, that unity is the price of victory . . . Not a cosmetic disguise, but living, working unity of people, of a movement, of a party, of a belief, of a conviction that wants to win.

These words provided the theme of conference, and they have been echoed on labour movement platforms ever since. Nobody, however – and least of all Neil Kinnock – imagines that party unity and a will to win, even if combined, as he went on to say, with 'fidelity to socialism', will be enough to produce a Labour government at the next election. Too much has happened for a windfall victory, based on Tory mistakes and the reassertion of Labour virtue, to be possible.

The seriousness of Labour's predicament may be seen from a few disturbing facts. To deprive the Tories of their majority, Labour needs a bigger swing than any British party has obtained since the war; to win outright, with an overall majority of one, we need a swing more than twice as great as any achieved since 1945. Even a small swing, however, would reverse a remorseless downward trend in Labour voting. Thus, in the Tory victory year of 1959, 62 per cent of manual workers voted Labour. In 1983 (when the Tories' share of the poll was actually 7 per cent less), only 38 per cent did so. More ominous still, as Doreen Massey showed in a devastating survey a few weeks after the poll, Labour's support is now concentrated in declining, rather than expanding, sectors of the economy. In other words, while Britain's industrial base withers under Thatcher, so does the Labour vote – increasingly restricted to regions of traditional industry and the depressed inner cities.[1] In short, we are still alive, but only just. In 1983, Labour's position began to look perilously similar to that of the disintegrating Liberal Party in the 1920s.

What is to be done? If the working class fragments, surely the fragmentation of working-class politics is also inevitable? One response has been defiant and robust. The working class has changed, but it is still there, argues Eric Heffer: 'It is a different working class . . . What Labour has to do in the William Morris sense is to go out and make socialists.'[2] We need not disagree. On the other hand, we do need to know how this vital task is to be performed, and why we should expect to be better at it now than in the recent past. It is wishful thinking to imagine that old-fashioned doorstep politics can influence the result anywhere except in the tightest marginals.[3] After the 1979 election, only one voter in seven could remember being canvassed by *any* party, according to a MORI poll, while the proportion of electors attending public meetings was one in thirty-three.[4] Nor is there evidence that, for the Labour Party at least, new-style community politics has much effect on votes one way or the other. The Labour Party, wrote Tony Benn in *Arguments for Democracy* (1981), is 'being transformed into a campaigning movement, and is no longer the narrow electoralist machine which it had become over the years of revisionism.' Again, we should applaud. But as a strategy for winning power in the short term, the transformation has yet to prove its worth. Party modernization is also often pressed. Eric Heffer writes of Labour bringing 'its propaganda and organizational rhetoric up to date', and few would dissent from a suggestion

which conference, with the backing of the NEC, rightly
endorsed.[5] Yet we may wonder what is likely to be achieved
in practice, even if a national newspaper is established, given
the power of the propaganda machines arraigned against us.
Radical literature is limited in its readership to a tiny minority
of the converted, while trade unions, formerly the source of
political campaigning strength, have been weakened indus-
trially by the present government and may soon be crippled
politically to boot.

How then are we to make socialists, or at any rate Labour
votes, in sufficient numbers? One solution that has had
currency among people with less faith in Labour's campaigning capacity than Heffer or Benn is that we should link up, on
the basis of an electoral pact, with the Liberal/SDP Alliance.
Supporters of this proposal see two advantages. First, they
claim that an electoral arrangement would be directly beneficial in terms of seats; second, they maintain that a broad
anti-Thatcher front, like popular front movements abroad,
would create its own distinct appeal. Some of the implications of this suggestion have been discussed by Raymond
Williams in a stimulating *New Socialist* article re-published in
this volume. Williams argues against a 'coalitionist' approach
on broad ideological grounds. We will return to his analysis
later, but first we need to look more closely at the arguments
in favour of a pact, and the possible consequences of such an
undertaking in electoral terms.

The first considered advocacy of some kind of arrangement across party lines came from people whose political
distance from the Alliance was greatest: members of the
editorial board of the Communist theoretical journal, *Marxism Today*. In the September 1983 issue Bob Rowthorn set
the ball rolling:

> Drawing together the anti-Thatcherite forces cannot be
> reduced to a party question. It is not a matter of persuading
> everyone to vote Labour – or Communist – at the next
> election, though we might wish this was the case. Rather the
> labour movement must seek to engage in action and dialogue
> with forces outside its own ranks . . . The problem is to build
> a new progressive coalition of opinion amongst the people

against the Thatcherites, even if for the moment that assumes a somewhat defensive character.

It was not Rowthorn, however, but the left-wing labour historian and philosopher Eric Hobsbawm who made the argument a talking point far beyond the normal readership of *Marxism Today*. Without coming out explicitly in favour of an alliance, Hobsbawm suggested pointedly that recent continental experience merited inspection. In France and Spain, socialists had entered 'common electoral fronts of all who are, for one reason or another, opposed to reaction, interested in reforms, and prepared to sympathize with progressive appeals'. He concluded that if Labour proved incapable of winning back its former supporters on its own, 'it will have to learn how to lead a broad front of other parties or their supporters in backing Labour's policy'.[6]

Whether or not Hobsbawm was actually advocating a pact or just talking about the possibility of having one as a last resort, became a matter of debate in itself.[7] However, a taboo was broken. Meanwhile there were parallel murmurings within the Alliance, especially among some of the more wistful members of its SDP wing. Where Marxist pragmatists wrote in general terms, SDP empiricists did their sums. In the spring of 1984, Evan Luard, former MP for Oxford (and for a time a Labour minister), identified 35 English seats in which the Alliance came second to the Tories by a smaller amount than the Labour vote, and where – assuming static voting patterns – the government was in theory vulnerable to a Labour–Alliance pact. On the reasonable assumption of some swing away from the Tories, the number of seats in the firing line would increase: a swing of 5 per cent, for example, would add 40 or 50 seats to the list. Nor need a pact be a purely expedient operation. Rejecting the notion of an unbridgeable gulf between Labour's left-wing and Alliance moderates, Luard indicated key areas of common concern. Both Labour and the Alliance, he suggested, were agreed on the need for more public spending and a higher PSBR; on support for the health and welfare services; and on the need for greater freedom of information, greater emphasis on civil liberties, better protection for the disadvantaged and reform of tax and social security. Based on these issues, a 'loose electoral arrangement, without policy preconditions' might be possible.[8]

Luard's calculations were of a fairly basic kind. Meanwhile, encouragement had come from a highly influential quarter: the world of academic psephology. On 23 March 1984, Professor Ivor Crewe, cartographer of voter 'dealignment', published a long article in *The Guardian* which gave statistical weight to the view that a pact might help both sides. Crewe's argument was based on key evidence: post-June 1983 poll findings that a high proportion of Alliance supporters would vote Labour in the absence of a candidate of their first choice. Hitherto, though a pact had obvious attractions for the Alliance (Labour voters with nowhere else to go were more likely to choose them than the Tories), the advantage to Labour seemed less self-evident because of uncertainty about the ability of Liberal or SDP leaders to direct their own vote leftwards in seats where Labour was the agreed challenger. Now this hurdle seemed to have been removed – paradoxically because in 1983 the Alliance had taken more of its vote from Labour than from the Tories. Crewe suggested that for political reasons a pact should be restricted to seats where one anti-Tory candidate (whether Labour or Alliance) stood a good chance, and the other evidently stood none at all. Making some carefully analysed assumptions about voters' likely second choices, Crewe then calculated that if 'no hope' candidates withdrew in selected seats, the swing needed to take away the government's overall majority might be reduced from the present formidable 5.3 per cent to as little as 1.6 per cent.

Shortly afterwards, the result of the May 1984 mini-election (local elections plus by-elections) seemed to reinforce Crewe's case. Predictably, the Conservatives lost support. Most of the detached Tory vote, however, went to the Alliance rather than to Labour – suggesting that, eleven months into Thatcher's second term and despite the change of Labour Party leadership, Labour was almost as far from achieving an independent victory as ever.[9]

So much, then, for the short-term tactical debate. We need to ask: do the arguments of Rowthorn, Hobsbawm, Luard,

Crewe and others have a future? Before answering, we should consider a point which Raymond Williams also makes: that they most certainly have a past. Subterranean historical layers, indeed, lie beneath much of the present controversy. Not only was an electorally powerful Labour Party, born out of a pact with the Liberals at the beginning of the century, but proposals for an alliance between Labour and both the political centre and extreme left were vigorously discussed in progressive circles during the Depression, and, ironically, were very divisive.

The parallel with the thirties is not exact. In 1983 Labour's parliamentary representation was relatively well protected by an electoral system which worked powerfully in favour of the Tories and against the Alliance. By contrast, in 1931 and 1935 Labour obtained a larger share of the vote (31 per cent and 38 per cent, compared with 28 per cent in 1983) but many fewer seats (52 and 154, compared with 209). Labour's disproportionately small share of seats before the war was one reason why the idea of an electoral alliance was repeatedly put forward – often linked to the idea of a broad opposition transcending party lines. In the 1930s (as in the 1980s), support for a pact came mainly from the outer extremes of any possible coalition: on the one hand the Liberal, non-aligned and even 'democratic' Tory centre; on the other the Communists and Labour left. While Harold Macmillan, then an anti-Chamberlain leader of 'middle opinion', called for 'a great popular political party' encompassing a wide spectrum of the left centre[10], the left called for a popular front on lines very similar to those suggested or implied by Rowthorn and Hobsbawm in *Marxism Today*.

From the outbreak of the Spanish Civil War in 1936 until Franco entered Madrid almost three years later, the campaign for an inter-party alliance of one kind or another was a revivalist political movement in itself. Victor Gollancz's hugely successful Left Book Club was based on it. Then, as now, the models were Spain and France: the club's first publication was by Maurice Thorez on the *Front Populaire*. In 1939 two leading left-wingers, Sir Stafford Cripps and Aneurin Bevan, were expelled from the Labour Party for publicly campaigning for a left-wing British popular front in defiance of NEC edicts. Meanwhile, National Executive members had themselves been involved in secret talks with Macmillan and Churchill about possible electoral pacts to help Tory rebels.[11]

Yet, significantly, even if interest in the possibility of an alliance was greater in the 1930s, in key respects the practical argument in favour of such an arrangement is much stronger today. Then as now advocates were motivated by the apparent impossibility of shifting a domestically callous and internationally dangerous administration without a political alliance among opponents. On the face of it, however, the chances of such an alliance having the intended electoral effect seem greater now. In both the last two pre-war elections, the popular vote for the national government was substantially more than half the total – that is, more than the vote of all the elements of a possible popular front (apart from Tory rebels) put together. In 1983, on the other hand, the government obtained only 42 per cent of the poll, holding office only because of the split in the anti-Tory vote. Indeed, looking back, it is remarkable that socialists imagined that the Liberals (with a mere 6.4 per cent of the vote in 1935) had anything to offer Labour at all. The modern Liberal–SDP Alliance, with the support at the last election of one voter in four, offers a very different prospect.

In the 1930s it was the Communists who made the running, and who – in the end – tainted the idea in 'respectable' progressive circles. Today, Communist influence is much reduced and most Labour opinion is hostile. But it is early days. 'In England the Popular Front is only an idea,' wrote Orwell as the pre-war movement gathered pace, 'but it has already produced the nauseous spectacle of bishops, Communists, cocoa magnates, pub-lishers, duchesses and Labour MPs marching arm-in-arm to the tune of "Rule Britannia".'[12] The same link-up between pragmatic left and compromising centre is to be seen in the current debate. The connection is a potent one, especially when supported by the apparent imperatives of the new electoral arithmetic.

This arithmetic, it should be stressed once again, is wholly without precedent; and it is the arithmetic which has caused the idea to be resurrected. What killed it after 1939 was not political opposition, but electoral circumstances. During the Second World War an actual electoral truce existed among the parties to the coalition (whose origins owed something to the pre-war popular front). At the end of the war, Labour was elected to office on its own and by 1951 the Liberals had shrivelled almost to vanishing point. Not until 1974 did the Liberals again become a significant force at general elections. In 1974, however, Labour was still capable of winning elections on its own.

In sum, the idea of an electoral pact or progressive front has roots. With support today (as in its previous incarnation) from both ends of the 'progressive' spectrum, it should not be taken lightly – especially in view of a statistical argument that seems stronger than at any time since the decline of traditional Liberalism.

Coalition as a last-ditch stand

In view of these considerations, ought the idea of a Labour-Alliance arrangement to be encouraged? Such a possibility should certainly not be dismissed in any spirit of vendetta, and it is possible to imagine circumstances in which it might become desirable. Nor should it be rejected, as Raymond Williams appears to suggest, on the grounds that it would involve some kind of pre-election agreement on policy. Unless one considers (for example) that the Wilson–Callaghan governments were as bad as Thatcher, the need to adjust our policy in order to meet former members of those administrations would surely be a small price to pay. There are, however, objections of a more fundamental nature.

The first is technical, and relates to the question of how voters might behave if their own ('no hope') candidate stood down. Here it is important to remember that Professor Crewe's assumptions, inevitably derived from past expressions of opinion, are assumptions – not predictions. To be fair, Crewe claims no more for them than this and offers a range of hypotheses, differently weighted. Nevertheless, any kind of extrapolation from 1983 or 1984 responses is very risky. We cannot take it for granted that second preferences will not change, depending on shifting perceptions of the major parties; nor that the highly fluid army of Alliance supporters will not contain very different people, with different residual loyalties, by the time the next election comes round. We should certainly take account of the possibility of a marked rightward shift in Alliance support – with disillusioned Thatcherites whose residual loyalties are Tory replacing former Labour supporters returning to their pre-1983 loyalty. In this event, a pact might actually benefit the government more than Labour. This may be less likely than the Crewe projection; but there is sufficient doubt to make the supposed electoral benefits to Labour highly notional.

The second objection also relates to pay-offs. Labour might, or might not, benefit directly from a pact. There is little doubt, however, that the Alliance would benefit to a very considerable degree, since Labour voters show greater willingness to regard the Alliance as their second preference than the other way round. In his *Guardian* article Crewe is coy on this point, neglecting to indicate how many seats Labour might hope to gain (Labour's supposed gain would be the reduction in Tory seats held on a given swing). His figures indicated however that a swing of (say) 6 per cent to Labour without any arrangement might give the Alliance 32 seats; with a fully operational pact, this could be raised to 88. 'A pact would not smuggle PR through the back door,' he claims, a trifle disingenuously, 'because Labour could threaten to put its candidates back into seats from which it withdrew.' Under such conditions, however, the parliamentary leverage of the Alliance would be such that its demands might well be irresistible, while its claim to 'major party' status in any subsequent election in which it chose to fight alone would gain immeasurably in credibility.

So far I have proceeded on a tacit basis of all other things being equal. If a pact was adopted, however, other things would certainly change. Hence my third objection is that a decision to embark on an arrangement with the Alliance would not be a neutral act: it would have political effects – not just in the sense of forcing a compromise on policy.

Political advocates, especially those on the left, have viewed this aspect with optimism. History comes into play, memories are evoked, there is a sense of banners unfurling. 'Popular Front' is a slogan which still has an emotive ring. The grounds for optimism, however, are slim. In the 1930s the electoral basis for a British popular front was non-existent (though a parliamentary alliance was briefly a possibility); yet a psychological case could be made. From 1935, when it obtained its largest share ever of the popular vote, Labour was on the electoral offensive. It is impossible to make such a claim today. For the Alliance, a popular front would be perceived as a breakthrough. For Labour it would be seen – rightly – as a prop, proof of infirmity.

The French analogy is thus inappropriate. It is not just that the French two-ballot system intentionally provides scope for second ballot alliances, without major sacrifice to the parties involved; or that, for a socialist party, an alliance of the left (involving Communists who could be expected to vote for the next-best left-wing option) is quite different from an alliance of the right (involving voters who might go either way); or that French socialists had *never* won an election on their own. It is also that the Socialist Party in France, unlike British Labour, was a party in the ascendant with its ally in the role of passenger. At present, Labour looks uncomfortably closer to the ghettoized French Communist Party.

Our conclusion must, therefore, be that electoral arrangements are one thing in conditions of advance but quite another if adopted as a measure of desperation. In the second case, a pact might well have the precise long-term effect which it must be our greatest concern to avoid – a permanent realignment of electoral support away from Labour.

Such a conclusion gives rise to an obvious rejoinder. Is there an alternative? If the chances of forming a majority government at the next election are barely altered by a pact, and the improvement in the chances of beating the Conservatives virtually impossible to calculate; if the 'moral force' argument behind the popular front idea is a chimera, based on false analogies; and if the most likely effects are to boost the Alliance, damage Labour's image and consequently undermine still further Labour's morale, then the answer is evidently yes. We may continue as a single party to pursue a strategy based on socialism without any sense of insularity.

In place of coalition

What, then, are we left with? The adverse trends of twenty or thirty years' duration, and the lack of any reason to believe that they will be automatically reversed. The danger, at this stage, is of slipping into the easy and misleading rhetoric of 'regeneration', with its resonance of prayer meetings and nineteenth-century methodist halls. Unfortunately, socialist sermonizing has not merely been restricted to the orations of political leaders. The tone of the pulpit is also a characteristic of the writings of intellectuals who, in some cases, feel called upon to offer guidance to an organization they had previously spurned. Such writers issue exhortations and injunctions to an anthropomorphized Labour Party, backed up by warnings about the consequences of continued misbehaviour. Thus Gareth Stedman Jones, in one of the more interesting instances of the genre, appeals to the Labour Party 'to rethink the social alliances upon which it could be based', in order to reverse its present involution.[13]

The Labour Party, however, is not a person. Nor, contrary to the apparent belief of some people, is party conference a collectivity of separate but like-minded members. The present reality is not of a Labour Party capable of acting as one, or a leadership able to impose its view, but of sources of power or pressure – conference, NEC, PLP, shadow cabinet, CLPs, municipal Labour groups, trade unions – with members, interests and ideals that sometimes overlap but may also conflict. Widely seen as a corporate body, Labour is actually more a social group, or perhaps an identity. Thus, to urge the Labour Party to regenerate, rethink, or adopt new commitments, is really just to shrug off an individual responsibility.

It is particularly ironic that those who believe most passionately in the participatory aspects of socialism should feel that their own task is complete when they have delivered their own views. Here we must return to the essay by Raymond Williams, whose pertinent analysis admirably illustrates the point. Williams argues that it would be foolish not to seek 'some mutually beneficial electoral arrangements' if Labour's policies are to be broadly the same as those of the Alliance. If, on the other hand (as he hopes) they are to be genuinely socialist, such arrangements must be excluded. In the past, however, 'nominal socialist commitment' has co-existed with 'actual liberal/social democratic policies'. Hence what is needed in the next four years is 'a radical reconstruction of all the main directions of policy in the light of the most open and informed contemporary socialist analysis'.

In a series of broad sweeps Williams spells out what the new main directions of policy should be: co-ordinated or integrated policies with other left governments, forcing the pace for a co-ordinated socialist reconstruction of a group of European economies, a much more developed process of democratic planning and control, and so on. This kind of politics, he firmly concludes, 'is, I am sure, the only immediate and practical alternative to the politics of overt or covert coalition'. ('Covert' coalition, in Williams's terms, is the kind of Labour government that has held office in the past.)

Having listened respectfully to the lecture, we scratch our heads and wonder what to do with it, while Professor Williams, pleased to have done his bit for socialism, returns to his books. The impression is not unlike that conveyed by a large and high-powered Fabian Society seminar held in London a short time after the election defeat. Expert witness after expert witness rose, delivered an incisive critique of Labour administrations past and the Labour Party present, before rushing off to catch a train to another world, sadly and righteously aware that his or her advice would not be heeded.

But this is not to do justice to Williams whose essay contains a crucial point. 'The long neglect of fundamental research and political education has produced an uneven but unmistakable mixture of half-formed policies and half-convincing protests,' he shrewdly remarks. 'In one linked area after another what we really have to discover – and as far as possible agree on – is what [the] intellectual argument actually is: the fully contemporary intellectual argument for socialism.' Trade unions and their research departments, the Socialist Society, the Fabian Society and political education officers, he suggests, are particularly well placed for the job of discovery. With this we may heartily agree. We may also feel, however, that the theoreticians who belabour us for our moral and practical weaknesses should also feel an obligation to lend a hand. The point is not a trivial one. In the heyday of Labour Party policy-making before and during the Second World War, it was the socialist philosophers themselves (some of them philosopher-politicians or philosopher-civil servants) – men and women like Cole, Dalton, Durbin, Jay, Laski, Tawney, Wootton – who knuckled down to the hard, detailed work of researching and drafting. Today there seems to be an implicit division of labour. It is certainly not enough – and Williams is far from being alone in this – to set an agenda and leave others ('The true intellectual resources of the labour movement have never been so rich') to break stones.

Agenda setting must in any case follow not proceed the investigative task. Williams's approach looks suspiciously like the orthodox Labour Party policy-making of the post-, not pre-war, era: first fix on your solution, then uncover reasons to justify it. If we agree with Williams (and with Bryan Gould in an excellent *Guardian* article[14]) that the trouble with Labour policy is not that it has been too socialist but that it has not been socialist enough, the first step must be to jettison the symbolic baggage which Labour has accumulated and which has gained the label socialist largely by association. We must start afresh, not with policies drawn from the old stock, but with first principles. It is astonishing, for example, how little consideration was given to the most basic socialist principle of all – equality – during the recent fratricidal war in the Labour Party. A wide-ranging reassessment of first principles could focus on persuading the whole labour movement to co-operate in achieving a real economic re-distribution. In this process, a range of traditions and analytic tools – Fabian and Marxian – could be brought into play, in fruitful combination.[15]

We certainly should not be frightened of the voters or take

heed of those who suggest that we should mould our policy to fit the opinion polls. There is evidence that Labour's handling of, or attitude towards, key problems has been regarded unfavourably by the electorate. This is understandable, since in very few areas has Labour had a coherent or consistent policy at all. 'Extremism' is a word given currency by the press, but what has characterized our commitments has been not their extremism but their weary lack of originality, and the lack of conviction that lay behind them. As the nation's problems deepen, we need not assume that the electorate will fail to respond – as, for example, it responded in 1945 – to a clear-headed radicalism that knows it can deliver.

Nor should we forget that electoral volatility provides opportunities as well as dangers. As the authors of a study of the 1983 election have observed, turbulence in voting behaviour 'offers the promise of big shifts to the advantage of any party that can take positions and adopt a style of campaigning that is most attuned to the electorate at the moment'.[16] In other words, an electoral hurdle that might have been insuperable in the stable fifties and sixties becomes less daunting in the stormy eighties. The accelerating rate at which voters desert traditional loyalties, moreover, has affected the Tories almost as much as Labour. As recently as November 1981, opinion polls gave the Tory government only 27 per cent of the popular vote.[17] Of key importance is evidence that for Labour as well as for the Conservatives, 'lost' voters have a propensity to return; and that (as Professor Crewe and Särlvik put it), support for the SDP is shallow as well as wide:

> [N]either the class divide nor the ideological cleavage in the party system, represented by Conservatives and Labour, have vanished . . . Both parties will need to take into account that they are appealing to an electorate in which social group loyalties mean less than they used to, where many fewer voters than in the past have any strong sense of party allegiance, and where many more are inclined to take an instrumental view of voting.[18]

For how long will electors continue to regard a vote for the Tories as 'instrumental'? A Harris poll in the *Observer* (6 May 1984) suggested that while people do not yet blame the government for the recession, growing numbers believe that the government has made things worse for them and their families rather than better. Here, undoubtedly, is Labour's chance: making possible the recapture of its own former 'loosely attached' following, not yet firmly committed to any other party. To achieve this, what is necessary is not a shifting of ground towards the formulae of our opponents but a perception of the real needs of the poor and of the relatively disadvantaged majority.

The model of electoral behaviour which portrays voters as desiccated machines, checking policy alternatives against prejudices and selfish private wants, is as inappropriate as the model which presents them as infantrymen in a partisan army. The reality is deeper and more challenging. Voters are capable of excitement, enthusiasm, hope, optimism, inspiration. It is for Labour – all of us – to produce policies, and a political atmosphere, which may spark these emotions. At times of electoral ferment all parties walk dangerously, yet these are precisely the conditions that make voters available for conversion, and hence make possible the socialist landslide that mass unemployment Britain so urgently requires.

Notes

[1] D. Massey, 'The Contours of Victory . . . Dimensions of Defeat', *Marxism Today* (July 1983).

[2] E. Heffer, *Marxism Today* (November 1983).

[3] See A. Bruce and G. Lee, 'Local Election Campaigns', *Political Studies* (June 1982), pp. 247–61; B. E. Cain, 'Blessed be the Tie that Unbinds: Constituency Work and the Vote Swing in Great Britain', *Political Studies* (March 1983), pp. 103–11.

[4] D. Butler and D. Kavanagh, *The British General Election of 1979*, (Macmillan, 1980), pp. 294–6.

[5] See the 1983 party conference debate on organization in *Report of the Annual Conference of the Labour Party 1983*, pp. 46–56.

[6] E. Hobsbawm, 'Labour's Lost Millions', *Marxism Today* (October 1983).

[7] See Hobsbawm's own survey, and answer to his critics, 'Labour Rump or Rebirth', *Marxism Today* (March 1984).

[8] E. Luard, 'A pact with Labour *could* pay', *New Democrat* (March/April 1984).

[9] J. Curtice, C. Payne and R. Waller, 'Labour recovery uncertain at the polls', *New Statesman*, 11 May 1984.

[10] Cited in A. Sampson, *Macmillan – A study in Ambiguity* (Penguin, 1967), p. 42.

[11] See B. Pimlott, *Labour and the Left in the 1930s* (Cambridge University Press, 1977), chapters 15–18.

[12] *New English Review*, 17 February 1938.

[13] See chapter 1, p. 21 in this volume.

[14] B. Gould 'In search of the popular face of socialism', *The Guardian*, 4 May 1984.

[15] See *Fabian Essays in Socialist Thought* (forthcoming, Heinemann, 1984).

[16] I. McAllister and R. Rose, *The Nationwide Competition for Votes: The 1983 British Election* (Pinter, 1984), p. 218.

[17] D. Butler and R. Waller, 'Survey of the Voting' in *The Times Guide to the House of Commons June 1983* (Times Books, 1983), p. 258.

[18] B. Särlvik and I. Crewe, *Decade of Dealignment* (Cambridge University Press, 1983), p. 338.

15

And Now for the Good News

DOREEN MASSEY, LYNNE SEGAL and HILARY WAINRIGHT

Over the last few years there has been much outpouring of admiration for Margaret Thatcher and much wide-ranging vilification of the Labour Party, the labour movement, and the left. A lot of this criticism came, inevitably, from expected sources, the *Daily Mail* and the *Sun*. But much of it also came from the left. It has taken a number of forms. Bob Rowthorn used his one half-hour of television time to attack the left, not the right. Similarly Stuart Hall's article in *New Socialist* (May/June 1983) accused the left as a whole of a lack of vision. It was his particular contribution – though one of the more thoughtful – that stimulated this article.

The effects of such criticism are still being felt. On the one hand the admiration for Thatcher and the belief that she has touched basic undercurrents of British opinion has allowed the debate to be shifted on to her terms. On the other hand the widespread pessimism, which has prompted some necessary rethinking on the left has also sanctioned acceptance of strategies which entail a move to the right. In brief, these strategies propose an anti-Thatcher alliance formulated in such a way as to mean continual accommodation to the centre and centre-right. It is Eric Hobsbawm's version of this strategy (*Marxism Today*, October 1983) – the most recent and fullest statement, and one clearly influential with Neil Kinnock, which we address here. We focus on the Labour Party but the issues are, of course, of much wider relevance across the left in general. What is ironic is that we share with the critics many of the same starting points – yet we have come to different conclusions.

We believe that it is necessary to make 'alliances' – indeed 'alliances' are central to the strategy we are suggesting – but alliances with whom? And on whose terms? Hobsbawm would like Labour to become 'once again' the focus for all those who want democracy. We agree. But when was it such a focus? And who is now making all the running on that front? It is the new local authority initiatives and the left – not the right – of the Labour Party which are most concerned with the issue of democracy. It is the left that is leading the fight for democracy in the unions.

Hobsbawm wants the Labour Party to appeal to women, *all* women, 'across class lines'. But it is hardly the old right of the Labour Party – or the Communist Party – which can claim to have addressed women as women or to have taken them seriously. No, once again it is the independent left which has been in the forefront, in so far as any attempt has been made to construct a feminist politics, within the Labour Party.

Hobsbawm says that we must 'take account of quite reasonable demands of bodies of people who are not satisfied that at present they are adequately met by Labour'. But who is he talking about? 'Home-owners, people who are dissatisfied with their children's schooling, or worried about law and order.' We agree that there are real issues here. But is it not symptomatic that he does *not* mention single-parent families, blacks and homeless people alongside the home-owners? He writes that it is necessary to appeal to all workers, not just some of them. We agree. He says 'the strength of the labour movement has always been that it could represent *all* parts of the working class – and did not discriminate against any.' To us as women this came, to say the least, as something of a revelation!

Proponents of strategies like Hobsbawm's have made use of women's declining support for the Labour Party to suggest that it must address the 70 per cent of women who do not vote Labour. In doing so they have drawn upon feminist dissatisfaction – even despair – over the way trade unions have represented men's interests so much more successfully than women's, and have proceeded to criticize trade union militancy itself. It is certainly true that the unions have pursued strategies through collective bargaining which have benefited those in full-time skilled jobs (of whom the majority are men) at the expense of those in low-paid and part-time jobs (of whom the majority are women). However, it is not a retreat from trade union militancy that is required but trade union militancy in pursuit of new and non-radical strategies which serve the interests of women. Women workers need higher wages, just as men do. They also need shorter working hours and an equality of conditions, rights and job security between full- and part-time work. Only then will women, and any men in their lives, be able to combine waged work with domestic responsibilities and share the caring for dependants. Within our present sexual division of labour, from which men benefit both at home and out at work, women have all sorts of special needs and interests. But, for all his emphasis on the need of the Labour Party to appeal to women, Hobsbawm has not seriously addressed himself to any of them.

The reason for enumerating these points is that they help reveal what underlies such a strategy. Beneath the rhetoric of alliance lies indeed the Alliance: moving right. It apparently assumes that the rest – the homeless, the low-paid, the unemployed, the blacks, the unilaterists – will vote Labour (which seems for this strategy to be the only important measure of socialism) because there is nowhere else for them to go. But even that we now know to be wrong. Many of them did not vote at all in 1983, and for good reason.

It is not that we do not want to attract home-owners and the more affluent to our ranks – we do. But Hobsbawm's strategy proposes an alliance based on unacceptable terms. Here is no re-thinking of what socialism can mean in today's world, no new vision. What we have instead, tacked on to a complacency about 'the old labour movement', is the selective adoption of a few policies which seem to have been popular when used by other people. No rethinking. No going back to the problem – decent housing, for instance – and trying to create new solutions. It is not reformation; it is capitulation.

What the Hobsbawm strategy essentially does is to attack the work of the left in the unions and the Labour Party and completely ignore the radical message of feminism. People did not vote Labour in 1983, Hobsbawm writes, 'because they felt the party did not represent their interests and aspirations adequately or effectively'. Quite. But that was not a product of the early eighties, as Hobsbawm deliberately implies. The Labour Party has had many years in power in the last two decades. Remember Wilson? Remember Callaghan? For twenty years the Labour Party has not been representing the aspirations of what ought to be its constituency. (What was different in 1983 was that there was a choice of party.) Hobsbawm ignores this record, just as he paints a glowing picture of the Labour movement as he pretends it was.

In contrast to all this, we argue that what is being built now, on the left, at the grass roots, is far more of a *real* coalition than anything proposed by Hobsbawm and company. It is not enough; but it is innovative and socialist. Not only does Hobsbawm's strategy ignore these initiatives, it *depends* upon ignoring them. In that sense, the overwhelming denigration of the left in earlier analyses laid the basis for these strategic moves to the right.

There are massive criticisms which can, and must, be made of the recent performance in Britain of 'the left' broadly defined, and of the Labour Party in particular. We do not want in any way to deny that. There *is* a lack of vision, an overwhelming defensiveness, a refusal to be bold and to confront the scale and nature of Labour's defeat. It is important to recognize the seriousness of the problem which the left faces and the deficiencies it must confront. But in this article we want to begin to counter the present tendency to wallow in defeat. It is the job of socialists not merely to write Olympian articles on the unmitigated disaster of it all and call from on high for alternatives, *but to set about developing and bringing into public view the initiatives from which a socialist vision is already being fashioned.*

The victory of Thatcherism has been devastating, but it is neither complete nor invulnerable. Nor is it simply that there are just pockets of resistance left, where the present and the past continue to be defended. There are also places where something new is being built. We want to help make these initiatives more widely known and more central, therefore, to discussions of strategy. Two things in particular characterize the examples that follow. First, they attempt to change the terms of the existing political debate; and second, they illustrate the growth points at the base of resistance to Thatcherism.

Changing the terms of the debate is essential, since Thatcher's attack has been successful precisely because there *was* so much to criticize. Nationalized industries are unresponsive to both worker and consumer. On a day-to-day level many people do experience the welfare state as undemocratic, impenetrable and even hostile – not that Thatcher's state is any less so, of course. We don't want the old, social democratic state back either. If the public sector is to be defended, whether it be the National Health Service or local authorities, we have to rethink from the beginning what it is about the public nature of provision which should be attractive and beneficial – a publicly available resource to be drawn upon rather than the heavy hand of the state. This is a major task, but in some places the challenge is being taken up. Furthermore, the importance of political demands from the base ought to be evident: real contact with and experience of alternatives has to be central to any strategy for the left. This is not just because we need to combat that view of socialism as nothing more than central-state planning, the grim legacy of the Wilson years. It is also necessary quite simply because it is the way we will reach people. It is the level at which the real impact of Thatcherism is being felt. And it is also one way to beat the media – to take a different route. Finally, it is at the base – in the factories, offices, hospitals and communities – that at least a part of the power and the skills to implement socialism must be built.

We will begin by looking at the experiences of the local authorities, particularly those in the major cities. The issues raised around the provision of local services are decisive for socialism – a fact which Mrs Thatcher has been quick to recognize.

The Labour Party and the left now have crucial bases in

many of Britain's big cities. The reason that such local authorities are under attack is not simply because they are big spenders (why go to such statistical acrobatics to avoid penalizing high-spending Tory councils?) but because *they have the potential to show that there could be an alternative*. The upholding of local autonomy must not simply be 'defensive'. And for once the left – or a section of it – is attempting to change the terms of the debate. Campaigns to defend local authorities are being built around new forms of local democracy and, increasingly, in terms of an emerging socialist alternative which several of their new initiatives illustrate. A range of innovative local authorities are trying to illustrate and develop this alternative in two ways: first, in activities over which they have (for the time being) direct power as both policy-maker and employer – (for example, transport; second, and equally important, in the way they have gone beyond the traditional role of local government to strengthen and support trade union initiatives both in the public sector and in private industry. These developments contain the potential for a powerful and novel alliance between the political power, however precarious, of social-ists in local government, and the extra-parliamentary power of trade union and community campaigns. Our second category of examples, therefore, covers new ideas and experiments going on in industry and in the public sector beyond local government. We are not attempting to cover all the areas where resistance is enriching socialist strategy and extending its popular base. Though outside the scope of this article, the peace movement provides further evidence for our argument.

The local state – changing the terms of the debate

When we consider what has been happening to the provision of local government services, the first thing to emphasize is that the working class did not vote for the dismantling of state services. Indeed, Thatcher was forced continually to lie about her commitment to the NHS before the 1983 election. People are unhappy with existing services, but they are not prepared to see their complete destruction. This is probably the principal area in which arguments for a different, caring, sharing or *socialist* society can still be heard. Such arguments now come most strongly from the more left-wing Labour councils spearheaded by Liverpool, Sheffield and certain metropolitan authorities – South Yorkshire, the West Midlands and the GLC. This is why Thatcher is determined to cripple these areas of local government. They reject the strategy behind Tory policies of 'privatization' – commercial priorities rather than collective responsibility for meeting people's needs in every areas of life.

Further cuts in central government support to municipalities and legal limits on local rate increases are going to make confrontation inevitable. What is important is that in the defence of local government it is the issue of *democracy* and *accountability* which is central. Further national interference in local government both prevents accountability of any sort and removes all possibilities for democratic control. Yet, as we are all aware, it is the very structures of local government which currently restrict any popular participation in how they are run. We are at all times kept in ignorance of how, when and what we will receive, in relation to the services we need. (Though we are always made to feel that for what little we get we must be truly grateful!)

Some socialist councillors are now arguing that they can only build support in their community to defend local government if they can make services responsive to people's expressed needs. On this basis, many of the old structures are *not* worth defending. It is for this reason that London boroughs like Islington, Hackney, Brent and Camden have pushed ahead with local decentralization plans – attempting through public meetings and discussions to increase local participation in planning their use of resources – and have talked about the type of society which would be able to provide the services we need. This is also why the GLC and Sheffield Council, for instance, are developing an approach to economic planning based on supporting proposals and initiatives from working-class and community organizations.

In Walsall, where decentralization was first initiated by a

left Labour council elected in 1980, 33 neighbourhood offices were set up with housing departments and repair teams more localized and accessible than before. These offices proved so popular that an anti-Labour coalition, which came to dominate the Council in the spring of 1982, has been unable to dismantle them. But decentralization is not intended to be merely a matter of making councils more accessible. What is important about the idea of decentralizing local services is the attempt to change their nature, to demystify and democratize them.

This brings to light enormous problems. At the moment, even elected councillors have very little power in determining municipal policies. Administration is firmly in the hands of non-elected senior officers, unused to consulting anyone, including councillors, before completing policy documents. Any attempt at genuine democratization would have to tackle these top layers of the rigidly hierarchical local bureaucracy, with councillors creating working groups determined to influence local policy. There is also the danger that decentralization and consultation could serve – like participation schemes of the past – merely to monitor and control discontent rather than to build people's confidence and determination to fight for and defend the services they want. They will strengthen resistance only if the independence of groups outside the council is accepted and supported. This must continually be reasserted, even though it is part of the thinking behind the creation of women's committees, ethnic minority and police monitoring groups, which have been established in some left Labour councils to give support and work with groups outside the official structure. It is also the thinking behind council funding of many women's and gay centres, trade union, community and resource centres.

In spite of the enormous problems and constraints, however, there are examples of how to challenge and change the hierarchical and undemocratic assumptions and social relations of existing social provision. The Centre for the Disabled in King Henry's Walk, Islington, North London, works on the principle that the disabled people themselves should run it. It takes disabled people out of hospitals and other institutions and provides helpers who work with them individually with the eventual goal of enabling them to move into some sort of sheltered accommodation in nearby flats. Not surprisingly, it is residents from this centre who fought for and won the Dial-a-Ride transport service for the disabled, now operating in Islington, Camden and other London boroughs. What is clear to us is that the confidence to live creatively, to resist and change things, cannot be separated from the push towards real democracy. Such local experiments can be the starting-point for a much wider debate about the institutions of political democracy. They also have fundamental implications for how we should think about economic strategy at a national level. Their practical experience can point the way to resolving some of the basic problems of defining socialist democracy: What kinds of representation will provide for the fullest form of popular control? What should be the balance between central direction and self management in various circumstances? How far can parts of the existing state be used to strengthen and support new, more democratic forms of political power? For socialists working with left local authorities, these theoretical issues are now being raised as urgent practical problems.

Nor is it just services. In certain local authority employment strategies, too, there has been an important reformulation of issues. Take the question of paid and unpaid labour. The GLC has endorsed demands to treat domestic work as an essential part of the economy. This has great potential significance for women. For although women have won more independence and a degree of autonomy, their economic and domestic disadvantages remain – in fact, they get worse. Britain is still unable to provide anything like adequate care for its young, old, sick and dependent people (not to mention its male workers) except at the expense of women. Yet up to now the Labour Party, almost as much as the Tories, has encouraged private rather than social responsibility for meeting people's personal needs, regardless of the strain on individual women. The GLC endorsement should assist funding for projects which aim to remove the isolation of domestic work. One example is the Norwood Children's Centre, which aims to combine provision for laundry service, cheap food and child care. Such projects could begin to benefit women by making the links between home and work. Crèches in work-places, nurseries, daycare and drop-in centres for the elderly and disabled could provide socially useful work, suggest one way of tackling women's inequality and also provide living examples of socialist rather than individualistic values.

These initiatives in local government have not come out of the blue, of course. Inside the Labour Party, they are the product of the long haul of a new breed of socialists. But their origins lie outside the party, in the work of independent feminists and socialists. Such initiatives will always have to be fought for, against the conservatism of traditional Labourism, which wants only to disown them. Both the Labour Party and the labour movement have to be continuously pushed and pulled along, from inside and out, before they learn how to do other than simply act on behalf of the male waged worker. The Labour Party embodies a tradition which was always patriarchal and paternalistic, and invariably suspicious of any movements outside Parliament and the trade union leadership. This is not a tradition which can rebuild a socialist movement strong and confident enough to resist the determination of the current Tory attack.

The defence of services will only be possible through alliances between councillors, trade unionists and campaigning groups. In the case of the metropolitan authorities such alliances will be necessary to defend the councils' very existence. Where local authority funds support trade union and community initiatives there are bonds of common material interest in the survival of the council, as well as a shared political commitment. Conflicts of interest are inevitable. But there are examples of co-operation. In the London Borough of Hackney, tenants' goups work with the direct labour organization to improve repair services. In Kentish Town, the health centres have set up consumer groups. In Haringey, The Womens' Project is carrying out local surveys of the type of resources most urgently needed in the area and feeding the results to the council. NUPE in London has drawn up a comprehensive strategy for fighting privatization and defending services.[1] It stresses the need to build unity between workers and users, and to develop alternative ideas to increase workers' and users' control over services. Local surveys and studies are important in this. *Brighton on the Rocks*, for instance, brings together a decade of work by community activists,[2] who monitored the tragic cost of council spending cuts in Brighton and the failure to provide for elementary social need. These cuts began to have their crushing effect long before Thatcher's triumph in 1979, with the Labour government's attack on council spending in 1974. The authors point the way towards an alternative plan for Brighton, based on democratic welfare and useful production. They come up with new proposals, such as that for 'area unions'. These ideas and the collective action they can inspire are not only strategically essential, but also contain enormous hope and potential for spreading socialist thought and values.

Union campaigns

In the unions, too – a long way from Congress House – there are activists extending the reach of shop-floor organizations and the scope of trade union demands in ways which could help to construct a popular alternative.

In most of the examples we describe, one or other of the major Labour local authorities is or has been involved, although the impetus for the initiatives has in each case come from trade unionists. The local authority connection is partly no doubt a result of our own bias in the selection. But the fact that trade union organizations turn to local councils for support indicates the political character of trade union initiatives at the present time, and the limits of trade union action on its own, especially when it concerns jobs. Similarly, the fact that several local councils have become involved explicitly on the side of labour comes from a political understanding that the forces they are up against – the big corporations, the government, and the recession – can undermine the employment initiatives of even the largest local authority, unless these initiatives have a strong trade union base.

The examples below are the initiatives of a minority. The

Michael Edwardes/Margaret Thatcher tactic of raising the political and material stakes of every threatened industrial dispute has had contradictory consequences. It has certainly caused fear and demoralization amongst the majority of trade union members, but in a minority it has prompted a more strategic, political reaction. In a political sense this minority represents an advance on the pragmatic, economistic shop-floor leadership of the 1950s and 1960s, though in most cases it has yet to win mass support for its cause.

The initiatives of this minority includes campaigns against privatization (which are gaining increasing support amongst the majority); making contact and exchanging information across national boundaries within multinational companies; establishing co-operatives out of struggles to resist closure; and pushing forward the social uses of new technology. The significance of such initiatives is not just that they are signs of a more sophisticated rank and file trade unionism in the work-place. As they develop, they could become a vital part of a convincing socialist economic strategy.

There are three reasons for this. First, these initiatives can illustrate and develop an alternative to the economics of the market. Take the campaign of the telecom unions against privatization. In the past, these unions have tended to accept management's approach to efficiency and productivity based on commercial criteria. The unions would simply argue about the number of jobs, within the economic framework. Now the campaign is challenging those same arguments about productivity and profitability – the very arguments now being used to justify privatization. The present campaign pushes to the fore the case for a telecommunications system which is a public service that should be run to meet social needs whether or not this brings in a profit. Similarly, several co-operatives supported by local authorities have begun to illustrate how industry, too, could be organized on the basis of social need. In Sheffield, a group of engineering workers have formed a co-operative making dehumidifiers for council houses. They worked on the design with local tenants and technologists at Sheffield Polytechnic, helped by finance from the council. They formed their co-op after losing a long struggle to keep their factory, Snow's part of the Elliot Consortium, open as a machine tool company.

In a small way, such examples of the public sector's ability to put to good use what the market has wasted, illustrate the case for a planned economy. Everyone involved in such initiatives would want to emphasize that all these initiatives can do is *illustrate* the argument. But the work of developing an economic strategy must build on such illustrations.

Secondly, many cases of political response by the trade unions show that it is the white-collar strata, commonly assumed to have no interest in such matters, who are actually in the forefront of applying socialist ideas to technological change. At ICL, for example, white-collar trade union representatives from different factories started meeting regularly in the late seventies to devise strategies for defending their jobs. Now they are discussing how to design software that will be useful to trade union and community organizations. A first step, they believe, is to educate the labour movement in how it can turn computers to its advantage, how software could be designed for its benefit. As part of this education the ICL combine is now working on a pilot project of software for a computer to be used by trade union and community resource centres.

Finally, most of these initiatives, in effect if not intention, point to the mechanisms for implementing socialist industrial policies. This is important for the present debate about a left-wing programme and the causes and lessons of electoral defeat. The unpopularity of the left is not so much due to popular disagreement with left ideals (if they've ever heard of them), as to an absence of any apparent strategy for putting them into practice and therefore a feeling that they are pie in the sky.

Take the problem of multinationals. A group of workers threatened by management policies in any one factory can be paralysed by even the thought of the global power and resources they are up against. There are, however, several examples of trade unionists beginning to build the contacts and share the information which can overcome this sense of powerlessness. In Kodak, local authorities and trade unionists in France and England have begun to achieve an international co-ordination which will at least help resistance to get off the ground, even though it is unlikely to ensure its success.

In the case of the co-operatives supported by the GLC, Sheffield, Leeds, the West Midlands and other local authorities, we can glimpse the possibilities and difficulties of workers' self-management, provided, we and those involved give ourselves the time to reflect on and generalize from their experiences. These examples and the support given by some authorities to workers fighting redundancies and privatization also illustrate a new kind of state intervention: instead of 'state run capitalism', it is state intervention to support the actions of labour against capital. This brings us back to one of our starting points; the need to convince people that there is an alternative to both the bureaucratic state and the jungle of the 'free' market. There is no better way of convincing people than by the propaganda of practical examples.

From local initiative to national strategy

These are just some of the ways that new ideas, experiments, 'new visions', are being created even in the midst of Labour's defeat. They are only beginnings, localized and far from perfect – our own examples, we are aware, are highly concentrated on London – but the point is that they exist.

There are a number of reasons why it is important that we keep hold of this. First, panoramic views of the left which ignore such initiatives denigrate the energy and imagination of many people. Second, and perhaps of most immediate danger, sweeping dismissals which represent the left as something that contains no positive ideas, no imagination, no hope for the future, also imply that there is nothing left to defend. This is not true. Certainly Thatcher recognizes that there is much left to attack. And it is important that the experiments which are under way are defended in the most imaginative terms possible. Third, the promulgation of such mass pessimism does not just document defeat, it helps reconcile people to it, even helps to bring it on.

But there is also a wider reason. Recognition of the kind of initiatives discussed here poses a direct challenge to the proposals currently emerging from a section of the labour movement – the Great-Moving-Right-Male-Left-Show. The shifts by Hobsbawm and company do *not* mean that we on the left should simply go on the defensive and dig in, immobilized in old strategies. We do need a new vision. What we have argued here is that some people are trying to get on with creating it. To ignore these beginnings is to lay the ground for solutions such as Hobsbawm's.

It is important to consider for a moment why some local authorities are demonstrating this potential and what its significance is for national strategy. This ability to illustrate an alternative both to Thatcherism and to Labourism is based on the feminist, anti-racist, anti-nuclear and more generally socialist ideas emerging throughout the sixties and seventies – partly as a reaction to the failures of Labourism. In the GLC and Sheffield, at least, many of these ideas are being backed with real resources and, at least partially, being put into practice.

This is taking place at a time which makes such an experience both extremely important for the future of socialism in Britain and extremely problematic in terms of the limits on how these ideas are put into practice. It is occurring at a time when, with the exception of CND, the extra-parliamentary strengths of the labour and other movements is extremely weak. Yet the ideas now being developed with local authority resources grew out of realizing the limitations of purely parliamentary democracy, and are based on or inspired by new forms of democratic, extra-parliamentary power. This has created the contradictory situation in which policies seeking to empower social and industrial movements are being carried out at a time when the existing power of these movements is flagging.

An outcome of this situation is a new kind of alliance between the industrial (broadly interpreted) and political wings of the labour movement. Unlike previous periods of trade union weakness, such as the thirties, it is not an alliance in which industrial and social organization *is substituted by political – parliamentary – action*. Rather, it is an alliance in which political – in this case local authority – resources and powers are made use of *to strengthen, support and give a voice to industrial and extra-parliamentary action*. This will have an important effect on the kind of trade unionism in the public and private sectors to emerge out of the present recession. It will strengthen the more political, less economistic trends.

The experience of present-day local authorities with socialist aspirations does not provide a model for national government. The conditions under which a socialist national government would be possible would be very different. For instance, such a government could not come about merely as a result of the left winning control of the national Labour Party in the way that they won control in London. It would need the backing of strong, sustained, extra-parliamentary action – or at least the preparedness to take such action. But the left local authorities do provide a laboratory out of which important guiding principles for redefining socialist policies and relations with different groups of people can be learnt.

At present, however, there are few signs of any national political force learning from local experiments. The Labour leadership tends to play down the potential of the local authorities to illustrate alternative policies. Instead it concentrates on a narrow defence of democracy in terms simply of the right to elect representatives. This is, of course, a very basic right and it must be defended, but in the local authorities under threat it has become the basis for extending democracy far beyond the right to vote. Hobsbawm's analysis would lead to the prediction that the left local authorities will not be able to win popular support if they persist with their radical policies – a view which is apparently endorsed by the Labour leadership. The opinion polls and mass demonstrations in London and Liverpool provide the best response to such an attitude.

We cannot rely on the experiments spreading to national level simply by the left influence in local authorities filtering upwards – or 'across the river', as they say. It will be very difficult for the left to gain the same kind of position nationally, through the Labour Party in its present form. The leadership and make-up of council Labour groups has a far more direct relationship with constituency Labour parties than Labour's parliamentary leadership. Moreover, the trade union establishment is directly and indirectly a very conservative influence on the leadership in Parliament, whereas trade union officials have very much less power at local authority level. The success of the left in achieving control over many constituency and ward parties has therefore had a much more direct impact on Labour's position within the local state than is currently possible at national level. Our concern to highlight local initiatives is *not* based on any version of the slogan 'The GLC today, Whitehall tomorrow'. The development of a national strategy will be much more complex than the simple sum of components of local experiments!

What we should be doing is putting all our effort into strengthening, popularizing, arguing and advocating. Using every access we have to the media and putting more resources into our own forms of communication, we can broaden the knowledge of these initiatives and the power behind them and turn it into a national challenge. Such initiatives begin, at least, to present some vision of an alternative future.

Notes

[1] See Dexter Whitfield, *Making it Public* (Pluto Press, 1983).
[2] *Brighton on the Rocks: monetarism and the local state* (Queenspark Books, Brighton, 1983). There are many other examples – the Merseyside Socialist Research Group, Centerprise, the Strong Words Collective in Durham, the Coventry Workshop.

Part 6
New Departures

16

New Deal for Europe

NEIL KINNOCK

Britain's future, like our past and present, lies with Europe.
But for us as socialists, it will still only lie within the EEC if
the Common Market can be transformed to measure up to
our wider vision of Europe's own future. We want a *square
deal* from the Common Market, and a *new deal* for Europe.
We want a wider, stronger and more generous Europe for
Europeans rather than for the United States or Soviets,
multinational power, finance capital or agri-business.

All the parties of the European left, and socialist governments throughout (Western) Europe, are united behind the
principle of joint economic recovery. Socialists are taking the
lead in the peace movements in all the West European nations
which are campaigning for a European security zone, free of
nuclear weapons. These are the two most critical issues for
Europeans today, but both are missing from the Common
Market agenda. So, too, are the fundamental reforms of the
EEC which the Labour Party agreed at our 1983 conference –
and which Andreas Papandreou, Greece's socialist Premier,
and others are also demanding.

A European Bretton Woods

The European Economic Community is not *European*: it
contains only some West European countries and excludes
East European countries not only from membership but also
from the political dialogue which must occur if we are to
achieve closer economic co-operation and military détente. It
is not *economic*: it is a food price-fixing system with a
common external tariff. It is not a *community*: it is bitterly

divided and in a state of continuing internal crisis. Where Europeans should co-operate, the 'community' aims to integrate, reducing major political imperatives to the lowest common denominator of compromise.

No progress has been made on joint economic policies to counter the economic crisis of the last ten years, and to generate the wealth which will enable Europe to make its proper contribution to the conquest of hunger and fear in the rest of the world. The EEC fiddles with farming subsidies while unemployment in the member states creeps nearer still to 20 million. In January 1983, President Mitterand of France proposed a major reform of international monetary institutions and the IMF to bring about a strategy for renewal, regeneration and recovery. His proposals were blocked in the summer at the Williamsburg summit by Mrs Thatcher, Chancellor Kohl and President Reagan and their opposition has made it difficult for any single European country to pursue policies for expansion and recovery. Europe has to speak with its own voice and act with its own resources if the United States will not endorse a global recovery programme. We need a Euro 'Bretton Woods' on the lines of the wartime conference at which John Maynard Keynes won the essentials of his case for world co-operation in recovery. If the United States will not endorse such a programme for a genuinely new international economic order, Europe could and should get on with its own proposals and its own programme. West Europe generates some two-thirds of the world's manufactured exports, and about half the world's trade. Yet the Community is muscle-bound by its self-imposed monetarism.

A new Euro Bretton Woods should take initiatives to harness multinational finance capital. It should aim to achieve the conditions for modern full employment policies in Europe and positive policies for the rest of the world. We know about the butter mountain and wine lakes of the EEC. We know one worker in ten in the Community has no job. That is because governments are failing to use the mountain of money now lying idle in property or in the stock market, or invested in more vigorous economies such as the United States. Because of unemployment resulting from the recession, governments in the EEC have lost tax revenues and had to make benefit payments at a total cost of around £50 billion *a year*. A slump is immensely expensive and that money could clearly be more creatively spent on generating the employment of people and other productive resources than on sustaining depression. Most European governments have taken the negative course and become agents of stagnation. By taking a new initiative to put those assets to work, we could invest in modern technology, improved training, industrial and social infrastructure and community services. That would begin to rescue Europe's economies from decay and dereliction, especially since the growth provoked in each of our countries by such policies would reduce the bills of slump, stimulate our own economies (and that of the USA) and reverberate as a rise in demand and revenues for the countries of the Third World.

To some extent the remedies exist within the present EEC structures but the scale is inappropriate to the task. While the Common Agricultural Policy costs about £10 billion a year, borrowing from the European Investment Bank is only £1.8 billion, while the social fund, regional fund and industrial research spend less than £1 billion each. The expansion of the borrowing and lending activities of the European Investment Bank, together with changes in the pattern of EEC expenditure, would provide an important facility for financing the growth which each European economy needs.

Developing democracy

We need joint policies for economic democracy and for the control of multinational corporations so that the economic strength they represent can be used constructively to help in the economic, social and cultural regeneration of our countries. The power implications of commercial ownership, development, movement and practice are not new. Only the international conglomerate scale and the adjustment of tactics which it requires are new. At every stage of capitalism a new power of commerce has arisen in a locality, a region, a state. And eventually the extension and exertion of that power has collided with the interests of the community.

Democracy has always had to draw up new rules for the conduct of commerce and the exercise of economic power. We have never made rules that are as effective as they should be; we have not used the extension of public ownership as intelligently as we should have done to complement the legislative changes in rules that subordinate commercial power to democratic authority. Those are challenges which remain for all of us in every democratic country. And now a further challenge exists. In the age of multinational capitalism, democracy must be multinational too. That would not have been fully achieved by the Vredeling proposals for worker information and participation, and it will hardly be advanced by the remnants of those proposals which eventually survived the amendments of the anti-socialist groupings in the European Assembly. But it is still important to strive to secure any progressive changes that can be obtained, and to support joint policies by like-minded left governments in Europe for the accountability of multinational capital.

Planning trade

Jointly, we also need to develop the planning of trade. We have to acknowledge the right of a country which pursues policies for full employment to protect itself against the effects of policies in other countries which do not. The purpose of planned trade is to ensure that each country which benefits its own people through the stimulation of demand, at the same time benefits its partners. And clearly the joint planning of our trade implies joint planning towards economic expansion and response to new technological developments.

The regeneration of our economies cannot be sprung from the so-called 'social market economy' now espoused by the SDP. A system which is policed by high interest rates, regimented by public expenditure cuts and dependent for discipline upon mass unemployment, is simply incapable of producing trade expansion. Recovery from international recession will come from the co-ordinated and planned response of economies – inside and outside the EEC. The socialist parties of this continent have already shown that they can offer the means of operating that regime of growth.

Combating Third World poverty

A further key area for joint activity by European socialists is in combating the poverty of the majority of the world's peoples. As Willy Brandt's reports have made abundantly clear, and as anyone who has seen the skeletons of starvation knows, we in Europe have a direct moral obligation and practical interests in transforming our relationships with the rest of the world. At least a million people in Britain and millions elsewhere are dependent for their livelihood upon exports to Third World countries. But the decline in this trade – 2.5 per cent last year for Britain alone – contributes significantly to recession. The main cause of the decline is the poverty of Third World countries. That poverty is being accelerated by our European trade and agriculture policies and turned into cataclysm by the fact that Third World countries are having to use revenues gained by higher commodity prices, or by higher sales, to service their debts to Western financiers rather than buy the goods of Western producers.

Our goal should be that every national government achieves the UN target of allocating 0.7 per cent of Gross National Product to aid – a proportion which Holland and Scandinavia already exceed. The interests of trade and humanity combine to illustrate the need for that increased commitment. Within the EEC we must improve the Lomé Convention when it is discussed later in 1984, to achieve a *global* framework which transcends Europe's old colonial ties and concentrates upon the poorest countries and regions.

But most of all, we as socialists need to intervene in a co-ordinated manner in the international summit conferences and meetings of the United Nations Trade and Development Conference to promote strategies for world recovery. As the debt burden of the third world reaches some $660 billion, socialist policies must reject the deflationary remedies of monetarism which feed slump with slump and, by keeping the Third World in penury, deprive the developed countries of customers as they deprive the peoples of less-developed countries of life.

A new Messina Conference

Can such international co-operation and development be achieved in the framework of the present Common Market – limiting its global role through Lomé; stuck in the mud of its agricultural policy; staggering from one budget crisis to another? Our blunt answer – not least following the failure of the Stuttgart and Athens summits – must be 'no'. Confined by out-of-date treaties, the Community is in a political cul-de-sac. It can develop a new deal neither for Europe nor for the rest of the world. These are the reasons – positive not negative – why the Common Market needs a fundamental review both of its principles and methods of operation. We need to take an overview both of the limits of the present Community framework and of the scope for a wider, more genuine form of European co-operation. We need a new start – a return to the drawing board of demands made by the parties and peoples of Europe itself. Some of these issues have already been stressed by Andreas Papandreou. In his speech to the Strasbourg Assembly last December he suggested that the time has come for 'a new Messina Conference' to 'reclarify our ideas about the important problems of our time'.

Almost 30 years after the meeting at Messina which laid the framework for the EEC, anyone who is frustrated by the institution as it has developed, who resents its inflexibilities and opposes its supernationalism, can be prepared to consider such a suggestion. A new conference would have to be flexible and wide ranging to lay the foundations for a genuine community of Europe, freed from the market-economy philosophy of the Rome Treaty or directives from a Brussels bureaucracy. In a spirit of rumination and in an effort to advance from the economic trench warfare which the unchanging EEC provokes, I consider that a 'new Messina' would have to decide:

(1)   whether to reject, revise or rewrite the Paris and Rome Treaties and replace them with a new framework for European economic co-operation;

(2)   how to relate the institutions of Western Europe (EEC and EFTA) and those including Western Europe (OECD and the United Nations Economic Commission for Europe) to today's needs and tomorrow's responses;

(3)   how to restore the initiative in policy formulation to European governments and parliaments on their own agendas;

(4)   whether all European parties should be invited to send representatives to an Assembly of Europe;

(5)   whether all European governments, including those not now in the EEC, should be invited to join a European Council which sets its own agenda on issues raised by its own peoples and parliaments;

(6)   whether the Council of Europe, to which national parliaments throughout Western Europe at present send representatives, should not be superseded by the new all-European Assembly.

If the new framework for international European co-operation, as suggested above, can be blocked in the short term by governments in some countries, and even if a new Messina Conference is unlikely in the near future, progressive parties and governments can still begin the process of discussing and delineating the conditions for the economic recovery of Europe, which must be achieved if we are to tackle the urgent problems facing our peoples and societies.

Freeing Europe from nuclear arms

Not least, Europe must play a role in détente and disarmament. From the Nuclear Test Ban Treaty of the 1960s through the UN special session on disarmament in 1978, it appeared to many that the superpowers had come to realize the risk of a nuclear holocaust and were ready to draw back from the brink. The 1978 special session stressed both that détente must be renewed and that practical steps should be taken for the establishment of nuclear-free zones. The Madrid conference of the Socialist International in 1980 adopted the ultimate goal of Europe itself as a nuclear-free zone.

There are fewer grounds for hope now. We are living in a second cold war. Most people are aware of the deployment of the Soviet SS20 medium-range missiles. Some realize, as Denis Healey has stressed in the House of Commons, that such ground-based missiles were always countered by the submarine-based Poseidon missiles of the United States and that there was no medium-range 'missile gap' overall. The CIA has recently produced 'revised figures' admitting that there is no such missile gap and that, if anything, the United States has an overall superiority in nuclear delivery power. Meanwhile, however, the Reagan administration has pushed ahead the deployment of Cruise and Pershing missiles in Europe. Although the former SPD Chancellor Helmut Schmidt is credited with the speech calling for their deployment, less attention has been paid to his admission since then that he had no idea at the time of the speed of delivery of the Pershings on targets in the Soviet Union, or the threat which they would represent to the Soviets.

It has been US policy to stampede Europe into accepting the new 'first strike' strategy, on grounds of Soviet nuclear superiority. Or as Admiral Gene Larocque has put it: 'Americans assume that World War III will be fought in Europe just as World War I and World War II have been.' European countries should reject such a strategy. It is not a matter of blaming one or other of the superpowers for the arms race. It is a matter of denying them the right to launch the third world war from Europe. This is why the next Labour government should and will refuse Cruise and US nuclear bases in the United Kingdom, as well as proceed with the adoption of a non-nuclear defence policy. It is also why, in welcoming a freeze, we none the less do not accept that freezing the present nuclear arms level can be anything other than a first step towards negotiated nuclear disarmament between the superpowers.

Nuclear weapons are a threat to European and world

security when their proliferation in each howitzer, aircraft and short- or medium-range missile lowers the nuclear threshold. Our policy of nuclear disarmament is a strategy, not a tactic. It will be a positive part of serious progress towards Europe as a nuclear-free zone. It is because we are already shaping joint policies with other European parties and governments – many of them outside the EEC – that we can fight a campaign which counters militarism and the slump syndrome with the rational and radical prospect of development, security and nuclear disarmament.

Reforming Europe

In 'Campaigning for a fairer Britain' – the document adopted at Labour's 1983 Annual Conference – we said that we would fight the European elections, but demand fundamental reforms in the Community. If they could not be achieved, we would reserve the right, like any other nation, to withdraw. Our demands must be as follows:

(1)   The CAP is intolerable. We need a new system of support which relieves the burdens on British tax-payers and consumers and ends the misallocation of produce and the waste inherent in the present system.

(2)   Britain cannot accept the continual outflow of invest-ment and employment imposed by membership, without any compensating improvement in our trade position.

(3)   Economic expansion is crucial. Even from opposition, Labour must actively promote policies throughout Europe which make sustained recovery possible – for developed and third world countries.

(4)   To achieve economic expansion, Europe must have the means to mobilize the finance to sustain recovery and spending on jobs and welfare.

(5)   There must be fundamental reforms in a wider sense: a project for a new Community – a new Messina Conference.

(6)   There must be progress towards European nuclear disarmament.

Our future, like our past and present, lies with Europe for historic and geographical reasons. But it will still only lie with the *EEC* if the Common Market can be a source of tangible value to the British people. The inspiration of the EEC as an organization to bind and stabilize the democracies of Western Europe was – and is – decent and desirable. But we could only realistically accept enduring membership if, at the very least, we suffer no significant material loss or disadvantage. That is really the position. It is not 'take all, give nothing' – that is neither plausible nor reasonable. But it is not plausible or reasonable either to accept 'give more, take less', especially when we begin – under present structures and with our present economic condition – from a situation in which we are not feasibly able to give more or feasibly justified in taking less.

Our position is not produced by nationalism or vanity. It is a product of the facts of economic survival for our country. Those facts are that unless we can achieve and sustain growth, a reasonable balance in manufactured trade and an end to the seepage of employment and investment that is disabling Britain, we cannot and will not have a resilient modern economic base. We need that dependable economic environment because we cannot meet even elementary requirements of care, opportunity and justice in Britain without generating wealth, and also because Britain will never make its proper contribution to the conquest of hunger and fear in the world without a viable domestic economy.

Socialism and recovery

Today the World Bank estimates that there are 570 million people who are undernourished, 800 million who are illiterate, 1,500 million who have little or no access to medical services and 250 million children who do not go to school. Every year 15 million children die of starvation. Amidst these terrifying statistics, official development aid amounts to $20 billion – world military spending to more than $450 billion.

In some countries, including Britain, industrial output has stagnated at the 1981 levels which – we were told – were the 'bottom of the recession'. Mass unemployment is epidemic in Europe. Trade stagnates as economic prosperity declines. The trading position of the poorest countries continues to deteriorate.

Socialists do not accept the cynical view common to Europe conservatism that the international recession is an affliction to be endured until it is healed by continued dieting. We know that policies of renewal are best achieved by common action. The Labour Party is already working with the socialist parties of Europe inside and outside the EEC to build a joint strategy for development. We must build a joint strategy at every level. I emphasize the point that our socialist commitment to overcome the problems of poverty, of international recession and of increasing international tension means that we must seek out the policies which unite us. We must challenge the despair and defeatism of deflation with renewal, regeneration and recovery. We must welcome the efforts of any government to reflate its national economy and to expand its trade. And thus our aim is to weaken the restrictions of Community institutions that enforce compliance with monetarist economic policy, rather than encourage economic growth; that impose protectionism of the worst kind in agriculture and require free movement of the most damaging kind in capital.

These are not the arguments of supplicants or isolationists. They are put by socialists to other socialists who realize that ideals of harmony and co-operation between nations and communities must, if they are to be durable, be translated into realities of employment and security. That is the difference between the faith of religion and the conviction of politics. The vocabulary of internationalism is made nonsense by the penalties of supernationalism. We do not breed understanding and mutuality between peoples through the EEC we now have. We breed hostilities through policies which, although masked by the grandeur of fine phrases, are operated by remote, bureaucratic institutions and impose disadvantages on producers and consumers throughout the EEC countries. As socialists, our family is humankind; our country is the world. But if that real internationalism cannot be seen to work as a new advantage, an extra strength, and an additional opportunity, it will provoke a revolt of nationalisms.

17

Out of Crisis –
International Economic Recovery

STUART HOLLAND

At the turn of the century, labour in Europe was international in organization while capital was mainly national. Today it is the reverse. Before the First World War, the international organization of labour was real and powerful. Capital felt threatened and showed it. Some claim that it went to war to avoid socialism; others that by mobilizing Europe's working class against itself, the war set back socialism in Western Europe for the rest of the century.

Today, 140 companies account for a third of Gross Domestic Product in the EEC countries. They dominate not only trade, payments and smaller firms but also governments and community institutions. In the quarter century since the Rome Treaty, the EEC is stuck in the mud of the Common Agricultural Policy, has no Common Industrial Policy worthy of the name and has left multinationals to proceed with monetary union on their own terms, through the Eurodollar and Eurobond markets. Meanwhile, monopoly is a game played worldwide by multinational capital, unrestrained by community institutions of European labour. Everywhere in Europe social advances hitherto considered part of the post-war consensus are being thrown back and for a decade the left has been on the defensive. Electoral gains in France, Greece, Sweden and Spain are in question.

It has become commonplace to put the blame on the worst economic crisis since the 1930s. But in key respects today's crisis is more profound and more severe than that of the inter-war period. For one thing, while incomes fell in the 1930s, prices fell as well and stayed low, unlike stagflation or slumpflation today. Further, while the main problem in the 1930s was investment to create jobs, investment today with new technology frequently displaces them. And in the 1930s capital was still mainly national rather than multinational in scope and scale, so that policies in a single country to reflate demand or protect trade had more chance of success. In addition, the investment horizon of firms was shorter than today: firms tended to respond to fiscal and monetary stimulus from national governments while today their investment planning horizon stretches longer than the lifetime of chancellors and most governments. Besides which, fuel and raw materials' prices were low in both nominal and real terms.

In the 1930s there also seemed to be clear and decisive alternatives to the slump syndrome: reflation through Keynesian demand management matched by welfare policies. On the twin pillars of Keynes and Beveridge, full employment and social progress gained real support. But today, governments have lost their confidence that demand management, indicative planning and direct intervention can assure full employment and social welfare. In some cases, they have tried to maintain that all was well until OPEC threw a slick on our economic prospects. Others maintain that the joint cause of the current crisis has been excessive wage demands. Few so far have admitted that post-war growth probably was unsustainable over the long term, whether or not inflation hit the world economy in the 1970s.

One factor was the demand structure of post-war expansion. This was based on armaments and aerospace, construction and consumer durables. Surging demand for the latter has given way to relative saturation. Most higher income consumers welcome their first home, car, refrigerator, washing machine and television. But they clearly do not need three of each. Nor do airlines need two planes for each passenger. Export demand in less developed countries cannot absorb surplus capacity in the supplying industries and major redistribution of demands has recently been ruled out of court by the IMF and international bankers. Armaments now are the only growth sector of the modern capitalist economy.

In some 'fast accumulators' of the post-war period, this led to a fall in capital accumulation. For instance, the rate of gross fixed investment in West Germany fell from 9 per cent per year in 1950–4 to 6 per cent in 1960–4 and less than one per cent in 1970–4. Investment had slumped *before* the oil price increases.

Most Western governments mismanaged the OPEC increases, revving the supply motor while slamming the demand brakes. Cutting domestic spending to reduce import costs, they failed to do simple sums on global export demand. Through subsidies and tax cuts they tried to stimulate investment and jobs. But they thereby undermined their fiscal base through a failure to tax effectively. Nominal tax was offset by a range of subsidies which meant that in Britain, by the mid-1970s, industrial big business was paying virtually no mainstream tax at all. Without effective taxation governments could not continue to increase public expenditure or welfare programmes and slamming the brakes on demand after 1973 condemned Europe to mass unemployment.

Faced with this compound crisis, Keynesian 'managed capitalism' has given way to pre-Keynesian monetarism, associated with Milton Friedman and the Chicago school. Stripped of sophistries, Friedman's message is that the crisis amounts to excess money supply through excessive public spending. To sanitize the scene he recommends: (1) reducing personal taxes to improve incentive; (2) cutting public spending and welfare policies; and (3) rolling-back the public sector in both nationalized industries and services. Friedman pretends that capitalism serves a sovereign consumer through competitive adjustment of demand and supply. But monetarists wholly neglect that the structure of supply world-wide has been transformed by multinational capital. It is not lack of incentive which prevents the entrepreneur in Birmingham Alabama or Birmingham England from competing on equal terms with IBM, but the monopoly domination of global markets which IBM has established.

Monetarism also misrepresents the nature of public spending in post-war capitalism. Basically, public expenditure in Western Europe ranges from a fifth to a tenth of total supply. As a result, between 80 and 90 per cent of public expenditure sustains rather than drains the private sector. Put differently, public demand for housing, health and education is almost exclusively supplied by private enterprise. Public enterprise either is minimal or non-existent in construction. The vast bulk of the wages and salaries paid in the public sector – including local and central government – go on personal consumption supplied by private enterprise in both industry and services, because of low public sector representation in the economy. Friedman totally ignores the inflationary problem arising from the trend to monopolistic concentration in recessionary economies. Between the wars, smaller-scale business could reduce prices during a recession because a higher share of its external finance came from the stock market. Shareholders could be reminded that times were hard, and dividends were cut or not paid.

But the bulk of finance for the big league corporate sector in the post-war period has been either through retained earnings or bank and bond borrowing, including a major increase in the Eurodollar and Eurobond markets in the 1960s and 1970s. Repayment of such funds – unlike shares – cannot be passed or avoided because of hard times. To meet these new fixed costs of borrowing – as well as to sustain profits and absorb imported inflation – big business naturally tends to increase prices. It also tends to raise prices to compensate for lost cash-flow through falling sales, so that deflation now causes inflation under new supply conditions. Reflation alone will not bring prices down. But it will reduce costs and is the crucial precondition to an effective counter-inflation strategy. If there is no effective counter-challenge to monetarism, the result will be catastrophic for both the developed and the less-developed countries alike.

The debt crisis

By the end of 1982, global debt lent by the private banks amounted to more than $1,000 billion, of which the less-developed countries owed nearly one third. That is apart from official lending and short-term credits, which raised the less-developed countries' total debt to nearly $500 billion.

However, this is still an underestimate, since the Bank for International Settlements figures exclude loans from Arab banks, and the World Bank figures exclude most military credits, bringing the Third World debt to about $660 billion. Then, towards the end of 1982, a tremor shook the private banks when three major countries effectively defaulted on their debts – Mexico in August, Argentina in September and Brazil in December. What went wrong?

First, the global economic recovery expected by many governments, including Britain, did not take place. The global recession was shifting into slump, thanks to the monetarist policies pursued in the developed countries of the North. Balance-of-payments problems caused key countries to cut back their development programmes. For instance, in 1981 Nigeria imported $700 million worth of goods, mainly manufactures. In 1982, that was cut back to less than $50 million. Other key OPEC countries, instead of being able to perform their initial recycling operations, left the league of big spenders. Iran did so because of the war with Iraq and the Ayatollah's regime. Argentina cut back on spending in an economic crisis aggravated by the Falklands war. Brazil was badly hit by the recession as some 60 per cent of its exports and 70 per cent of its manufactures went to developing countries most hit by the new phase of the economic crisis.

A second major factor is the scale and variation of interest rates on private bank lending to Third World countries, including Commonwealth countries. The North has a key responsibility for this. High interest rates in Britain and the United States, both pursuing monetarist policies affected the international banking system and LIBOR – the London interbank offer rate. The three-month Eurodollar rate was 5 per cent at the end of 1976 and nearly 20 per cent in March 1980. Average rates rose from less than 8 per cent in 1976 to nearly 15 per cent in 1981. Those are variations in the cost of borrowing which less-developed and Commonwealth countries can scarcely absorb with ease.

Monetarist deflation of global demand and trade, associated with high interest rates in the North, have crippled the development prospects of many countries of the South.

Morgan Guaranty recently estimated that the debt service ratio for Chile, Brazil and Mexico ranged from 115 per cent to 130 per cent and for Argentina to 180 per cent. An economy such as Brazil's, which is crucial for the trade of the South and other Commonwealth countries and not just for Latin America, now needs more than its total export earnings to service its debt.

In the Commonwealth itself, Zambia owes $4 billion, India $20 billion and Nigeria $13 billion. Elsewhere, in South East Asia, Indonesia, the Philippines and South Korea – the so-called miracle economies of yesteryear – now owe $22 billion, $21 billion and $40 billion respectively.

On the demand side, the Friedman formula represents beggar-my-neighbour deflation by leading world economies. The trade and payments system cannot recover through each economy trying to gain an export surplus by cutting public spending to reduce import demand. This just reduces other countries' exports. In many cases it has a worse effect than protection since it reduces trade, domestic production and employment, while protection may at least benefit domestic employment and income levels in the short run.

Clearly there are cost inflationary elements in the international economy, including the inflation in oil prices. None the less, OPEC prices stabilized in real terms through the later 1970s, and inflation was not simply due to the price of oil. Other commodity prices, with the exception of precious metals, depreciated markedly through the later 1970s after major increases in 1972–3 when shortages (such as Brazilian coffee) and speculations (on commodity markets) contributed to the initial price rise. It is clear that no policy for global reflation can neglect energy prices. This was stressed in the Brandt Report which gave a key role to the recycling of OPEC surpluses to regenerate the world economy. On the other hand, not all OPEC countries are massively in surplus. Expenditure programmes in the 1970s moved many of them into deficit, contributing to further OPEC price increases from 1979. Nor is it clear that the world can recover on the back of OPEC any more than it can rely on the 'locomotive effect' of being pulled out of the slump by the United States, Germany or Japan, all of which are now gripped by the crisis syndrome and in serious economic difficulties.

Reflate, restructure, redistribute

What can we do about this? Can we reverse the slump and avoid chronic structural unemployment, especially in view of the impact of new technologies? The issue is not Keynes versus Friedman but the socialist alternative to capitalist crisis. Its political economy has three main imperatives. Essentially, we must reflate, restructure and redistribute resources in society.

Reflation is imperative to reverse the beggar-my-neighbour slump syndrome. So far the EEC and OECD have failed to mobilize reflation policies while the IMF has imposed deflation on so many world economies that it has reinforced rather than reversed the slump itself. *Restructuring* is crucial in both developed and less developed countries alike if a global reflation strategy is not to result in inflationary pressures over the medium term. But such restructuring cannot proceed on the classic capitalist basis of joint reduction of costs and increased price competitiveness alone since it is partly this which contributes to the beggar-my-neighbour slump syndrome. We need to restructure in a different and more radical sense, involving relations between the public and the private sector and the power relations of the system itself, including private finance capital on a global scale and central banks and governments.

Redistribution is crucial for socialists world-wide. But it is also crucial for a strategy which goes beyond demand management. There clearly is a demand crisis, but this is at prevailing levels of income distribution between social groups and classes. Redistribution towards the lower paid and the unwaged could give a massive boost to demand and welfare – unlike Keynesian policies of raising or lowering unreconstructed income levels.

Redistribution of resources on an international scale,

rightly stressed by Brandt, has a central role to play in the recovery of exports and employment in the developed countries themselves. But there also is a wider role for redistribution: first, at the *structural* level – between different firms and sectors; secondly, at the *social* level – between the employed and unemployed, between men and women and towards unprivileged ethnic groups and minorities; and third, a *spatial* redistribution between regions throughout the world as well as within countries to classic problem regions and inner-city areas.

Sub-Technology and Employment

Effective planning implies policies which change decision-making at the level of individual firms.

Deflationary monetarist policies are primarily responsible for the current jobs crisis. But there is also the new 'technological' unemployment.

Evidence available from the new generation of mini computers based on the silicone chip indicates that these are mainly labour displacing rather than job creating. They include robotics in industry and word and data processors in services.

It has been forecast by the Manpower Services Commission in Britain, by Nora and Minc in France and by the Siemens Co. in West Germany that between 30 and 40 per cent of services employment in typing, data processing, clerical, design and related staff could be displaced by these technologies within the next ten to fifteen years. Individual studies of the application of these technologies in Britain confirm the forecasts at a micro level. This would be a devastating contraction of employment overall granted that in the post-war period, it has mainly been public and private services which have absorbed those workers displaced by technical progress in industry.

In industry the progress of robotics has been remarkable in the late 1970s in countries such as Japan and is likely to be similar in Europe and the United States in the 1980s. A report prepared for the Central Policy Review Staff of the British government in 1978 predicted that within thirty years Britain could produce all her projected material needs with only 10 per cent of the existing industrial labour force if robotics were extensively applied. In other words, the report projected 90 per cent technological unemployment. This report has been criticized on various grounds. Trade union opposition, management inertia and other factors could well offset it. But its message is none the less striking.

Some of the reaction to these forecasts is simply ostrich-like, claiming that such displacement of labour has never occurred before. But in fact it has occurred, throughout Europe and the United States, in the key sector of agriculture. From being the dominant employment sector in Britain, employment in agriculture by the turn of the last century was down to less than 15 per cent. In the EEC countries, agricultural employment was still as high as 25 per cent in the 1950s, but now is less than 10 per cent. In Britain the sector now accounts for only 2.5 per cent of total labour and in the United States only slightly more.

While it is possible that the new products such as mini-computers and data processors may create new employment opportunities on a significant scale, it also seems highly unlikely that they will create significant net employment. Major technological unemployment now appears more clearly on the agenda than when Marx wrote of rising technical and organic composition of capital in the 1860s.

Such factors indicate that there is no simple solution to the crisis of contemporary capitalism. The crisis is in substantial part due to the 'beggar-my-neighbour' policies of deflation imposed by monetarist governments who are seeking to restructure capital through depressing wage costs. But reducing wages reduces demand and thus sales and profits. Moreover, the *structural* crisis of technological unemployment also takes the form of a *social* crisis.

For instance, it is clear that a major contraction of both industry and services employment will have specific social distribution. In Britain it is conventional to distinguish five social classes in the accounting of social statistics. Available evidence indicates that the new technologies will impact on middle management such as draughtsman, designers, technicians and those managers with 'routine' jobs. But the *main* impact of the technologies will be on the lower skilled, semi-skilled and unskilled workers in both industry and services, i.e. those categories in British terms which constitute the main part of the working class.

It is also evident that the impact of technical progress will not be regionally neutral. Distinguishing more-developed countries from intermediate regions and less-developed regions, evidence already available indicates that the main effect for technical progress in relatively labour-intensive industry is to displace labour in those areas and regions which were part of the nineteenth century industrial revolution, i.e. those which already are less developed. Intermediate regions in metal manufacture and engineering are especially prone to impact from robotics.

The categories adopted to describe regional distribution are relative. Thus they should not be conceived in a literal geographical sense. An intermediate or less-developed area by current standards may well be an inner-city area in a major metropolitan region. This certainly is the case with inner London, where there are more unemployed today than in a classic 'problem' region such as Wales, and where the out-migration of capital, combined with technical progress, has resulted in the loss of more than half a million jobs in manufacturing over more than ten years.

The prospect of technical progress causing grave social tensions because of the distribution of job losses should not be underestimated. The Northern Ireland case is instructive. In this region of the United Kingdom economy, unemployment for a quarter of a century after the Second World War was nearly double that of the rest of the UK, while unemployment among Catholics was double or more than double that of Protestant workers. In inner London or inner Liverpool, youth unemployment can be double the national average (during a period in Britain when youth unemployment now is higher than at any time in the 1930s). Meanwhile, youth unemployment among ethnic minorities, such as those in the black community, can easily be up to double that for youth unemployment as a whole.

Myths spawn on such an unemployment. Attention tends

to be focused on religion or race, rather than on the structural causes of the unemployment and its social and spatial impact. A bias arises against public programmes to alleviate unemployment, even when these are marginal or cosmetic. Overall, the bias against public spending and public works programmes is reflected in the political support for monetarist policies, with their assumption that public spending drains private spending and private initiative.

But in reality, as already stressed, in the unequally mixed economies of Western Europe and the United States, public spending sustains rather than drains the private sector. For instance, in Western Europe as a whole, public enterprise typically represents less than 15 per cent of GDP. This means that for any injection of 100 units of public spending, 85 units (whether £-sterling, francs, lire or marks) is spent in and generates income in the private sector. The recent relative failure of public spending to sustain full employment has less related to its income generating effects than to the effects of structural change through technical progress in the developed economies, and its social and spatial distribution.

The contradiction is especially clear in the area of housing policy. In England and Wales more than 90 per cent of the public housing built is constructed by private enterprise firms. Therefore more than £90 of every £100 cut in the government's spending on the nominally public sphere of council housing is in practice cut away from the private construction companies. Meanwhile, speculative capital is pouring hundreds of millions of pounds into inner-city office development in projects which will mature during the 1980s in a period when the impact of micro-technologies such as data and word processors is reducing the demand for office staff and with it the demand for office space.

A policy aiming to counter the effects of new technologies on the structure of employment and its socio-spatial distribution cannot, therefore, in any way neglect the primary importance of public spending. On the other hand, a policy of reflation must also take account of technological restructuring, its social distribution and the related spatial location of income and employment.

There is a clear case for social redistribution *per se*, i.e. a move of wealth from an upper class and a redistribution of income between the middle and working classes. But, again, the available information on the impact of technical progress indicates that such classic redistribution now also will need to be accompanied on a major scale by redistribution between sectors of activity and cities and regions. Social distribution of income itself is related to employment, even in a society of sizable benefits and social security. Such a redistribution, if serious, cannot neglect structural and spatial effects. Real-life opportunities are related not only to social class but also to the region or area in which one is born, and the available local employment.

In a clear sense this makes a radical response to the current crisis more than ever relevant. Only policies for major redistribution are likely to be able to offset or resolve the structural, social and spatial implications of technological change in the coming decades. In reality this makes imperative policies for not only *public spending* on an unprecedented scale but also *economic and social planning*, and *a new public sector* including not only nationalized industry and services of the traditional model, but also new regional, municipal and local enterprise in the public sector (whether directly owned by the state authority or by workers' co-operatives). It also necessitates negotiation of major changes in the economy and society: shorter working time and higher personal or social incomes made possible by the increased productivity from major technical progress.

In some firms, industries and services this will mean a 35-hour week. In others it may mean a 35-week year such as that enjoyed by many academics in higher education institutions. Introducing 'sabbaticals' or longer paid holidays for working people will cause both structural and social change in the system, and will not avoid the problems of lost overtime, productivity bonuses or other benefits which – not least in the French case – resulted in reduced worker support – or outright opposition – to a 35-hour week. Clearly, such change can only be achieved in democratic fashion if it is with rather than against the workforce. But in reality this means not only industrial democracy at the place of work, but also an economic democracy extending to the wider issues of the distribution of resources between and within sectors, social groups and classes, and different areas and regions.

Such economic democracy implies that the planning necessary to adjust to the impact of technical progress cannot be from the 'top down', imposed in a technocratic manner by elites. Such elites may well forecast the impact of technical change but cannot anticipate either the full range of social needs or the social resistance to specific forms of change. On the other hand, such economic democracy cannot be simply from the 'bottom up'. There is no way in which workers in an individual factory or company can themselves independently gain an overview of the impact of technical change on the whole economy and society.

Forecasts must be made on the best possible evidence of overall distribution of the effects of technical progress. But the inputs for such forecasting at the top or centre of the system must themselves come from the base. Moreover, the base cannot simply be the place of work, but must also include those either unemployed or about to become unemployed in the near future through the impact of technical change, as well as the elderly and retired.

This social dimension to redistribution will need to be matched by the spatial dimension if the economics of regional deprivation is not to be complemented by the politics of protest, mystifications and violence. The expansion of investment and those few jobs about to be created cannot simply occur in the more developed regions and areas of the system if the social and political cohesion as a whole is to be maintained. There are many mechanisms for the representation of such interests, of which direct regional representation is only one. Crucially, there must be a link between the regional level and what is occurring at the national level in terms of the social and regional distribution of resources.

Above all, the economic planning involved in seeking to adapt to the consequences of technical progress must itself be a process rather than an administrative fiat or act. If the aim of economic progress is social progress and the development of the individual within the whole, then economic planning must itself increasingly become a process of social negotia-

tion of changed options for the economy and with it for
society as a whole. This, in turn, implies social control.

New European dimensions

Already key parties of the European left are committed to
policies to reflate, restructure and redistribute resources as
part of their medium- or long-term programme. This
approach is the core of the case for economic recovery laid
out in the March 1984 Manifesto of the Confederation of
Socialist Parties of The European Community. For many
parties it involves not only a commitment to equalize
personal incomes but also to reduce employment hours.
Most parties of the European left are also committed to
increasing social income and social services as well as
extending social control and public enterprise in the economy. Not least, with reason, socialists want to plan rather
than leave the economy to the hazard of market forces.

Effective planning implies policies which change decision-
making at the level of individual firms. This has been
conventionally conceived as the relation of macro and micro
economic policies. But the new multinationals have a major
effect on the macro economy while also dominating the
scope and market share of minor micro companies. In
Galbraith's vocabulary, and in a real sense, they are a
planning system in their own terms. Internationally, little or
nothing has been done to bring this multinational private
sector under public accountability and control. The United
Nations and OECD have formulated codes of conduct for
multinationals, as have international trade union federations
but they have voluntary status and are not enforced.

Yet new dimensions for the possibility of effective planning and accountability over the big business sector are now
on the agenda of the European left in individual countries.
While differing in name, form and in some cases content,
they none the less focus on the need to gain public
accountability and economic democracy through a new
planning framework. Some of these new forms of planning
emerged under state capitalist governments in the form of

contracts between big business and the state. Programme contracts were introduced in France in 1968 with powers for the government to gain direct information on the cost, profit and pricing schedules of big business as part of a counter-inflation and export promotion programme. In Belgium such contracts were introduced in the late 1960s with the aim of gaining more direct leverage on both the multinational big business sector and public enterprise planning. Similarly, in Italy in 1968 under a centre-left coalition government, programme contracts with leading private enterprise – as well as direct controls of public enterprise location – were introduced with a view to off-setting the increasing divergence between the north and south of the country.

Such policies in some cases clearly amounted to a public relations exercise between private big business and the government. A key limit in the programme contracts approach was their voluntary status in relation to the private sector. In spite of warnings made at the time, the Labour government from 1975 decided that planning agreements should be voluntary only in the private sector and failed to implement them (with the notable exception of the plan for coal) in the public sector itself. None the less, there were two major changes in the focus of planning on the big business sector in Labour's programme in 1973. The first was simple and crucial: the principle for trade union negotiation of such planning agreements, moving beyond wage bargaining with an opening of the books on costs, profits, prices and forward plans. The other main emphasis was on bridging the gap which had emerged between the micro and macro sectors of the economy with the rise of the new big business sector.

A similar transformation of planning was happening at the same time in France. The Socialist Party's programme for the last election stated that new agreements would be 'the main plank' of its industrial policy jointly with an extension of the public sector. In June 1982, as part of its reform of French planning procedures, the government in France introduced new planning agreements which closely parallel Labour Party policy; in September of the same year, the PASOK government in Greece did the same. In Portugal the planning

agreements approach was introduced by a range of measures
with both public and private companies. In Belgium the
Socialist Party is reformulating the previous programme
contracts approach with greater powers for economic
democracy and public accountability. Austria already has the
means for worker accountability on the boards of companies
and close supervision of corporate planning in an economy
where 45 per cent of enterprise is publicly owned. In West
Germany the Social Democratic Party is committed to
'investment co-ordination' in the big-business sector, with
trade union involvement and an opening of the books to
government.

The similarities between these new approaches are much
clearer than any differences. Besides which, the various
means envisaged for implementing such agreements or
involving worker representation – in contrast with the lowest
common denominator approach of the European Community – is part of the strength of the new approach to
planning and industrial democracy. They reflect a real base in
labour movements and parties of the left in different European countries, rather than hollow proposals from community institutions, or other international agencies (see table
17.1).

Thus the convergence of the planning-by-agreement
approach in key European countries now has the potential to
answer monetarist 'supply siders' with social control by
governments and unions of the big business sector. Real
advances are being made. But the left in government – and
trade unions pressuring governments of the right or centre –
must advance its gains by relating the planning agreements in
one country to the same multinationals in different countries,
taking the case from the national base to the international
joint agenda. Not least, the left in Europe also needs to relate
its strategy for transforming 'supply-side' power to joint
pressure to restore and redistribute demand in the European
economy.

The international constraint is real, as Labour governments
know, and as the French socialists have experienced. But the
response does not have to be deflation, spending cuts or
monetarism with a human face. It may well be that we have

**Table 17.1   Planning by agreement:
the European convergence**

British Labour Party	Planning agreements Labour's programmes 1973, 1976 and 1982
French Socialist Party	Long-term programme and legislation, June 1982.
Greek Socialist Party	Prime ministerial statement and legislation, 1982.
Portuguese Socialist Party	Planning contracts in legislation since mid-1970s.
Belgian Socialist Parties	Planning contracts legislation plus revisions in progress
Austrian Socialists	Legislation on company planning and opening books to trade unions.
West German SPD	Investment co-ordination, long-term programme commitment, 1975.
Italian Socialist Party	Planning contracts since centre-left government in 1960s; new planning agreements since 1981.

to go it alone if a Labour government were not able to persuade enough countries to undertake a joint reflation to promote our mutual recovery. Aided by self-sufficient energy, and to avoid deepening slump and social tensions, we would need to take powers through planning agreements and supplementary measures to plan and control our trade.

However, without reflation on a major scale there is no hope of getting out of the crisis. Acting on its own, a government of the left in Europe might be able to increase production and real income by between 3 and 5 per cent and begin to reduce unemployment. But even assuming negligible retaliation from other countries on import controls, planned trade by one country during a world slump is one-sided. Not least there would be massive pressure from financial institutions working against any reflation in one country large enough to register a significant impact on jobs and incomes in the short-term.

With 'better-my-neighbour' reflation, trade, spending and production will be stimulated in the rest of the world. But the reflating country can only hope to recoup a fraction of the general increase in trade. The net effect is a dramatic deterioration in its balance of payments. For each 1 per cent gain to its own production and income the country could lose 0.5 per cent of GDP on its balance of payments. To put it another way, for every 100,000 jobs created by unilateral or go-it-alone reflation, the country's trade could deteriorate by some 5 billion dollars. No European country could go far in creating jobs and raising income if this were the cost.

By contrast, if several European countries jointly reflate, the 'better-my-neighbour' reflation becomes mutual. The countries concerned would not only in part compensate each others' losses in trade, but the gains to income and employment in each country would be greater and the net costs to their governments' budgets would be correspondingly reduced. For example, if all governments in Western Europe engaged in a joint reflation, each 1 per cent gain of income might involve on average as little as a 0.2 per cent deterioration in their countries' trade balances, and they would recoup about three-quarters of the initial budgetary costs through higher tax receipts. They could certainly go much further before running into major financial constraints.

If all the West European economies were to reflate immediately they could create several million jobs in a few years, with more if the United States were pulled in. If short-term relations in Western Europe were combined with restructuring and redistribution, it is feasible that we could jointly abolish involuntary unemployment in the 1990s. The advantages of such joint reflation over going it alone are obvious. For one thing, on the better-my-neighbour basis, increased imports in individual countries would tend to be offset by increased exports to other economies also expanding their trade. Setting joint targets of 1.5 million new jobs each year would mean raising the growth of total production and real income from the present average of around 2 per cent a year to around 5 per cent a year. This would be no more than the growth rate enjoyed in the 1960s and early 1970s. If other parts of the world were reflating their economies simultaneously, then the size of the *direct* stimulus to spending in Europe in the first two years would need to be of the order of 3 per cent of total income (GNP) – an increase of some 100 billion dollars as an annual flow.

These illustrative figures are not academic. They are part of the *Out of Crisis* project, published in the spring of 1982.[1] The project includes members of the executives of the socialist parties of Portugal, Spain, Italy, Greece, France, Belgium, the Netherlands and Sweden, with strong interest on Labour's own National Executive, as well as other European parties of the left and trade unions. If the project has strength it is partly because of the readiness of the European left to transform the crisis through better-my-neighbour reflation rather than succumb to the slump syndrome.

European recovery

In February 1983, the European Parliament commissioned Michel Albert, former head of the French Plan, and James Ball, director of the London Business School, to draw up a report for European recovery. Commissioned a month before the launch of the *Out of Crisis* project and published some three months after it, the report supports arguments for European economic recovery, with stress on better-my-neighbour recovery of spending and trade. More conservative than the *Out of Crisis* project, it argues that it would be enough to gain a 1 per cent increase in the gross domestic product of the member countries over a period of three years to begin the process of recovery. This is less than the 3 per cent increase recommended in the *Out of Crisis* project through an annual net expenditure of the equivalent of US$100 billion a year. The *Out of Crisis* project also stresses that such a recovery would need to be sustained for a decade, creating some 20 million jobs, before one could claim that the economic crisis in Europe had been overcome.

The European Trade Unions Institute has shown how a 1 per cent of more initial recovery of the European and OECD economies would achieve a cumulative effect. The initial 1 per cent expenditure – through multiplier effects – would accumulate to 3 per cent for Western Europe as a whole after two years. In this respect, the ETU analysis bridges the gap between the 1 per cent recovery of the European Assembly scenario and the 'maxi' recovery scenario of the *Out of Crisis* project. But if the OECD countries only fulfilled the UN target of 0.7 per cent of GDP in aid to less-developed countries, this would not only help the South but would create up to 2 million jobs in the North.

Initiatives for recovery have come from the United States, too. In May 1983, a major statement on the imperative for economic recovery received the support of nearly 150 Democratic members of the House of Representatives. This project was prepared by Gar Alperovitz, a progressive Democratic economist associated with the Centre for Democratic Alternatives in Washington. Echoing the emphasis made by Neil Kinnock on the need to 'produce our way out of slump', the project stresses a 'high production strategy to rebuild America'. The outcome of some two years of research, the National Economic Recovery Project includes a group of 75 members of the House of Representatives organized in some 16 task forces to specify policy options for recovery. The American project directly parallels the European *Out of Crisis* project in proposing alternative programmes for recovery. In employment terms this implies a reduction of the unemployment rate from just under 10 per cent in 1983 to just over 5 per cent in 1987. Challenging the Reagan re-estimates on budgetary deficits, which anticipate a US fiscal deficit of $175 billion by 1987, the 'maximal' recovery target proposed by Alperovitz and endorsed by the US Democratic congressmen aims at halving registered unemployment in the United States and reducing this deficit to $75 billion by 1987.

We cannot realistically expect a Thatcher government or a Reagan administration to endorse this kind of recovery. In practice, they blocked it together at Cancun, Mexico, by mouthing platitudes about recovery while doing nothing thereafter to promote one. But we can propose that like-minded nations undertake joint recovery programmes in their mutual interest, irrespective of the global development veto of Ronald Reagan and Margaret Thatcher.

Moreover, the United States *needs* a strong international recovery – just as the Third World does. For instance, a European recovery of a 3 per cent addition to annual output growth rates would result in the addition of $12–15 billion, or 4–5 per cent a year to US visible exports, and $30 billion and 1 per cent a year to US GDP. Such a mutual interest in recovery between Europe and the United States clearly is critical in the short term, granted the extent to which a sustained US recovery is in question. While the recovery potential of the United States economy may be underesti-mated, it is probable that the recovery will 'blow out' by the second half of 1985. The present situation is that if US output continues to grow by current rates throughout 1984, the US current account deficit could well increase by $30–40 billion. Put differently, a 'mini' European recovery would not contribute significantly to sustaining economic recovery in the United States. By contrast a 'maxi' European recovery could be crucial, both for the United States and for the less-developed countries of the South.

The political implications are suggestive. A 'maxi' re-covery statement may be the one offer Europe may make to the United States which it cannot easily refuse – even under a Reagan administration. How likely is this in the last analysis? How can the European left hope to succeed where the French government failed in gaining sustained recovery? Precisely, in part, by being a European left rather than a left within one country, or a minor Atlantic partner offering capital with a human face. Precisely by being a left open to all of Europe and a wider world rather than confined by the Common Market. Precisely by arguing for the maxi budget which will help the world spend its way out of slump rather than only for mini budget rebates on a food-price policy. If even some like-minded left governments can jointly face this global challenge on the lines of the recovery programme spelled out in the 1984 manifesto of the Confederation of Socialist Parties, then not only Europe but also the world would have a chance of surmounting the current crisis.

Note

[1] Stuart Holland, (ed.), *Out of Crisis* (Spokesman Books, 1982).

18

Reconstructing the Mass Media

JAMES CURRAN

Given the enormous amount of time and emotional energy the Labour movement has devoted to denouncing the shortcomings of the mass media, it is surprising that it has had so little influence on mass-media policy. Nearly all the key political decisions about the ownership, organization and funding of the mass media have been taken by Conservative administrations, even though Labour has been in power for approaching half the time since 1945.

Thus Conservative governments introduced commercial TV in 1954 and commercial radio in 1972. What minor changes Labour administrations made were all within the framework of broadcasting policy established by Conservative ministers. Significantly, this framework is only now being challenged – by a radical government on the right rather than the left.

Press policy in Britain has long been based on the conservative principle that it is best to have no policy at all. Labour ministers have been at one with their opponents in resisting press reform in any shape or form – including sensible and constructive measures introduced by reforming administrations in other Western European countries.

The one exception to this conservative record provides little to boast about. In 1965, the Wilson administration introduced a law to restrict the acquisition of newspapers by the big press groups. The law was so feebly worded that it failed to prevent a single take-over bid by a press chain in the next twelve years, even though this was a period when the big press groups bought up more than 50 newspaper companies. Dismayed by this record, the Royal Commission on the Press urged the government to strengthen anti-monopoly press legislation in 1977. This advice was ignored by the Callaghan administration with the result that Murdoch was able to add *The Times* and *The Sunday Times* to his media empire in 1981 without even a reference being made to the Monopolies Commission.[1] The Wilson government's attempt to restrain the growth of press monopoly has thus been totally ineffectual.

Only in relation to the cinema can Labour claim to have made a significant impression on media policy. Yet even here, its record is notable for its lack of success. In the late 1940s, Harold Wilson introduced a film bank, the National Film Finance Corporation, and a new form of subsidy, the Eady Levy, in order to build a vigorous, British cinema industry. Twenty years later, a government committee chaired by Wilson concluded mournfully that Britain's collapsing cinema industry was so totally dominated by America that it had become, in effect, an offshore island of Hollywood. The Thatcher administration has since decided to deny Wilson's film bank direct government finance and is currently assessing the role of the Eady Levy. A support system that has failed is perhaps rightly on trial.[2]

Why have Labour governments been so unsuccessful in their approach to media reform? One partial explanation is that some Labour politicians have been reluctant to attempt serious reform in this area for fear of souring their working relationship with media. For example, Clement Attlee was against even appointing a Royal Commission on the Press in 1947 partly because he thought it would turn the press against the government. For much the same reason, James Callaghan used his personal influence as premier to bury the reforming minority report of the third Royal Commission on the Press, written by the union leader, David Basnett, and the Daily Mirror's assistant editor, Geoffrey Goodman.

Some senior Labour politicians have also been reluctant reformers out of conviction. For example, the Labour Party promised in its October 1974 election manifesto to introduce an open government 'measure to put the burden on the public authorities to justify withholding information'. The Labour government of 1974–9 failed to fulfil this commitment largely because leading Labour politicians either had second thoughts, were uncertain about how best to implement their promise, or thought it was misguided in the first place.[3]

But these explanations tell only half the story. Most leading Labour politicians are adept at delivering ritualistic denunciations of the media without having thought very deeply about how to remedy the problems they complain about. It is this lack of considered commitment to specific reforms, combined with a rather selective understanding of the workings of the media, which largely explains why so many distinguished Labour politicians have been so ineffectual as media reformers.

The New Communications Revolution

Nothing illustrates more clearly the limitations of Labour's approach to the mass media than its continuing preoccupation with Fleet Street at a time when the most important mass medium, television, is about to be transformed. In the next five years, the majority of the population will have their own video recorder; they will also be able to pay for additional channels broadcast direct to their homes by satellite (DBS); and, in some affluent areas, they will be able to subscribe to anything up to thirty TV channels relayed by cable.

These developments are being promoted by the government in a way that will further undermine the independence of Britain's media. During the last three decades, a small number of multinationals have gained control over much of Britain's media. Television is, however, the medium least subject to the stranglehold of international conglomerates. This is partly because of the size of the public sector in broadcasting but also because the IBA has insisted on allocating TV franchises only to consortia with a local connection in the regions they bid for.

This restriction on the expansion of multinational corporations is now being relaxed. The new cable TV network will rely heavily on programme services provided by the leading communications giants. A remarkable coalition of global media magnates from Twentieth Century Fox, Columbia, Home Box Office, Thorn-EMI and Pearson-Longman (through its subsidiary, Goldcrest) have set up a new programme company, Premiere, to service British cable TV. They will be competing against another programme company, TEN, bankrolled by UIP Pay-TV, Visionhire and BET. And Rupert Murdoch has launched a rival TV company, Sky Channel, to service cable TV not only in Britain but on the continent as well.

Multinational communications conglomerates are also well represented among the consortia owning cable TV stations. For example, the Canadian-British conglomerate, Thorn-EMI, with interests stretching from a record factory in Peking to the ABC cinema chain in Britain has gained major interests in three out of the eleven franchises awarded in 1983.

At the time of writing, intense behind the scenes lobbying is also taking place over the development of direct broadcasting by satellite (DBS) services in Britain. Originally intended to be pioneered by the BBC, it now seems likely that DBS on the British channels will be developed by a consortium of the BBC, ITV companies and new interests – including multinational conglomerates which have been excluded hitherto from having a substantial ownership stake in British TV.

The communications conglomerates are thus about to increase their domination over information and cultural production in Britain. Yet, already, the leading five corporations in each media sector now control over 90% of national newspaper circulation, over 80% of women's magazine sales, over 60% of paperback book sales, record sales, and cinema admissions and over 50% of the video market.[4] The further expansion of the communication giants is a threat to the diversity of Britain's media. It is also a threat, as we shall see, to the long-term future of British television as a major centre of production.

The Threat to British Television

It is widely assumed that British TV is safe from competition because it is so good. This complacent view ignores the main reason why British TV dominates its home market. It is one of the most ruthlessly protected broadcasting systems in the Western world: only 14% of programmes on British TV are allowed to come from outside the EEC.[5] Yet audience research regularly shows that the strictly rationed American programmes on British TV are among the more popular programmes shown in Britain.

The received wisdom that the future of British TV is assured also fails to come to terms with the dynamics of the international TV trade. British TV is vulnerable because it will be heavily undercut by American TV companies. In 1982, ITV spent on average £40,000 on one hour of programming, while the BBC spent £30,000 and Channel 4 £24,000. Yet, all these organizations could have filled the same one hour time slot with a popular American programme costing as little as £2,000.[6] This is because American TV companies can spread their overheads and production expenditure over a large volume of international sales and sell at only a fraction of cost price. In the face of competition of this sort, being 'good' is not enough.

The new TV media will punch a large hole through the protective wall that has sustained British television. They will transmit mainly cheap American material, since they are not subject to import restrictions, and will expose British TV to real competition on its home ground for the first time in its history. This challenge will materialize gradually and undramatically. Cable TV will spread more slowly than was originally thought likely; the new DBS channels will have an as yet unknown impact; and the purchase of video recorders while expanding rapidly, will complement as well as compete with the established networks. But the cumulative effect of the new media will almost certainly be to fragment the audience for TV, and erode the financial base of British TV production. If a substantial number of viewers are diverted away from BBC and ITV, the revenue of both organizations is likely to decline. BBC will find it more difficult to justify an increase in its licence fee, while ITV companies will have a falling share of advertising expenditure. With declining resources, both networks will be forced to make fewer programmes. They will also come under strong economic pressure to import more cheap programmes as a way of cutting costs and making up for the shortfall in production.

This is a familiar pattern which has been repeated in many other countries.[7] Indeed, the global hegemony of the American TV conglomerates is merely part of a more general trend in which cultural production in the West has come to be dominated by a small number of corporations.[7] The big seven American 'majors' controlled in the late 1970s 70% of the Western film market. Five multinationals, mostly based in the United States, controlled an estimated 63% of the Western record market in 1977. The developing global information 'software' and video film market has been dominated from the start by a small number of multimedia conglomerates. If Britain's media are further colonized, this would be merely a continuation of what is now a well-established, world-wide trend.

Threat to Diversity

Although the new media will make available more programmes, paradoxically they are likely to diminish the cultural and ideological choice of programmes available to the British public.

If the new media grow at the expense of British TV production, as seems likely, fewer TV programmes will be made which reflect the cultural and social diversity of British life. American soap opera and cops and robbers films will be transmitted (and endlessly repeated) at the expense of new productions from the stables that produced *Boys from the Blackstuff* and *Tinker, Tailor, Soldier, Spy*.

Of course, the new media will provide access to many enjoyable American programmes, and some of the British TV productions that will fall by the wayside in the new conditions of competition will be no great loss. But a further effect of the new media will be to create a two-nation TV system in which the quality of the universally available TV services will deteriorate as their revenues decline in the face of competition from the new subscription services.

The character of British mainstream TV is also likely to change. In order to ward off the threat posed by American TV corporations enjoying large economies of scale, British TV is likely to become increasingly oriented towards the global mass market. In this way, it can aim to stay competitive by spreading costs. This is a familiar strategy attempted by all the failed leaders of the British cinema from Korda to Grade. Its consequence has usually been to manufacture more films of inferior quality.

The emergence of cable TV is also likely to recast British TV more in the right-wing mould of Fleet Street. Apart from its news service, cable TV will be exempt from the obligation imposed on public service broadcasting to be impartial. The new Cable TV Authority will also have a much less active oversight role than the IBA. Although in theory the bias of individual programmes on cable TV will be mutually balancing, no attempt has been made to 'balance' the ownership of cable TV, which is solely controlled by big business consortia.

The familiar claims made for cable TV also turn out to be misleading. To judge from American experience, interactive systems will not normally be available with cable TV due to low subscriber take-up. And cable TV is not coming 'free'. On the contrary, it is being heavily underwritten by tax payers – including people who cannot afford to pay the subscription for the new service.

New Approach

The new communications revolution will not provide a market solution to the shortcomings of Britain's mass media. It will not increase the media's diversity; improve its quality; or enfranchise new working class interests within the media. Indeed, if anything, it seems likely to make some things worse, rather than better.

Consequently, we need a new strategy for the mass media which serves the public interest rather than the present fragmentary and amorphous policy developed in response to pressure from industrial interests. What is proposed below is a new approach – a programme encompassing all the media. Its main objective is to create a more diverse mass communication system that reflects more adequately the variety of attitudes, values and cultural interests within the community. To achieve this, it is necessary to reduce the major conglomerates' domination of the media; assist new voices to be heard, which are excluded by the high costs of market entry; and strengthen those parts of Britain's media which are worth defending.

Anti-Monopoly Measures

The growth of communications giants with a global reach stretching around the world now represents a serious threat to democracy.[8] The dangers inherent in this trend are graphically illustrated by the rise of Rupert Murdoch who controls through News International over 30 newspapers and magazines extending from San Antonio, Texas, to Brisbane, Australia with an aggregate circulation of 20.5 million in addition to extensive book publishing and broadcasting interests in three continents. He rules most of his media empire like a personal fiefdom, rewriting editorials, deluging editors with copies of articles from the new right, raging against the publication of left-wing comment, above all, personally vetting the senior appointments in his media enterprises. Working for Murdoch, if you do not conform to his now extreme right-wing views or do what he wants, is to put your job in jeopardy. Stafford Summerfield, the successful editor of the *News of the World*, twice packed the personal papers in his office and, thereafter, kept his 'suitcase handy' in expectation of being summarily dismissed. Harold Evans, the distinguished editor of *The Times*, chose to resign rather than be 'subjected to a thousand humiliations'. Murdoch's prestige paper, *The Australian*, has had thirteen editors in just fifteen years. A barrage of ineffective protest about the way Murdoch's media have deliberately lied or misled has come from the Australian Broadcasting Tribunal, the Australian Press Council, the British Press Council, and numerous outraged journalists and broadcasters. Rupert Murdoch is a new phenomenon: a media magnate with global power who makes his predecessors like Lord Northcliffe or Randolph Hearst seem harmlessly parochial by comparison.

In order to counteract the threat represented by global media moguls like Murdoch, as well as by smaller concentrations of media power, a number of anti-monopoly measures should be introduced.

(1)   No group or individual should be allowed to own more than 3 national newspapers *or* more than 10 local daily papers *or* more than 50 local weekly (paid or freesheet) papers within the United Kingdom.

(2)   No group or individual should be allowed to own over 10% of shares in more than one ITV company or franchised cable TV company or local radio company.

(3)   No group or individual should be allowed to own *voting* shares in both press and broadcasting organizations.

The enactment of these measures would lead to a considerable unscrambling of media conglomerates. Murdoch would be divested of one national newspaper and major interests in one radio station; the Thomson Organization would have to sell four local dailies and four local radio interests; the Pearson Longman subsidiary, Westminster Press, would have to sell over 50 local weeklies and interests in two radio stations; the Industrial and Commercial Finance Corporation would have to sell off interests in one ITV company, while Thorn-EMI would be confined to one cable TV franchise; a substantial number of other enterprises would have to decide whether to be mainly broadcasting or press corporations.

This frontal assault on conglomerate power will produce a predictable howl of outrage. But a number of countries have made a start in curbing the growth of media concentration. As long ago as 1947, the Hollywood majors were compelled by law to sell their cinema chains. The Springer media conglomerate hastily sold off five magazines in Germany, in the late 1960s, to evade the anti-monopoly measures proposed by the Gunther commission. The French government is currently introducing an anti-monopoly law which will lead to the divestment of the Hersant press empire. There is no reason why what has been initiated by reforming administrations in France, Germany and the United States cannot be followed up in Britain.

Media Bank

But anti-monopoly law will accomplish little unless it is accompanied by other measures. By itself, it will achieve little more than a game of musical chairs in which divested media will be sold on the open market to other substantial financial interests.

The character of the media will also remain fundamentally unchanged unless steps are taken to prevent high market entry costs from excluding all but the rich and powerful from owning substantial commercial media.[9] It is not simply that the acquisition of viable media corporations is prohibitively expensive. Beginning with an acorn and turning it into an oaktree is an unrealizable ambition for most people with limited financial resources, however talented, in the main sectors of the commercial media. The cost of establishing even a local evening paper, operating with new technology in a town with no direct competition, amounts to well over 3 million.[10] More ambitious projects like a local cable TV station or a new national Sunday paper require even more capital.

A Media Enterprise Board needs to be established, which should provide loan finance for two purposes: the acquisition of divested media and the launch of new media. It should be funded directly by the Exchequer. But its establishment should be accompanied by the introduction of a tax on all advertising which, even if set as low as 1%, would yield a gross annual revenue of over £10 million.

One purpose of the Board will be to prevent the assets and employees of a divested company from being automatically sold like a job lot in an auction to the highest bidder. The Board should fund realistic bids by workers to take over their own company or establish the company as a public trust.

The Board should also assist some individuals and groups with limited resources to start new companies across the full spectrum of the media, providing always that they seem likely to succeed and that they own no other media. Local radio is one sector of the media where the Board should become involved, not least since new initiatives in local radio are relatively cheap to fund. The development of cable TV provides an opportune moment perhaps to fund an alternative programme distribution company servicing cable TV. Film production is now more worthwhile to selectively fund because TV provides an efficient distribution system for films reaching a large audience. Market openings exist for new press launches that would extend the diversity of the press.

For reasons of historical accident, seed finance for new media launches is confined in Britain to film. However, there is no rational reason why film should be privileged in this way. In Sweden, seventeen new papers have been launched since 1976 with the help of funds from the Press Subsidies Council – with only one failure to date. In Australia, a comparable body to the Media Enterprise Board is being set up with a remit to fund, in particular, new national minority journals as well as film production. Again what has been pioneered by the left elsewhere can be developed in Britain.

What kinds of continuing support the Media Enterprise Board should provide is open to question. One problem is that the media conglomerates will offload their least profitable ventures, when they become subject to new anti-monopoly legislation. In many cases, these have long been subsidized by the public in the form of tax losses set against company profits. Public subsidies have thus been spent not according to public interest criteria but according to the public relations needs of major corporations.

Another problem is that funding from the Board could be abused for narrowly partisan advantage. One way of circumventing this is to allocate support according to set criteria which are invariably applied regardless of the media's content. But the trouble with this approach, as is forcibly illustrated by the experience of Sweden, is that it entails injecting money into dying ventures and the scale of the subsidy tends to escalate in an effort to keep sinking media afloat. A preferable and more economic approach would be for the Board to provide back-up finance for those ventures which appear likely to be successful. For this discretionary approach to be acceptable, it would be important to ensure that people from all the leading political parties are represented on the Board and that its activities are subject to proper parliamentary scrutiny.

Open Market Access

Open access is usually discussed in terms of creating minority programmes for worthy causes. What is needed is something less paternalistic and more far reaching: widening access to the market so that radical media can compete on equal terms with mainstream media.

All publications should have the legal right, as in France, to be displayed and sold in the newsagents of their choice, subject to a handling charge on returns. This would greatly aid the development of minority magazines, many of which find it difficult to get properly distributed.

Unequal market access, arising from the fact that affluent readers generate more advertising than low paid ones, should also be tackled. Its most damaging consequences are in the national newspaper press where newspapers have been forced to close down with far larger circulations than their rivals with a more up-market readership. The easiest and cheapest way to counteract this is to introduce a variant of a scheme already in operation in France: any newspaper with a circulation of over 20,000 and less than 500,000, which receives less than 25 per cent of its revenue from advertising, would be automatically eligible for a grant to compensate for its shortfall. The effect of this scheme would be to encourage the launch of new quality papers not oriented towards the elite market – and to give them a fair chance of surviving with sales as low as that of the *Guardian* or *The Times*.

The IBA should be encouraged, through revised terms of

reference, to distribute at least some franchises to non-profit making organizations in the next round of allocations for TV and radio. By being so exclusively oriented towards big business consortia, the IBA has helped to exclude alternative approaches and viewpoints from the senior command structure of both commercial TV and radio.

The new Cable TV Authority should not exclude trade unions from obtaining franchises. It should ensure that cable TV operators include some genuinely local, controversial programme material. And without detracting from cable TV's freedom to be committed, the Authority should ensure that a balance is maintained between partisan programmes.

Redefining Public Service

The single most effective way of sustaining British TV production is to impose a quota on foreign programmes transmitted by cable TV, even if this quota is considerably less restrictive than the one currently operating on ITV and the BBC. The government should also restrict the transmission of imported programmes on the British DBS channels. This will prevent British TV production from being undercut by American TV companies, even if its effect will be to impose a brake on the rapid development of cable TV.

But British broadcasting needs to be improved as well as defended. The governing bodies of the broadcasting organizations should be recruited from a much wider spectrum of political opinion and more varied social background. (For example, 56 out of the 85 Governors of the BBC appointed between 1928 and 1976 were graduates – 40 of them from Oxbridge.)[11] The politically appointed representatives on the BBC Board of Governors, IBA, Fourth Channel and Cable TV Authority should also be more assertive in resisting political pressure from governments. Probably the only way to achieve these twin objectives of a more independent and more mixed representation on broadcasting authorities is for some members to be appointed by nomination from accredited interest groups.

There is also a strong case for separating the organization

of radio from that of TV. The direction of BBC radio, in particular, needs a thorough shake up. The BBC's local radio stations are usually of a very low quality. BBC's radio current affairs coverage is markedly biased to the right – much more so than its TV counterpart. And the middle class, cultural paternalism that marred the BBC's popular radio channels until the invigorating impact of the pirate radio stations of the 1960s is now gaining an increasing hold on Radio 1 and 2.

A central part of the public service tradition is that the media should be accountable to the public in more ways than merely through the operation of an imperfect market. A legal right of reply should be established, as in France and West Germany, allowing for the prompt correction of factual misrepresentation. The Press Council and Broadcasting Complaints Commission (expanded to cover all broadcasting organizations) should also become more genuinely independent of the media they deal with by being publicly financed, and they should have the legal right to insist on the publication or transmission of indictments, if serious complaints are upheld.

At the same time, excessive state restrictions on freedom of expression should be lifted. Our national security law is currently being abused to limit the release of information to the public because it could be politically embarrassing to the government. The scope of Section 1 of the Official Secrets Act on the betrayal of defence secrets to the enemy should be limited, and Section 2 of the Act should be abolished. A Freedom of Information Act should be introduced to provide legal access to government records, with a high court judge to investigate and determine government claims to privilege. Contempt of court should also be abolished in cases without a jury.

Conclusion

Labour's sorry record on media reform exemplifies the party's Janus-faced posture on so many things – a combination of fundamentalist socialist rhetoric in public and timorous caution in office. In this area, at least, Labour should promise rather less and deliver rather more.

There is nothing in the programme outlined in this essay which is automatically unacceptable to the broad centre of public opinion which Labour must appeal to, if it is to form a majority government. The most controversial part of it, perhaps, are its proposals to scale down the major monopolies. Yet this has been advocated as much by people with centrist political views – such as Lord Crowther and Professor Jeremy Tunstall – as by people from the left. Indeed, it has been the telling protests of centre-left editors like Harold Evans and Donald Trelford, rather than the more predictable jeremiads of left politicians, which have begun to prepare the ground for a popular campaign against the abuse of media power.

This programme is bound to be attacked on the grounds that it will introduce state censorship through the back door. But the main element of the programme – anti-monopoly measures, a media bank, guaranteed right of distribution, advertising deficit grants, programme import quotas, right of reply and freedom of information laws – have all been implemented already by reforming governments elsewhere. In not one instance has any of these measures led to covert censorship by government.

These proposals can doubtless be improved upon. But what needs to take place is a widespread debate on the left about what practical reforms should be implemented to reconstruct the media. Indeed next time you hear Labour politicians attacking the media, you might ask them what they propose to do about it. If they propose nothing concrete, they are wasting your time as well as their own. More to the point, they are also signalling that nothing much will be achieved in this area when Labour is next elected to government.

Notes

[1] Harold Evans argues persuasively in his *Good Times, Bad Times* (Weidenfeld and Nicholson, 1983) that the take-over of Times Newspapers was technically in breach of the Fair Trading Act. But the Thatcher government would never have been able to stretch the meaning of the Act, if it had been reformed along the lines proposed by the Press Commission.

[2] Margaret Dickinson provides a devastating analysis of the failure of Labour's film policy in J. Curran and V. Porter eds., *British Cinema History*, Weidenfeld and Nicholson, 1983.

[3] For an interesting account by two radical lobbyists of how the Labour government dragged its feet, see Rosemary Delbridge and Martin Smith, 'The Secrecy Debate in Britain' in their jointly edited *Consuming Secrets*, Burnett, 1982.

[4] J. Curran and J. Seaton, *Power Without Responsibility: The Press and Broadcasting in Britain*, Fontana, 1981. Revised edition forthcoming, Methuen, 1984.

[5] The IBA now exempts limited categories of programme from its 14 per cent quota.

[6] *Report of the Inquiry into Cable Expansion and Broadcasting Policy*, HMSO, 1982

[7] Jeremy Tunstall, *The Media are American*, Constable, 1977.

[8] See, in particular, the pioneering study by G. Murdoch and P. Golding, 'For a Political Economy of Mass Communication' in J. Saville and R. Miliband, (eds.,) *The Socialist Register*, Merlin Press, 1973; A. Matellart, *Multinational Corporations and the Control of Culture*, Harvester Press, 1979; H. Schiller, *Who Knows: Information on the Age of Fortune 500*, Ablex, 1981; and G. Murdoch 'Large Corporations and the Control of the Communications Industries' in M. Gurevitch, T. Bennett, J. Curran and J. Woollacott eds., *Culture, Society and the Media*, Methuen, 1982.

[9] It is often argued that excessive labour costs, caused by union opposition to new technology and overmanning, is *mainly* responsible for high entry costs in the national press. This is not borne out by the investigation of the last Royal Commission on the Press See, in particular, its *Interim Report*, HMSO, 1976.

[10] Establishment costs were estimated between two and three million pounds as long ago as 1977 in N. Hartley, P. Gudgeon and R. Crafts, *Concentration of Ownership in the Provincial Press*, Royal Commission on the Press 1974–7, Research Series 5, (HMSO 1977).

[11] Asa Briggs, *Governing the BBC*, BBC, 1979.

19

Rethinking Defence

MARY KALDOR

Since the 1983 general election, there has been a good deal of talk within the Labour Party and within CND about the need to develop a credible non-nuclear defence policy. In particular, how do the people of Britain reconcile this demand with membership of NATO, since NATO is at present committed to a strategy based on the first use of nuclear weapons?

The question is not merely technical. Technically, we could choose to be a non-nuclear nation and withdraw all forces assigned to a nuclear role within NATO. Technically, the North Atlantic Treaty does not commit us to any particular strategy or any specific military task. But in practice the question is a political one about the whole process of nuclear disarmament in Europe and the significance of the American 'nuclear umbrella'.

Much of the discussion about alternative defence policies is obsessively technical – how to substitute missile-firing infantry men for nuclear artillery, or small conventional submarines for HMS *Invincible*, and so on. Yet in peace time, and that is what we are concerned to maintain, defence policy is primarily a political signal. It is built on perceptions about the kind of contingencies a nation might face in which force might be used. These perceptions depend partly on the international situation – how we relate both to potential enemies and to allies; and partly on domestic factors – how to translate domestic political positions, such as Atlanticism, into foreign policy. In order to think about an alternative defence policy, we need therefore to think about an alternative foreign policy.

Britain's current defence policy is closely integrated into overall NATO strategy. Before the Falklands war, 90 per cent of Britain's military spending was allocated to NATO. NATO strategy rests fundamentally on nuclear deterrence, in the different variants that have been adopted over the past 35 years. Nuclear deterrence can be described as the strategic expression of the bloc system. It is a kind of state of no war/no peace which is somehow supposed to be maintained indefinitely. It is an imaginary enactment of World War III (which must never actually take place) in which the antagonists are NATO and the Warsaw Pact. The underlying rationale of both blocs is the *possibility* of this imaginary war.

For NATO, deterrence is primarily nuclear: conventional forces are viewed as the first rung in the ladder of escalation to nuclear war. Although, of course, Britain possesses so-called independent nuclear forces, deterrence is largely seen to rest on the American presence in Europe. Indeed it can be argued that deterrence is a way of reminding Europeans of the American victory in 1945. In this imaginary enactment of World War III, the Soviet Union charges across the north German plains in a conventional *blitzkrieg* and the Americans come to the aid of the Europeans with a glorious (and hideous) form of strategic bombing.

It is important to remember the political significance of this nightmare. When NATO was formed in 1949, the immediate military threat from the Soviet Union was thought to be minimal. The idea that the protection of Europe would rest on America's atomic monopoly was viewed, to use Michael Howard's term, as a form of 'reassurance'. He argues that it was reassurance in the face 'of widespread fear, not of Soviet military attack on Europe, but of disintegration of the whole political and economic structure that would make any such attack unnecessary'.[1] From its inception, the Atlantic Alliance was viewed as the defence of a 'way of life'. In other words, NATO could be viewed as a way in which ruling groups of a similar political outlook within Western Europe obtained support from the United States and each other. This is what is now known as Atlanticism. Atlanticism was not just an international philosophy – it had to do with the commitment to free enterprise economies and the domestic political struggles of the 1940s with left socialist and communist parties.

With the recovery of West European economies and the relative economic decline of the United States, real political and economic differences have emerged between West European and American governments. These differences have to do with trade, policy towards the Third World, East–West policy, and so on. And they have increasingly been expressed in differences about nuclear strategy. This is because the American emphasis on the significance of nuclear weapons is also a way of reasserting American leadership in the alliance. In particular, the growing trend towards nuclear war-fighting as opposed to war-deterring exposes the dependence of European lives on American decision-makers. To put it another way; the various instruments of American foreign policy – aid, trade, money – have been weakened as a result of America's economic problems and this has led to an increasing emphasis on military power, particularly on nuclear weapons.

Perhaps because the Soviet Union was always economically weak, the military element was always more important in its relations with its allies. Of course, this relationship was different in kind from that which prevailed within the United States and Western Europe. The former rested on crude force; the latter depended on the development of a kind of political consensus – which is now breaking down.

The Soviet Union is often said to lack a concept of deterrence in the Western sense. It is certainly true that there is no clear distinction between nuclear war-deterring and nuclear war-fighting. Rather, there is a broader concept of deterring war in general because Soviet forces are sufficiently large 'to repel (or at least absorb) any attack and then go on and win the war'.[2] These include both conventional and nuclear forces. There is no question that the massive Soviet conventional presence in Eastern Europe, the nature of Warsaw Pact military exercises and forms of joint military training represent the main mechanism for maintaining Soviet control in Eastern Europe. Soviet writers have explicitly referred to the 'internal function of a socialist army . . . as a psychological deterrent against anti-socialist forces.'[3] Some commentators have argued that the development of a

Warsaw Pact military-political doctrine in the late 1950s was determined by the need to prevent independent policies of territorial defence, as in Yugoslavia and Romania. And some have even gone so far as to suggest that Warsaw Pact military exercises are, in fact, rehearsals for military intervention.[4]

The nuclear institution

Present forms of deterrence depend on continued hostility between the blocs. To be 'credible', as the strategists like to put it, nuclear planners have to prove that they actually intend to use nuclear weapons. Limited nuclear war doctrines are, in fact, a logical consequence of deterrence. Nuclear planners, in effect, have to perpetuate and even exacerbate near war conditions. As Anders Boserup has pointed out:

> The reprisals envisaged by the strategy [of deterrence] are, by definition, wholly disproportionate in their effects and militarily pointless. While one can hope to deter hostile actions by threatening to massacre millions of innocent people, it makes no sense whatever to carry out the threat when the time comes, not even if it can be done with impunity. For deterrence to be credible, not rational political judgement but insane vindictiveness or some unthinking 'doomsday' device must be seen to be in control . . . What some writers characterize as the 'excesses' of nuclear deterrence are in fact its requirements: hostility and paranoia, recurrent sabre rattling, military and political dispositions which promote instability and encourage escalation and a continuing arms race.[5]

Behind this conceptual problem lies a political problem. If the raison d'être of each bloc is the threat of the other, and if at least part of the reason for the bloc system is to hold together groups of nations (whether to 'defend a way of life' in the Western sphere or to preserve 'a security belt' in the Eastern sphere) then any tension within the blocs is inevitably externalized and expressed in terms of the military threat. As internal dissension increases, so does the tension *between* the blocs.

Historically, the problem of 'credibility' has been raised by the actual occurrence of wars or by threats to the stability of the bloc system. It was revolutions in Latin America and South East Asia, as well as growing political independence in Europe that introduced doubts about American willingness to engage in nuclear war in the late 1950s. When the presence of an atomic howitzer did just manage to prevent the Chinese from taking Qemoy and Matsu in 1957, the question immediately arose: what if it hadn't? That discussion paved the way for the doctrine of flexible response and the increased readiness to engage in limited conventional war which led to Vietnam.

The Vietnam war represented a tremendous blow to American credibility. The new emphasis on nuclear war-fighting has to be understood in the context of American frustration, in the face of uncontrollable conflicts and grow-ing defiance from West European and Third World leaders. One can speculate about a similar process occurring in the East. The entropy of centrally planned systems, the pressure for reform in East European countries, the dissatisfaction of ordinary citizens in the East with the failure of living standards to grow, may well provide an impetus to recipro-cate the new cold warism of the West.

This is the problem that caused the erosion of détente. For détente was predicated on the continued existence of the blocs. It was a kind of guarantee of mutual non-interference, a way of avoiding the risks of ideological hostility. Yet the possibility of interference, and of renewed hostility, were conditions for the continuation of the blocs. Why should Western Europe concern itself with defence, why should Poles be disturbed about 'anti-socialist' infiltration, when Soviet and American leaders hug each other? Moreover, the very exchange between East and West allowed by détente introduced new aspirations for change, especially in the Eastern bloc, that could not be contained within the bloc system. Indeed, for the Western bloc, détente itself became a cause of contention as in the case, for example, of the gas pipeline.

Before discussing the alternatives to nuclear deterrence, it is important to mention the other factor that has contributed to the formation of NATO strategy. The whole complicated system of deterrence is produced by scientists, engineers, workers, soldiers, bureaucrats, politicians and others. The institutions within which they operate generate an autonomous dynamic geared to the development and production of ever more advanced weaponry and ever more 'worse case' justifications. Longstanding relationships between the armourers and the armed forces have to a large extent dictated the particular pattern of military roles and the types of technology designed to fulfil them within the broader framework of deterrence. The relationships differ in the East and West. In the West, the combination of independent or private arms manufacturers and a relatively conservative military establishment has led to the development of ever more grotesque and expensive weapon systems, like aircraft carriers or multi-role aircraft. In the East, the emphasis on quantity or on particular types of equipment like artillery can be explained in terms of the dictates of equally conservative military establishments combined with the inflexible quantitative planning indicators that guide the state enterprise. In fact, precisely because the military and industrial institutions in both East and West were shaped for the most part during the Second World War, military technology tends to have evolved in a linear extension from the technology of the 1940s. This has shored up the idea of World War III as a bigger and better version of World War II. In effect, it is the institutionalization of the bloc system.

Towards an alternative

The political aim of an alternative defence policy should be to avoid war through *lessening* the confrontation between the blocs. Such a policy would have to provide convincing conventional military protection to society, without at the same time posing a military and/or political threat to other countries. The term 'defensive deterrence' has been used to describe a defensive conventional posture which would exact a 'high admission price' – that is, an unacceptable human, political and economic price, from a potential aggressor – and yet could not be used for offensive purposes.[6] In place of the in-built alarmism and vindictiveness of retaliatory nuclear deterrence, the aim would be to develop an alternative defence policy which explicitly builds upon existing and possible future constraints against the use of warfare as a means of settling conflict. The idea is to narrow the arena of warfare in international relations, and to de-emphasize the perceived significance of military power. Since the current bloc system is, in fact, defined in military terms, this would also help to initiate the process of phasing-out the blocs. In other words, if nuclear deterrence is the expression of the current bloc system, then an alternative defence policy must be compatible with or make possible an alternative international order. In effect, it must be based on a non-aligned or non-bloc minded foreign policy.

Non-alignment is not the same as neutrality. Neutrality may, in fact, presuppose the continuation of the blocs. Countries like Sweden and Austria (and even France, which is not strictly neutral) are arming to protect their neutrality in the event of a war between East and West. In such a war, a primary objective of both sides will be pre-emptive invasion, in order to ensure that the territory of the neutral country is not taken by the enemy. This is the main military contingency which military planners in neutral countries expect to face. Indeed, military thinkers in neutral countries often support 'nuclear deterrence' or 'preserving the balance' in order to protect their own positions. Neutrality, in this sense, would necessitate a strong frontier and/or territorial defence of Britain – not perhaps as strong as Sweden or Switzerland because of Britain's fortunate geographical position.

I do not accept the argument that the defence of British territory would be expensive. It would actually cost much less than our present defence policy since we spend so much currently on the defence of West Germany and the Eastern Atlantic. But such a defence policy would also entail an increased militarization of British society – the reintroduction of conscription, an increase in military installations in Britain, and so on. We have been fortunate to avoid the militarization of Britain up to now.

Whether or not the goal of non-alignment, in the sense of phasing out the blocs, can be best pursued outside NATO would depend on the realpolitik of the situation. If Britain were to leave NATO, this could help diminish the confrontation between East and West by increasing the political space between the blocs. However, it could also have the opposite effect; if other NATO countries, particularly West Germany, were to increase their own armaments and play a more dominant military role, this could greatly increase tension within and between the blocs. On the other hand, if Britain were to remain in NATO and join with like-minded political forces in Western Europe to reorientate NATO strategy towards a defensive conventional posture, this could well have a more profound influence in diminishing tensions in Europe and making possible the ultimate phasing out of the blocs. Much would depend on our relations with these like-minded forces, especially in West Germany. Would withdrawal from NATO strengthen or weaken the support we could provide to anti-militarist movements? The choice is, for the moment, hypothetical. The immediate task is to oppose dangerous trends in current military policies and to oppose bloc thinking. For that will determine the political circumstances in which an alternative defence policy might be carried out and whether such a choice exists in practice.

The effort to reorientate NATO strategy towards a defensive conventional posture should be sharply distinguished from ideas about increasing the conventional emphasis of NATO strategy that are currently being touted in influential circles on both sides of the Atlantic by such people as General Rogers or David Owen. These ideas advocate increased conventional armament, including offensive elements such as armour and strike aircraft and even such systems as conventionally armed long-range Cruise missiles. In other words, the increased conventional emphasis will be achieved *not* by reducing nuclear weapons but by increasing conventional weapons. Moreover, some of the advocates of increased conventional capabilities are proposing 'non-nuclear weapons that approach the destructiveness of low-yield (2–5 kiloton) nuclear weapons'.[7]

NATO is proposing to withdraw some short-range battlefield nuclear weapons, such as atomic demolition mines and artillery. NATO officials fear that such weapons would be 'self-deterring' because they would be used on NATO territory. Instead, NATO will emphasize intermediate range nuclear weapons like Cruise and Pershing-II which are to be used against Warsaw Pact territory. Further, according to the new US Army doctrine *Airland Battle*, nuclear, chemical and conventional war-fighting is to be more closely integrated in future.

Any reductions in nuclear weapons are, of course, to be welcomed. But their significance depends on whether they can initiate a *political* process of reducing tensions between the blocs and allow for a political loosening within the blocs, so as to make possible further steps towards disarmament and security (in the fullest sense) in the future. A conventional arms race, and in particular a shift from short- to intermediate-range nuclear weapons, would nullify the political consequences of reductions in nuclear weapons and could, in fact, prove highly *destabilizing*. The emphasis on offensive conventional weapons, together with developments in the strategic arms race and the rhetoric of the Reagan administration, could well be used by hawks in the Kremlin as evidence that NATO is planning an attack on Eastern Europe. Moreover, since nuclear weapons do represent a symbol of the American presence, a conventional arms race might be associated with, or seen to be associated with, the emergence of a new West European bloc, dominated by West Germany. This would represent an increased menace to the Soviet Union and could also exacerbate conflict with the United States. The consequence of Soviet conventional armament would, in turn, be seen to increase the threat to the West and provide a mechanism for greater oppression in Eastern Europe. These developments could make war in Europe *more* likely. And in such a war, nuclear weapons would surely be used, whether NATO possessed 6,000 or 4,000 nuclear weapons.

This is why it is important to be absolutely uncompromising about our opposition to NATO strategy. We should oppose *any* escalation in the nuclear arms race in Europe. And we should oppose any increase in offensive conventional armaments. We should pose as an alternative a defensive conventional posture for NATO. This need not differ substantially from NATO's present conventional posture. At present, NATO has a defensive conventional posture. It would be desirable to remove some obviously offensive elements – long-range strike aircraft, for instance, or maritime intervention capabilities such as aircraft carriers. And it might be desirable to strengthen some defensive elements – anti-tank or anti-aircraft weapons. It would also be a good idea to eliminate 'baroque' (expensive and over-sophisticated) weapon systems. But such changes should be accomplished with present or lower defence budgets. Such a policy probably ought to include a declaration of 'No First Use'. This would necessitate a change in NATO strategy and would therefore open up new possibilities for nuclear disarmament. But it could also be used – and indeed *is* used by some of its proponents – to justify increased conventional armament, and the shift from short- to long-range nuclear weapons. This is why it is more important to emphasize the priority of withdrawing nuclear weapons.

The argument that NATO could now provide an effective conventional defence is unconvincing. I would argue that there is now a rough conventional balance in Europe which has actually moved in NATO's favour over the last ten years.[8] NATO has a numerical superiority in some categories, such as manpower, anti-tank weapons, helicopters (for which US experts claim an eight-to-one kill ratio against armour). The Warsaw Pact has a superiority in others – tanks, artillery and anti-aircraft weapons. The Warsaw Pact also has huge logistical problems. Most authoritative sources would agree with the conclusion of the International Institute of Strategic Studies, that 'The overall balance continues to be such as to make military aggression a highly risky undertaking. Though tactical redeployment could provide a local advantage in numbers sufficient to allow an attacker to believe he might achieve tactical success, there would still appear to be insufficient overall strength on either side to guarantee victory'.[9] In fact, to carry out the kind of *blitzkrieg* strategy that NATO expects from the Warsaw Pact, the Soviet Union would need a massive superiority which it manifestly does not possess.[10] More importantly, the Soviet Union could not count on the reliability of Warsaw Pact armies in the event of war.

What could we do to oppose current NATO strategy and to pose an alternative? It is important to identify and publicize our collective roles in NATO and build support among sympathetic groups within other NATO countries for alternative ways of carrying out these roles. In effect, we could use our collective contribution as leverage for shifting NATO strategy as a whole. In this way, we could expose the true nature of NATO and the way in which it undermines natural sovereignty. This might at some future date create the political environment for withdrawal.

In addition to our independent forces, we have three main roles within NATO: defence of the UK home base; defence of the Eastern Atlantic and Channel areas; and the British Army of the Rhine, which is part of the Northern Army Group in the Central Region. We also have some Royal Marine Commandos in Norway, a number of ships in the Mediterranean (Britain usually provides a ship and some RAF Nimrods for NATO's On-Call Force Mediterranean when it is activated), plus regional reserve and specialist reinforcement forces for possible deployment in Norway, Denmark, North East Italy, the Atlantic Islands and the border areas of Greece and Turkey. Not committed to NATO are forces deployed in Hong Kong, Cyprus, Gibraltar, Berlin, Belize and the Falklands.

Clearly, a first priority is opposition to Trident and Cruise missiles and the phasing out of British nuclear weapons, including American nuclear weapons on British territory or used by British forces. If Britain were committed to a non-nuclear defence policy within NATO, it would be difficult for us to allow our forces to co-operate with other forces preparing to use nuclear weapons. We would therefore need to attach certain conditions to the continuation of our collective roles within NATO. These conditions could be related to the interests of socialist parties and peace movements in the countries concerned. For example, we could insist on the removal of battlefield nuclear weapons from the Central Region, oppose increased offensive conventional armament, call for the withdrawal of Pershing-II and non-deployment of cruise in West Germany, and join with peace movements and socialist parties in Holland, Belgium and West Germany, our partners in the Central Region, to draw up a plan for the removal of other nuclear weapons from Germany. In the Atlantic, we could co-operate with the Dutch and the Danes in opposing the use of nuclear depth charges and new offensive naval doctrines. In Norway, our demands could relate to the Nordic nuclear-free zone; in the Mediterranean, we could demand the establishment of the Balkan nuclear-free zone and the removal of Cruise missiles from Sicily. By discussing and drawing public attention to the way in which Britain is implicated in current NATO strategy, by linking our demands to those of other like-minded groups in NATO, and by pointing out alternatives, we would lay the basis for a possible negotiating stance within NATO at some future date.

Destroying the cold war myth

Such co-operation with like-minded forces in other NATO countries to reorientate NATO strategy only makes sense as one element of a foreign policy which aims, first and foremost, to overcome the confrontation between the blocs and to create political space in both Europe and the third world so that nations are much freer to pursue their own domestic policies. In particular, we need a new conception of Europe that includes both halves of the continent. At present, the East-West conflict is presented as a clash of social systems. The political image of the confrontation as 'freedom' versus 'totalitarianism' as the imaginary World War III, is an extremely powerful form of ideological conditioning. We need to be able to put across an alternative version of the East-West conflict; as a mechanism for our own oppression – in a way in which the superpowers preserve their spheres of influence by instilling fear of the 'other'. We need to develop the idea in people's minds that we have a common interest with the peoples of Eastern Europe in eliminating confrontation and the immense burden of threatened nuclear war. We could perhaps remind people of an alternative historic memory, the European resistance against Hitler and the goal of a democratic socialist Europe. The idea that the 'threat' is Reagan and Andropov and their joint collusion in the arms race, and that World War III is not a bigger and better Hiroshima and Nagasaki, is already gaining ground.

A defensive conventional posture for NATO would contribute to this conception. It would mean a certain political disengagement of Western European countries from the United States, as well as a diminution of the military confrontation between East and West. This could allow for a reciprocal disengagement by the Soviet Union from Eastern Europe and thus help to initiate the process of ending the division of the continent. It is a policy of transition from Atlanticism to non-alignment. Any attempt to achieve disengagement of Western Europe from the US without a diminution of the military confrontation and without a new conception of Europe could lead to a kind of West European Gaullism, a new European bloc mentality, which could be even more dangerous than the present situation. In other words, any attempt to shift NATO strategy has to be part of an attempt to achieve a political rather than a military alternative to the confrontation in Europe.

But it should also attempt to develop a people's détente and to encourage the idea that the peoples of Europe, both here in Britain and in Eastern Europe, have no interest in continued confrontation. The Labour Party and the peace movements could make use of their position as opponents of the cold war, to support those groups in East European society that are creating the possibility of a loosening of the Eastern bloc. Already, some elements of the peace movement have provided support to the new peace movements in Hungary and East Germany as well as Solidarity in Poland or Charter 77 in Czechoslovakia. Support for these groups serves to rebut charges that opponents of the cold war are pro-Soviet. Yet, at the same time, greater public knowledge about the situation in Eastern Europe could help to allay fears about the Soviet 'threat'.

The policy of overcoming East–West conflict should also guide an alternative foreign policy in other parts of the world. European countries ought to be able to support those political forces in the Third World seeking an alternative to incorporation in the East-West conflict. At the same time, so as to avoid the development of a new Euro-imperialism, the form of our relationship with the Third World needs to be changed. For example, we ought to downgrade, even to the point of elimination, the military element in that relationship.

An alternative defence and foreign policy has to be accompanied by an alternative to the institutional framework of the cold war – the military-industrial relationships, both in Britain, and within NATO as a whole, that profoundly influence the pattern of weapons procurements. If politics is to be in command, then these relationships have to be shifted irreversibly. In particular, a policy of conversion or diversification of defence industries does not so much follow from disarmament, but rather represents a necessary condition for reducing the pressure from existing military policies and creating the opportunity for alternative strategies. The basis for a conversion policy would need to be established through intensive discussions throughout the defence industry, with the relevant trade unions and with local communities and, where necessary, with trade unions in other countries involved in collaborative ventures such as Tornado.

These proposals are founded on the assumption that disarmament and alternative defence policies can only be achieved through the political process. By criticizing existing NATO strategy and making demands that are consistent with the stated goals of NATO – demands which may well appear more rational to many innocent adherents to NATO than present NATO policies – we widen the political spectrum of support for our alternatives, both within Britain and within other NATO countries. We also expose the gap between the stated goals of NATO and the underlying political assumptions. And we popularize an alternative political vision in which a real peace is achieved by eliminating the existing military blocs – the causes of confrontation – and breaking the bond of fear which binds individual nations together. The hold of World War III over the popular imagination must not be underestimated. If the myth can be undermined, it will be possible to create an environment in which the 'withering away' of the blocs becomes a reality.

Notes

1 Michael Howard: 'Western Defence in the 1980s: Conditions for Consensus', *Foreign Affairs* (Spring 1983).
2 Michael MccGwire: 'Soviet Strategic Weapons Policy, 1955–70', in Michael MccGwire, Ken Booth, John McDonnell, (eds.) *Soviet Naval Policy: Objectives and Constraints* (Praeger, 1975).
3 Quoted in Christopher Jones: 'Soviet Military Doctrines and Warsaw Pact Exercises' in Derek Leebert, (ed.) *Soviet Military Thinking* (George Allen & Unwin, 1981).
4 Ibid.
5 Anders Boserup: 'Nuclear Disarmament: Non-Nuclear Defence', in Mary Kaldor and Dan Smith, (eds.) *Disarming Europe* (Merlin Press, 1982).
6 See *Defence Without the Bomb*, Report of the Alternative Defence Commission (Taylor and Francis, 1983).
7 J. M. Shuttleworth: 'RUSI Forum: NATO's Forward Defence Strategy', *Royal United Services Institute Journal* (July 1983).
8 See Mary Kaldor: Is There A Soviet Threat?' in Michael Clarke and Marjorie Mowlam, Debate on *Disarmament* (Routledge & Kegan Paul, 1982).
9 *The Military Balance 1982–83* (ISS, 1982).
10 John J. Mearsheimer: 'Why the Soviets Can't Win Quickly in Central Europe', *International Security* (Summer 1982).

20

Beyond Bullock

KEN COATES

The institution of mass unemployment as a permanent economic fact has naturally transformed the prospects for collective bargaining. But this does not mean that trade unions are left entirely without resource. Undoubtedly, because collective bargaining has been the main method of trade union advance during the whole period of full employment following the Second World War, political action has been somewhat undervalued as a mode of activity. To some degree, as successive governments have legislated in order to control wage levels, trade unions have assumed a rather defensive mentality at the mention of the word 'law'.

This trade union sensitivity is understandable in the light of the constant sniping by governments (and by establishment economic doctrine) against the rights of free collective bargaining – a trend which has been maintained throughout the post-war period. Orthodox logic has sought to express the problem created by the Keynesian revolution and the assumption of 'demand management' functions by modern governments in a necessary chain of baleful consequences, which have often been represented schematically in sloganized form. The argument has gone like this:

Full employment + free trade unionism + free collective bargaining
= inflation + balance of payments crises + stop–go monetary and fiscal policies + low rates of investment + low productivity + more inflation and so on, in the familiar pattern of a vicious circle.

On the left hand side of this mock equation are three factors, all of which have been repeatedly undermined by governments of various persuasions, at different stages. Every governmental curtailment of these conditions threatens trade unionism in one way or other. Full employment survived longest, until the breach with Keynes announced by Jim Callaghan in the 1970s, the early version of monetarism pursued by Denis Healey which followed it, and the subsequent whole-hearted application of that doctrine by Margaret Thatcher. Trade union freedom has been successively put in question by Harold Wilson (*In Place of Strife*, 1969), Edward Heath (the Industrial Relations Act, 1971), and Mrs Thatcher (Employment Acts of the 1980s). Attempts to erode free collective bargaining have been the most consistently pursued of all three strategies; between 1939 and 1983 only 16 of the 44 years have been entirely free of any form of government intervention in the process of wage bargaining. It is in this way that legislation in the field of labour relations has acquired distinctly negative overtones for most trade unionists.

Even so, during the 1960s and 1970s there were some notable, if always limited and sometimes ambiguous, advances in labour legislation (covering health and safety at work, employment protection, redundancy payments, equal pay, sex and racial discrimination and other issues). The ambiguities and limits of these measures might have been fewer had the trade unions not, in their defensive posture, seen the legislative method as distinctly secondary to collective bargaining amongst their modes of work. The effect of legislation was also indirectly beneficial in a number of ways about which unions were at first quite naturally ambivalent. For instance, the threat that procedural agreements might be made legally enforceable provoked the much needed modernization of such agreements, removing some very archaic practices and unfair procedures from a ramshackle industrial relations system. For all this, the main weight of trade union effort, even during the earlier years of the social contract, went into direct bargaining on wages, hours and working conditions.

One majority legislative commitment of the Trade Union Congress was frustrated. But had it succeeded, it would have raised collective bargaining to a new level. The commitment to formal structures of industrial democracy, enabling accountable trade union representatives to be elected on to the boards of companies, reached a high point in the earliest years of the 1974–9 Labour government. The TUC had been persuaded of the need for counter proposals to put against the draft for a European company law, which sought to generalize a modified version of the German system of codetermination. British trade unions objected to German *Mitbestimmung* on three grounds of principle. First, they believed that any elections for worker directors should be held through the established trade union machinery, in order to avoid a situation in which the workers' voices could be divided through divergent or even contradictory channels of representation. Second, they objected to the intrusion of company works councils which might undermine the unique representative role of the British shop-steward system.

Third, the unions did not wish to participate in a minority role. They saw working people's involvement on company boards as an extension of normal collective bargaining in which there are two possible 'votes' – 50/50 or 100 per cent. A 50/50 vote is a 'failure to agree', and constitutes a veto. A 100 per cent vote facilitates harmonious action. Most radically, the TUC insisted that the 50/50 board, with its enshrined veto power for the trade union side, should assume legal supremacy in company law, overriding the authority of the shareholder's meeting. With a wealth of supporting arguments, the TUC prepared a succession of drafts for industrial democracy laws, and Labour came to office pledged to legislate along these lines. The most significant apostasy of that government was its refusal to do any such thing. Instead, Harold Wilson set up the Bullock Commission to report on how such legislation could be framed, and then procrastinated for long enough to ensure that action on Bullock's recommendations became impossible. Wilson was undoubtedly prompted to follow this course of action by some blatant threats from the City and the CBI of a 'strike of capital', should the TUC proposals be enacted.

The actual proposals of the Bullock Commission represented an important dilution of the TUC's original policies. Notably, Bullock recommended the creation of an intermediary group of directors to be nominated by consensus of both shareholders' and employees' representatives – such a group to hold the balance between the two sides. This was the famous '$2x + y$ formula' and was much discussed at the time, but it did not actually persuade any employers' organizations of the acceptability of such a reform. Indeed the employers maintained a strenuous lobby against the whole idea of legislating for industrial democracy. By contrast, the Bullock compromise was often cited by trade unionists as a reason for cooling their ardour for reform. The most important proposal of Bullock's team tended to be swamped by the commentary on the idea of an intermediary y group of directors. Basing itself no doubt on the strategic sense of Jack Jones – certainly the most far-sighted trade union leader of his time – the Commission had devised an arrangement of joint representative councils to co-ordinate the trade union input to company board elections. These joint councils would have provided a framework up to the company level which would have been a most notable legislative contribution to the development of trade union influence and unity, by generalizing and facilitating through legal authority the emergence of the equivalent of shop-steward combine committees.

The TUC's proposals for legislation on industrial democracy were an attempt to secure legislative expression for a vast secular movement based upon full employment. The growth of plant bargaining and of work-place initiative by shop stewards was founded on the decisive fact that employers were competing for labour. Attempts to subordinate shop stewards to managerial interests were recurrent throughout the whole period of post-war industrial relations, but they met with only the most ephemeral success. Full employment was the continual refresher of trade union independence, the stream from which trade union initiative was constantly renewed. Collective bargaining might be thought to have reached its highest point in this movement, which foundered in the rejection of Bullock's proposals. Now it has fallen far below that peak.

By February 1984 there were 3,186,000 people registered as unemployed, including school leavers. Cosmetic manipulation of these figures has removed many men of 60 from the statistics by relieving them of the obligation to sign on. As always happens, unregistered women are also invisible, and together with young people working on transitory schemes, the 'hidden' unemployed number well over a million people. With registered unemployment at 13.4 per cent of the employed population and rising, the meaning of many trade union practices is transformed. Not only are employers in many parts of the country no longer competing for labour, but workers are actually vying to hang on to their jobs. A reign of fear grips large sectors of the economy, in which shop-steward leaders such as Mike Cooley of Lucas or Derek Robinson of British Leyland may be sacked with impunity once employers become combative.

Bargaining advances have become far more difficult, while the very nature of trade union institutions is in some cases being forced to change. The shop stewards' movement of today is different in many ways from the self-confident, resolute and inventive movement of the early seventies. The dawning of 1984 found large sectors of British trade unionism crouched in abjectly defensive postures.

Legislation directed at the widening of democratic powers can only be effective when there is a resolute force for democracy which seeks such powers to achieve its social objectives. The most perfect charters for democratic reform are meaningless in the absence of such a real movement of people. For this reason, it makes little sense to reopen the argument on industrial democracy by stepping into its stream where Bullock stepped out. There is a major role for legislative change, in restoring and securing trade union rights and capacities, but this role will not be asserted unless we determine a careful order of priorities.

What kinds of laws do today's trade unions need?

Legal action is urgently needed to tackle two of the most acute problems resulting from the imposition of monetarist doctrines. Unemployment must be drastically reduced, so that the trade union movement can recover its creative capacity and begin to move towards playing a full part in the renovation of industry in Britain. And the victims of recession and savage cuts in public services need to be rescued from poverty, if social solidarity – on which effective trade union and democratic forces depend – is not to break down irreparably. It is possible to identify at least five main issues in which legislation can tackle these two overriding problems. During the referendum about Britain's membership of the EEC, and again later in the first general election to the European Assembly, innumerable promises were made by partisans of the Common Market. In every field of welfare, employment rights, health and social care, we were encouraged to believe that great improvements would follow British membership as superior European standards came to be applied in the backward United Kingdom. In the field of industrial relations the comparisons were particularly telling, since more advanced industries in Europe had already established better standards in a number of areas. People remember the promises of those times, which are notable examples of electoral hyperbole – much to be honoured in the breach, little in the observance. The five themes into which a trade union campaign might be concentrated are these: (1) a national minimum wage; (2) shorter working hours; (3) longer holidays; (4) equalization of trade union rights; and (5) development of industrial democracy.

A national minimum wage

At the beginning of 1984, the TUC had to revise its guidelines on low pay. Basing itself on the notion that anyone receiving less than two-thirds of the average male manual earnings is in jeopardy, the TUC recommends that negotiators treat £98 a week as the figure below which low pay is defined. For a family, such a level of weekly income may well hover very close to the official poverty line. None the less, very many workers – including a large number of government employees – receive far less than this.

The gap between the highest and lowest paid people has grown steadily wider during Mrs Thatcher's years of office. This results partly from generalized economic pressures during a vigorous slump in which the weakest have gone to the wall. But it also flows from deliberate policies enforcing monetarist prescriptions. Among the purposeful onslaughts on poorer people have been the abolition of the fair wages resolution, the undermining of wages councils – the running down of their staff and inspectors and the exercise of pressure to restrict their rates, especially for young people – and the wholesale encouragement of privatization of public services. There has been insistent propaganda from the more neanderthal ministers blaming unemployment on 'high wage rates' and insisting on the withdrawal from ILO conventions designed to protect poorer people.

Government ministers are not the only ones seeking to end the vestigial protection for low-paid workers. A *Times* leader on 20 December 1983 claimed that wages councils 'tend to price young people out of jobs' and should be done away with. There is a clear refutation of this unedifying argument: the earnings of young people have fallen relative to those of adults since the middle 1970s, while youth unemployment has risen rapidly and continuously. Wage cutting has been illegally imposed in the Young Workers' Scheme which provides employers with a weekly handout of £15 for each young person they retain on their books on a wage of less than £42. Employers willing to do this do not have to prove that the young people in question are newly employed, still less that they are undergoing training. The subsidy is available on the sole understanding that the young people receive only the lowest imaginable pay. The House of Commons Public Accounts Committee reported in December 1983 that 77 per cent of the jobs which qualify for a Young Workers' Scheme subsidy would have been necessary whether or not the subsidy was available. The small number of jobs created over and above these were costing the government almost £5,500 apiece. The easiest way for employers to qualify for a subsidy is to cut the pay of young people already on the books, or to take on new young employees while getting rid of older ones.

The Times refers to a research paper of the Department of Employment which suggests that a 10 per cent cut in the wages of young people might produce up to 100,000 jobs for young people. But 80 per cent of these jobs would be created by displacement of older workers. In fact, low pay produces low demand and itself contributes to the spiral of decline and slump.

The government's own view is encapsulated in a 1983 white paper on *Regional Industrial Development* (Cmnd 9111). It says:

> Imbalances between areas in employment opportunities should in principle be corrected by the natural adjustment of labour markets. In the first place, this should be through lower wages and unit costs than comparable work commands elsewhere. Wage flexibility, combined with a reputation for good work and a constructive attitude to productivity and industrial relations, would increase the attractiveness to industry of areas with high unemployment . . . The Government believe that wage bargaining must become more reponsive to the circumstances of the individual enterprise, including its location. Their policies for privatisation, together with a reduction in the power of trade unions to act against their own members' interests, should help to achieve this.

This is both a very open attack on the trade union principle of the rate for the job (the common rate), and another expression of the popular government belief that workers are 'pricing themselves out of work'. Mrs Thatcher herself has abrasively voiced this belief, as in this extract from a pronouncement in 1980:

> If excessive wage demands are granted, one of two things will happen. Either workers price their products out of the market and lose their jobs, or, if they are in a monopoly industry and can hold the country to ransom, end up by destroying the jobs of others.

Novice students of economics could identify the flaws in this argument as a useful, if not too difficult, early exercise.

A very large proportion of the low paid are women, and 1.5 million of them are public service employees. No doubt this accounts for the strong traditional support in the

National Union of Public Employees for legislation to establish an official minimum earnings level. However, other trade unions have been slow to support this call. One reason for their reluctance is that women workers are less fully organized than men, and inadequately represented on the governing councils and in the annual conferences of unions in which they make up a large part of the membership. But a more comprehensive reason for trade union reluctance to seek legislation on pay levels is quite simply that many unions feel such legislation might remove the pressure on low-paid workers to belong to a union. If such workers felt that their earnings were protected solely by government intervention, would they see the necessity to continue to pay trade union subscriptions? This argument has, over many years, been heard in the debate among farm-workers. They are covered by a wages council, which they often cite as sufficient reason to explain the low density of trade union membership in their industry. But whatever the explanation in such particular cases (and low-level unionism in farming has other causes), a *general* statute on minimum pay, for which the trade unions sustained a public campaign, would have a different effect on trade union consciousness; it would bring the issue out of the obscure, marginalized areas of wages council industries into the centre of political controversy and debate, the position which it occupies in countries like France. From the point of view of the Labour Party, this timidity on the part of affiliated unions has been a liability. Legislation would have been the quickest way to win support among legions of presently apathetic and non-political low paid workers. Hundreds of thousands of women's votes would mobilize themselves in its favour.

On the 12 April 1983, a bill was tabled in the House of Commons by Michael Meacher, Stuart Holland and a number of other MPs which offered an ingenious solution to the problem which had for so long divided the unions. The bill would establish a 'minimum fair wage', which at the time it fixed at £100 a week, based on a normal stint of 40 hours. Employers would be required to enter into negotiations with appropriate trade unions in order to implement this fair wage. Employers of part-time workers and home-workers would be compelled to concede a basic hourly rate proportionate to the minimum full-time wage. Negotiations would begin within 12 months of the passing of the Act, and would need to be completed within two years of that time. The Act would only apply to the wages of employees who were represented by a TUC-affiliated union at relevant negotiations. This stipulation at once removes the main trade union objection to a legal minimum wage, since it preserves the union's crucial space in representing its members' interests.

Of course, employers have always argued that a national minimum would squeeze out many jobs by pricing inefficient companies out of their markets. A fair wage Act would have met this argument by providing for government financial assistance to companies which could not otherwise implement the new law. If the implementation of the Act did lead to redundancies or the closure of the company, financial assistance would be made available, subject to an economic audit according to Treasury criteria, which would be agreed with the Departments of Industry and Employment and the appropriate trade unions. If the employer was reluctant to apply for such assistance, the trade union would be empowered to require him to do so – or alternatively to apply for assistance itself on the basis of converting the company to a co-operative or municipal enterprise.

A new British law to establish a compulsory basic wage would bring Britain into compliance with the European Social Charter, which lays down that 'all workers have the right to a fair remuneration, sufficient for a decent standard of living for themselves and their families . . . The exercise of these rights shall be achieved by freely concluded collective agreements, by statutory wage fixing machinery or by other means appropriate to national conditions.' Statutory machinery has operated in France since 1950 and in the Netherlands since 1945. In Belgium, there is a national minimum wage agreement between the trade unions and employers' organizations within the framework of the National Labour Council – a statutory body. All three countries have linked their minimum rates to the Consumer Price Index, but only in France and the Netherlands are there arrangements to modify the national minimum alongside general living standards.

Numerous analysts have commented on the influence of minimum wage legislation in France, especially during the most recent electoral victory of President Mitterand. Few can doubt that Mitterand's promise to raise minimum wage levels by 10 per cent under the existing French legislation played an important part in the changeover which brought him to office. The promised measure was duly introduced in June 1981. The new, larger minimum immediately benefited more than one-third of the labour in the clothing industry (although less than one-tenth had been covered by it before the increase). In the field of personal services, the new minima covered almost half the labour force after the increase, although less than a quarter had been protected before. In Britain, previous minimum wage protection has always been piecemeal, so that the absence of a statutory national figure has made it very difficult to generalize the protection of low-paid workers. The only significant improvement needed by the Fair Wage Bill is that it should state a clear and precise hourly minimum when it is prescribing for part-time workers. In every other sense, the Meacher/Holland draft provides a perfect instrument for dealing with that crucially significant part of Britain's economy directly attributable to low pay.

Working hours

Even though unemployment waxes, institutional overtime in British industry never wanes. In December 1982, while three million people were already out of work, British manufacturing industry worked 9.66 million hours of overtime. In December 1983, this figure had risen to 11.36 million hours, whilst the incidence of short-time had fallen from 1.61 million hours at the end of 1982 to 0.46 million at the end of 1983. If it became magically possible to outlaw overtime, a quarter of a million new jobs could be created overnight. The number would increase as working hours were reduced.

In 1981, the TUC adopted a motion moved by Clive

Jenkins of the ASTMS, instructing the General Council to campaign for a limit on the number of hours worked annually, reducing the working week 'by statute to a maximum of 35 hours', providing a 'minimum holiday entitlement of six weeks per annum, plus sabbatical leave after a stipulated number of years for all employees' and reducing 'the qualifying age for retirement pensions to 60 years'. In an eloquent support for this case, Clive Jenkins showed that engineering workers in Sweden were, at the time, working 1,500 hours annually, while in Belgium and Germany they were working 1,600 and 1,700 hours respectively. But 'the British engineering worker is working 1902 hours a year.'

We must face the fact that there are a number of difficulties about implementing the call for a statute to fix a 35-hour week. The TUC has been carefully monitoring progress, and publishing a regular progress report. By 1983, it had monitored 57 separate agreements reducing hours by varying amounts from 40 down to 39 or 36.5. Only one agreement was reported implementing a 35-hour week (it was in the exhibition industry) but this does not take effect until 1987.

The killer in this process is, of course, overtime. Overtime is concentrated and does not fall equally across the labour force. Therefore workers who are doing overtime are normally putting in far more than the average hours of overtime. Between April 1981 and April 1982, the average weekly hours of overtime per male manual worker actually rose from 4.5 to 4.9, having fallen the previous year. But average overtime hours per male manual overtime worker rose from 9.5 to 9.7 during the same period. The following year both these statistics fell back to 4.78 and 9.3 respectively. The TUC is well aware of this continuing, intractable problem. Indeed, in February 1984 it pointed out the fact that the percentage of workers who do overtime has actually been rising since 1981 from 46.8 to 49.8. The small decline in the number of overtime hours is more likely to reflect the depression than the results of trade union limitations. And in its scrutiny of these figures, the TUC tells us that 'the tendency . . . for the percentage of people working overtime to rise from April 1981 must be a matter of concern.'

The agreed basic weekly hours have been slowly declining, and manual male workers now average a 39.2-hour week, compared to 39.9 hours which they would have expected to work in 1979. Various conclusions have been drawn by TUC researchers from the movement of working hours during recent years. First, men who are manual workers work a lot longer than other people. They average a 44-hour week, of which 5 hours are overtime. But the average is misleading, because half the manual male workers do not work *any* overtime – which means that the other half, who do, average 9.5 hours of overtime a week. Women manual workers average 39.5 hours, of which only 1 hour is overtime. Only one-fifth of these women workers get any overtime at all, and so they average 6 hours of it a week. Second, non-manual working men put in some 38.5 hours, of which 1.5 are overtime; but only one-fifth of these people actually do work overtime, which means that those who do average 6 hours a week. Non-manual women workers are on a 36.5 hour week, of which only half an hour is overtime, and in fact only 12 per cent of these women get to work overtime at all, and they average 3 hours a week. Between 1979 and 1983 the total hours worked by men who were manual workers declined by 2.3 of which 1.6 were accounted for by a decline in the availability of overtime. Decline among other groups was very much less significant.

The TUC's campaign, and the efforts of affiliated unions, have effectively broken through the barrier of the 40-hour basic week, and it is clear that legislation could make a major contribution if only the unions could agree on how it should be framed. The problem is extremely simple to state and very difficult to solve. Trade unionists will not say 'thank you' for a law which cuts their earnings and, if overtime is forbidden, approximately half the male manual workers will be much worse off unless they are compensated for its loss. There is a very strong need for parliamentary draftsmen to consult with the TUC if the Congress resolution of 1981 is to be implemented. Meanwhile, concern with this matter grows throughout Europe.

In West Germany, the trade union campaign for the 35-hour week bids fair to become the most severe and important struggle in which that hitherto quiescent labour movement has engaged since 1945. Already British trade unions have promised solidarity with it. The German unions' case has been developed with characteristic comprehensiveness. They argue the job creation potential of a shorter working week, calling for commensurate new jobs to replace the hours 'lost' by the reduction in working time. They also point to the beneficial effects of such a move on health and safety, and on reducing the inequalities of domestic labour within family life as male workers, in particular, obtain more free time. They look forward to the liberating effect upon social awareness of a decisive breach in the customary trade union goal of 'eight hours' work, eight hours' sleep and eight hours' play'.

Longer Holidays

I have mentioned above that when Britain joined the EEC, heavy blandishments were held out to the British people. A cornucopia of benefits was expected. Perhaps the most prominent among these was the benefit of increased holiday time. It was pointed out that Europeans enjoyed far better holiday entitlements than British workers: that they had longer annual vacations and more of them; that their statutory holidays outnumbered ours, sometimes by two or three times. The same TUC resolution of 1981 which sought a statutory 35-hour week also addressed the problem of holiday starvation which afflict workers in British industry. But when we look at the problem with care, it seems very clear that legislation to standardize holiday entitlements is very much easier than legislation on weekly hours to be worked. Basic annual holiday entitlement in France and the Netherlands runs at five weeks, and in many enterprises in Italy this is also true. In West Germany 90 per cent of workers get six weeks' annual holiday, or more.

The TUC's official objective of six weeks' holiday is in fact a modest one, although it would represent a substantial improvement in the conditions of most workers. It would be relatively simple to legislate a statutory holiday entitlement of six weeks. It would even be feasible to legislate to enlarge the size of the labour force in every firm by an amount commensurate with the increase in holiday entitlement. To invent a simple example which embodies the principle: if we were to legislate to give every person an additional month's holiday, it might well be possible simultaneously to require every employer to expand his or her labour force by 10 per cent. This would at once create some two million jobs, even allowing for the fact that some smaller employers would slip between the mesh of a net which would have to be loosely strung. Any such large redeployment of formerly unemployed people would liberate vast sums of dole money which could be used to ease the burdens of those employers who fell into difficulties as a result. Here a similar principle could be invoked to that we have already discussed in connection with the Fair Wage Bill. Of course, some people will argue that a month's additional holiday is a dramatically over-generous improvement in conditions. In that case, we could opt for a fortnight's additional improvement, and a 5 per cent increase in the size of labour forces. Indeed, we could create a sliding scale, upwards or downwards, directly aimed at facilitating work-sharing.

Equalization of trade union rights

The Thatcher administration is associated with a blockbusting campaign to roll back trade union powers to the point where even the most docile conformity is viewed with suspicion. The Trade Union Bill of 1983 is only the latest in a series of measures which are imposing heavier and heavier state controls on the operation of trade unionism. The spirit of the King Bill directly contradicts Article 3 of Convention 87 of the International Labour Organization, which is entirely specific on this matter: 'Workers' and employers' organizations shall have the right to draw up their constitutions and rules, to elect their representatives in full freedom, to organize their administration and activities, and to formulate their programmes. The public authorities shall refrain from any interference which would restrict this right or impede the lawful exercise thereof.' The Trade Union Bill is imminently to become law and the unions will be compelled to structure their internal rule books according to a number of very tight governmental prescriptions. They may also eventually be compelled to accept the most rigorous control over contributions for political purposes, which will become illegal if they are not renewed in a decennial special ballot. Other organizations and commercial concerns have no such restriction on their system of choice about how to use their resources, and it is indeed difficult to find any precedent for so systematic an onslaught on political pluralism.

Taken in conjunction with the earlier legislation of Messrs Prior and Tebbit, the removal of key parts of the Employment Protection Act introduced by an earlier Labour government, and the dismantling of machinery for the protection of low-paid workers, the Trade Union Act 1984 represents only the latest stage of an uncompleted series of assaults on the industrial relations system since the Second World War. The government openly plans further raids which will include the banning of industrial action in 'essential' services and probably a widening of the ban on trade union membership in GCHQ to other military and mililtarized sectors of the security and arms economy. No trade union will be able to operate freely until such an attack has been reversed, and this will require more than a repeal of the offending legislation.

Some of the most obnoxious governmental onslaughts on unions have not even required legislation. Notably, the unilateral withdrawal of trade union rights at GCHQ in Cheltenham was the result of an administrative decision. Such decisions are being challenged in the international courts but this will take time. While this is going on, British trade unions must urgently consider their own constructive legislative proposals, not only within the framework of the campaign for the restoration of trade union rights in Britain, but also at the level of similar international action.

Development of industrial democracy

The argument for company law reform, to increase trade union involvement in industrial decision-making was, we have already argued, given a notable impulse by European draft legislation. As a result of preparing a draft statute for the structure of a European limited company, the British TUC became involved in a long debate that produced a far-reaching set of proposals and culminated in the Bullock Report.

We should note, however, that the legislative initiative from Brussels only worked to the extent that it provoked counter-proposals in Britain and other member states of the EEC. The weakness of attempts at legislation across the whole area of the EEC is that they invariably fall between two stools. Either they are seen as bureaucratic impositions, or they seek to establish a feeblest common denominator. This reinforces the belief that, in spite of all the federal rhetoric, the best possibilities of international action come from an agreed convergence. Separate member states which agree to take similar action can accomplish more, and do so more quickly, than all the machinery of Brussels. Even so, in this case the Labour government in Britain jibbed at taking the advice of British trade unions.

The joint effects of mass unemployment and harassment by illiberal legislation make it difficult to imagine that Bullock's proposals could ever be revived. A parallel set of proposals which featured in the Labour Party's campaign strategy in the early 1970s, and which has been generalized throughout Europe since, is the development of a series of 'planning agreements', aimed at bringing multinational corporations into a structured relationship with governments and trade unions. Within this framework, it would be possible to develop the kind of argument which has been increasingly heard for 'resource bargaining', in which unions press for the allocation of new investment in particular areas, or the expansion of employment provision in existing ones. Planning agreements were put forward in the British Labour Party's 1973 programme, and the refusal to implement them was one of the major apostasies of the Wilson–Callaghan administration. But the proposal was not for nothing. That it has been taken up and implemented by socialist parties in Greece, Spain and Portugal clearly demonstrates its continuing relevance. That it has been possible to tackle the influence of multinational corporations in such a similar way, over such divergent territories, shows that federalism is not the only model for international co-operation.

There exist a number of other sources of inspiration for legislative models of industrial democracy. In the EEC, there is a battle over the implementation of the Vredeling proposals for the opening of the books – of multinational companies in particular – to trade union scrutiny. Although this is another lowest common denominator, we should not overlook the possibility that it could stimulate not only a renewed debate in the British trade union movement on the requirements in this field, but also a more concrete channel for the development of a European level of trade union awareness. It is, moreover, an issue on which the British government and the CBI will find themselves increasingly isolated. In the past few months these two bodies have concerted their increasingly strident opposition and made the most incredible claims for the 'progress' made in British industry through 'voluntary' encouragement of 'employee participation'.

In Britain, the whole prolific experience and experiment in new forms of local, trade-union based economic planning and job creation through municipal enterprise, pioneered by the GLC, West Midlands and Sheffield Councils, needs to be incorporated in any comprehensive programme of trade union demands for legislative support and encouragement. Local enterprise boards, with trade union representation, local planning agreements, local sponsorship of workers' co-operatives and municipal economic enterprise, would greatly benefit from legislative enabling measures and from the allocation of investment funds which would enlarge their coverage. The labour movement debate around the TUC/ Labour Party Liaison Committee proposals for economic planning and industrial democracy has abated sadly since the election defeat of June 1983. It is not too early to revive it and to examine all the models on offer, including those from the 'Popular Planning' networks of combines and trades councils, and from the Institute for Workers' Control.

The very fact that the Conservative government has been so merciless in its onslaught on political pluralism and so determined to reduce trade unionism to a shadow, means that it becomes not only possible but also to a degree necessary for the trade unions to address themselves to the problem of company law reform. This is possible because Mrs Thatcher has removed many taboos and provoked people to think more radically. It is necessary because the weakening of trade unions by mass unemployment as well as legislative encroachments will mean that they will not easily resume some of their traditional roles while unemployment remains at record levels. The British Conservatives registered the quite unjustifiable claim that trade unions are a favoured type of organization because they have been entitled to certain immunities for behaviour in restraint of trade. How a trade union might operate without such immunities is not easy to imagine.

However, this onslaught by the Thatcher team has distracted people's attention from a far more powerful privilege which is enjoyed by every major capitalist organization: the principle of limited liability. The capacity to avoid personal responsibility for debts incurred on one's personal initiative is, by any standards, a remarkable advantage. Well over a century ago, the argument for this degree of licence was heard in the absence of an organized mass labour movement. Now it is time to reopen the question. As a modest first step, the principle of limited liability should surely be subordinated to an affirmative vote of employees at regular intervals. The easiest way to make this effective would be to require every company to submit to the Registrar, with its audited accounts, an annual statement of satisfactory labour relations. Such a statement would need to be endorsed by the relevant trade union organization. Failure to submit the statement would automatically revoke the privilege of limited liability, thereby rendering all shareholders responsible in full for any failure by the company in which they held investments. This moderate measure would strengthen trade unions during their convalescence from the gross debilities imposed by monetarism.

The Labour movement throughout Europe is being tested by a crisis which is as much political as economic. Attempts to resolve this crisis by arbitrary means can only succeed in making it worse. If we can keep clear heads through these present adversities, we can bring about a notable advance in the democratic organization of industry and society. Surely it is quite unthinkable that an age of microcomputers, lasers, and widespread robotics will for long conform to the prejudices of the more backward Victorians? There is a future in which human capacities can grow to match and outpace the results of invention. Already this future lives in the imaginations of multitudes of people. How long can it be prevented from asserting itself in our public order?

21

A New Starting Point

ANNA COOTE

It was in August 1981, while the politicians and economists were scattered about on beaches, that the Department of Employment chose to publish its remarkable report on the mental health of production-line workers.[1] Based on a study of women in three food factories, it sought to show 'how far mental strain and ill-health among industrial workers may be caused by the nature of their jobs, especially repetitive, machine-paced tasks.'

The researchers, from Lancaster University, established that almost all the women suffered mental stress, many of them acutely. However, this was caused not by their jobs, but by a combination of factors – chiefly their domestic responsibilities, which involved them in long hours of labour, subjected them to serious financial worries and made it hard for them to gain satisfaction from paid employment. Women with dependent children living at home suffered most, the report said:

> These women are caught up in a constant and unremitting round of activity throughout their waking hours. Their day begins early, about 5 or 6 am, and finishes late, about 9 or 10 pm, with little or no time for rest or relaxation, leaving them continuously tired and often emotionally exhausted. Many are responsible for the household budget and under financial pressure to make ends meet, which is a major factor in their going out to work.
>
> But employment has to be fitted in with household duties and childcare arrangements, which they and their families regard as unquestionably their responsibility. Factory work is often seen as the only job possible in the circumstances and entered into more from necessity than choice, although

outside employment of some kind was in almost all cases
considered desirable.

When information of this kind is set alongside the Alternative Economic Strategy it gives a hollow ring to the call for
full employment. Michelle Barrett has pointed out in *New
Socialist*[2] that women have not in our recent history ever had
full employment. But of course that is true only in relation to
paid employment. Most women are already *over-employed*.
The crucial consideration for them is not availability of
work, but what kind of work they do, how much of their
time they spend on it, how much they get paid for it (if
anything), and the degree of their economic dependence or
control. The AES does not address or control itself to such
matters.

How did we get into this predicament, where the left is
pinning its hopes – and indeed its reputation – on a set of
proposals that bear so little relation to the material conditions
and needs of more than half the population? Before we begin
to tinker with the details of the strategy perhaps we should
dig it up and inspect its roots. We shall find that in spite of its
radical pretensions, it is embedded in the same old-fashioned
patriarchal values that inform and distort all mainstream
political thinking today. We may conclude that we need a
new starting point, a new set of criteria, a new order of
priorities.

Patriarchal politics begin from and are focused upon one
relatively limited area of life: production. If women had
power to assert their own experience, as men have, we might
develop a different approach, one with a double axis:
reproduction and production. This would embrace unpaid
work as well as paid work, and relations within the family
and community as well as relations between labour and
capital.

Our starting point for an alternative strategy would change
accordingly. Rather than asking in the first instance, 'how
can we regenerate industry in order to create full employment?' we might begin with a different kind of question,
such as 'how shall we care for and support our children?' (I
mean this in the sense not of private domestic choices, but of

our collective responsibility towards the next generation.)
Much turns on the question, in particular the redistribution
of labour and wealth within the family. It does not eclipse the
aim of reviving the economy or of redistributing wealth
between labour and capital, but sets them in context.

If we take this as our point of departure, we shall have to
decide at the outset who should care for our children and in
what manner. Few would disagree that our present arrangements are inadequate, but the left has yet to develop a viable
alternative to the Tory strategy of sanctifying motherhood
and family life. Driving women out of the paid labour
market will not benefit children any more than it will benefit
mothers. Cared for almost exclusively by women, children
grow up with a limited picture of the respective characters
and capacities of males and females: this is one of the main
ways in which sex stereotypes become rooted in people's
minds.

While men continue to segregate themselves from children, they are cut off from a range of experience which
would broaden their understanding and no doubt alter their
political priorities (and which they might even enjoy). It
scarcely needs to be added that while women bear the full
responsibility for childcare, they are forced into economic
dependence, subjected to considerable stress and deprived of
the opportunity to explore their full potential. There is a
strong case, then, for arguing that children should be looked
after by men and women equally.

Moreover, children's lives are unlikely to be enriched if
they are confined to their own homes and the company of
their immediate family: collective childcare is a positive
advantage, not just a means of compensating for the absence
of wage-earning mothers. If there is anything wrong with
childcare facilities today, it is that they are under-resourced
and poorly organized. Even if they were flawless, there
should be no necessity for children to spend as much as 35 or
40 hours a week in them. We need a combination of
community-based and parental care. Our strategy might thus
combine generous resourcing for childcare facilities with a
commitment to re-organize paid employment so that parents
of both sexes can spend equal time with their children.

The arrangement of time spent in paid employment is a crucial factor if we are to change the current pattern of male absenteeism from childcare and other domestic responsibilities. It would be necessary to reduce working hours substantially, aiming perhaps for a 30-hour week, together with firm restrictions on overtime. This could put an end to the present distinction between 'part-time' and 'full-time' workers, which acts so much to women's disadvantage.[3]

It would help create new jobs, and it would *begin* to create the conditions in which men and women could participate equally in domestic work as well as paid employment. If a new government were to embark on a public spending programme aimed at reducing unemployment, could not the new jobs in the public sector be limited to 30 hours? It might enable more people to have paid work. And it might be combined with a system of incentives to reduce hours in the private sector, beginning in areas where the workload is contracting – not as an emergency stop-gap, but as a positive alternative to redundancy and a means of encouraging a permanent change in the pattern of working time.

These proposals obviously raise vital questions about pay. How can living standards be maintained and improved if working hours are reduced? The conventional response of the left is that any proposal for change which threatens the wage is unacceptable. Yet this springs from a fixed idea about the nature of family support – which is that each family has one main source of income, provided by a (male) employee bread-winner. It has been argued elsewhere that this notion of the 'family wage' is a false one which perpetuates female dependency and male control.[4] It discriminates against larger families, since the individual wage does not vary according to the number of children the wage earner has to support. It is no help to the families of the unemployed. And it is based on the concept of the family as an harmonious economic unit, which takes no account of conflicting interests within the family – especially those between women and men.

So we need to restructure family income. We can begin to do this by fighting for genuine equality between female and male workers, so that women are able to contribute as much as men. Since we know that laws *against* sex discrimination and unequal pay do little to achieve equality, we shall have to give priority to developing the campaign for positive action in favour of women – in education, training and employment, as well as within trade unions.[5] This need not entail discrimination against men at the point of entry to employment, but if it is to be successful it *must* break down the infrastructure of male privilege, and ensure that women have real equality of access to skill, to the means of organization and to all levels of employment. The reorganization of working time and the provision of childcare facilities are crucial to the success of positive action.

At the same time, we need an effective strategy against low pay. This will have to include an overhaul of the wages council system, and the introduction of a statutory minimum wage. The latter has been strongly resisted in the past, on the grounds that it interferes with trade union bargaining, and will tie wages down to the minimum. Against this it must be said that free collective bargaining has done nothing to solve the problem of low pay; that there are still four and a half million workers with earnings below that poverty line; and that the gap between lowest and average earnings is no narrower to day than it was 100 years ago.[6]

Positive action and an offensive against low pay would be two essential elements in the restructuring of family income. A third would be substantial increase in child benefit. It is hardly in the best interests of children to depend on their parents' wages as their primary means of support: those whose parents are out of work, who have only one parent or who have more than one or two siblings, are bound to suffer relative disadvantage. If we are to have greater equality between families, as well as secure support for children, we shall need to raise the level of benefit until it is commensurate with the real cost of supporting a child. This principle is already accepted in relation to one group of people who do not earn wages – pensioners. Could not the same principle be extended to children?

In addition, we need to ensure proper support for adults who have care of dependants. This can be met partly by extending the period of paid parental leave and making it available to the mother or the father, according to which one is absent from paid employment while the child is at home. For those not covered by parental leave, we need to devise a benefit which helps those in need, while not serving to keep women out of paid work (a 'stay-at-home' allowance), and which requires a minimum of policing (e.g. through a means test or cohabitation rule).

The services and facilities provided by the state are equally important. Our strategy should place a strong priority on extending the 'social wage', by providing better housing, transport, health care, welfare and social security, as well as introducing new services, such as community restaurants and laundries, to ease the burden of domestic work. Just as incomes need to be restructured in order to minimize the economic dependence of individuals within the family, so state provisions must be reorganized in order that they are not conditional upon membership of a traditional family unit. People who live singly, or with a partner of the same sex, or with groups of friends, must be free to do so without suffering social or financial disadvantage. The welfare state is based on an assumption of female dependence, and its rules and regulations reinforce patriarchal control. We need to transform the principles on which it is founded.

Of course, we cannot rely on the state as a benefactor any more than we can rely on employers. We shall have to struggle to win what we need, and no doubt we shall have to fight to preserve what we have gained. It is essential, therefore, that trade unions extend the scope of collective bargaining to local and national government in order to win improvements in the social wage – and that they invest no less energy in this than in bargaining with employers about pay and conditions at work.

I am not arguing for a list of utopian addenda to the AES. In the first place, these proposals cannot simply be added on to the existing strategy, because they will not work unless they are given political priority. When we have decided on the best way of caring for our children and the most effective means of supporting them; when we have resolved to re-allocate labour and wealth within the family; and when we have worked out how best to restructure paid employment and improve state services, *then* is the time to decide how to pay for what we need. There could be some redistribution among working people – for example, by abolishing the married man's tax allowance and using the extra revenue to increase child benefit. There could be a major redistribution of resources between different areas of public spending – for example by diverting funds from the 'defence' budget. And of course there must be a redistribution from employers to workers – for example, through taxation, by the introduction of a statutory minimum wage and by winning through collective bargaining (backed up by legislation if necessary) a substantial reduction in working hours without a commensurate loss in the value of earnings.

These proposals are not utopian: they are necessary and possible. They only seem far-fetched to those who presently stand at the centre of the political stage, believing that their own experience and their own interests are universal. It is a classic mistake that men make, to interpret their own view of the world as *the* view, around which women's needs and experiences revolve like so many satellites. To restructure family income in such a way as to free women from the economic control of men, and to base an alternative strategy upon the consideration of childcare and child support, is no more or less utopian than seeking to bring into public ownership certain sectors of the economy, or seeking to increase industrial democracy. It is simply less familiar to those who have been accustomed to formulating policy on the left.

Notes

[1] S. Shimmin, J. McNally, & S. Liff, 'Pressures on Women engaged in factory work' in *Employment Gazette,* 89 (8) (August 1981).

[2] M. Barrett, 'Unity is Strength?' in *New Socialist* 1 (September 1981).

[3] The dividing line is presently 30 hours. See A. Sedley, *Part-time workers need full-time rights* (NCCL, 1980).

[4] H. Land, *The Family Wage,* Eleanor Rathbone Memorial Lecture, 1979. See also, A. Coote & J. Cousins, *Family in the Firing Line* (NCCL and CPAG, 1981).

[5] S. Robarts, *Positive Action for Women* (NCCL, 1981).

[6] 'Low Pay 1980 Style' in *Low Pay Review,* 4 (March 1981).

Index

i.e. shows that socialists gain by giving up the material benefits of life in the modern capitalist sector.

A new movement will need to be created through example as well as analysis. Even with ~~the~~ success at these levels a final essential ingredient is missing if the movement is to become self sufficient, develop between generations and expand to affect national and international systems a compatible + creative education system needs to be designed and put into place.

This is the second point where the Labour Party needs to play a role. Without a national force capable of legislating for change at the system level any attempt at a socialist education will fail.

5.   socialism that places high priorities n
the solution of problems affecting the least
(individually) powerful members of the world community.

It appears an impossible task in the face
of the ~~various~~ success and enormous force
behind consumerism and the massive power
of accumulated capital. Yet there are signs
that all is not well within the capitalist
system of production and financial accumulation
both at the level of consumerism and at
the level of the underpinning financial mechanism.
In addition a ~~second paradox~~ hopeful trend
has emerged. The drop outs of the 60s
created unstable and dependent systems rich
in culture but weak in alternative mechanism
of production. The drop outs of today, along
with the throw-outs of advanced capitalism
in our inner cities, see the need for new
kinds of work and are prepared to experiment
with new forms of production organisation.
Worker owned coops are one of the most
hopeful phenomena to appear out of the
wreckage of the 70s. Socialists need to
study them, create them and work in
them. It will not be sufficient to
pontificate about them from the sidelines.

/ and a labour Government needs to support them through legislation

1. It does not seem to have occurred to these writers that any solution (other than catastrophe) to our predicament might well involve sacrifice by large sections of the population in the sense that great equality produced from the redistribution of growth is not only slow but is predicated on rates of growth for the modern world that will be ruinous both for the traditional world and the ecosphere. Socialists will need to get their satisfactions from solving problems, better social relationships and an enriched culture of cooperation rather than increased consumption of material things if they are to put forward solutions that can succeed.

The problems that confront the Labour Party and British Society cannot be understood in the context of analyses about electoral success and national party politics. The national systems are now so intimately intwined with international systems that the broader canvas needs to provide the background to the analysis. To approach this problem we will need to understand the mechanism of the 'tyranny of small decisions' which presently unites many social + economic systems which appear disparate

4 world and those resources freed by the
modern world to help overcome the
problem. Even today it would require enormous
inputs of energy and resources to stabilize or
solve this problem. The only existing remedies
are those in early 'modern world countries'
where resources from the traditional world
could be expropriated to fuel industrialism
and feed the population to the extent that
they individually felt the need to secure
their future through family limitation and a
reliance on promises of a prosperous secure
future based on increasing prosperity for their
fewer children and eventually a guaranteed
old age. It follows that while the mechanisms
and strategies are likely to be different
it will still require a massive injection
of resources from without (only the modern
world is available) to generate sufficient
trust to overcome this particular tyranny.

However, lest we forget, the modern world
is bound up in its own tyranny and still
strives for virtuous cycles of expansion to
fulfill the unsatisfiable appetite for higher
material standards. No resources are likely
to become available unless an enormous
reorientation is achieved in the modern world.
No less, is required, than a form of

2 The two worlds in which the tyranny of
small decisions has most destructive effect
are situated respectively in the ~~1st and 3rd world~~
'modern,' ~~developed~~' and traditional sectors of society.
In the modern sector the search for advantage
leads time & time again, as Hirsh has shown
to temporary advantage for the individual and
accumulating
~~collection~~ disadvantage for the collective whole
Once they are exhausted, old remedies are no
longer applicable and the modern world has
to generate new fields of endeavour and expansion
to off-set the loss. Each round in the spiral
places new strains on an overstrained ecological
a new complexity in economic & technical systems
system, and a growing instability in finely
balanced social systems. Each round makes
the modern world more susceptible to a
                                                        will
catastrophy that will not be mended and, pu[t]
an end to the 'progress' of humankind that
we have begun to believe is an inevitable
feature of human history.
                of inevitable progress
   That this view, is a myth and the ultimate
opiate is nowhere clearer than in the traditional
world. Here the structures of meaning and
hopes for stability are already in ruins and
the certainty of traditional belief displayed only
in the dignified stoicism in which people